THE BIG DROPS

The Big Drops

TEN LEGENDARY RAPIDS

Robert O. Collins and Roderick Nash

Color photographs by John Blaustein

SIERRA CLUB BOOKS | SAN FRANCISCO

The Sierra Club, founded in 1892 by John Muir, has devoted itself to the study and protection of the earth's scenic and ecological resources—mountains, wetlands, woodlands, wild shores and rivers, deserts and plains. The publishing program of the Sierra Club offers books to the public as a nonprofit educational service in the hope that they may enlarge the public's understanding of the Club's basic concerns. The point of view expressed in each book, however, does not necessarily represent that of the Club. The Sierra Club has some 50 chapters coast to coast, in Canada, Hawaii, and Alaska. For information about how you may participate in its programs to preserve wilderness and the quality of life, please address inquiries to Sierra Club, 530 Bush Street, San Francisco, California 94108

Library of Congress Cataloging in Publication Data

Collins, Robert O.   1933–
  The big drops : ten legendary rapids.

  Bibliography: p.
  Includes index.
  1. Rafting (Sports)—The West. 2. Rivers—The West. I. Nash, Roderick, joint author. II. Title.
GV776.W3C64   797   78-5821
ISBN O-87156-217-0

Maps by Edwin A. Gustafson

Drawings by Pat Fish

Book design by Anita Walker Scott

Printed in the United States of America

First Edition

To Nat Galloway, the best of the first

CONTENTS

Put-In   1

Acknowledgments   7

Chapter *One* | Clavey Falls   8

Chapter *Two* | Rainie Falls   24

Chapter *Three* | Hell's Half Mile   38

Chapter *Four* | Warm Springs   60

Chapter *Five* | Satan's Gut   76

Chapter *Six* | Redside   102

Chapter *Seven* | Big Mallard   125

Chapter *Eight* | Granite Creek   142

Chapter *Nine* | Crystal   158

Chapter *Ten* | Lava Falls   179

Epilogue: Honor Roll   207

Selected Bibliography   208

Index   212

It is difficult to find in life any event which so effectually condenses intense nervous sensation into the shortest possible space as does the work of shooting, or running, an immense rapid. There is no toil, no heartbreaking labor about it, but as much coolness, dexterity, and skill as man can throw into the work of hand, eye, and head—knowledge of when to strike, and how to do it, knowledge of water and rock, of the one hundred combinations which rock and water can assume—for these two things, rock and water, taken in the abstract, fail as completely to convey any idea of their fierce embracings in the throes of a rapid as the fires burning quietly in a drawing-room fireplace fails to convey the idea of a house wrapped and sheeted in flames.

Sir George Back (1834)

"Put-ins" are where river trips begin, where you put your boat in the water and go with the flow. They are exciting places, hopeful places, often nervous places. Come to a put-in with good equipment and river know-how and you have at least a fighting chance of running a Big Drop.

Big Drops are big rapids, whitewater, places where rivers go wild. They have been around as long as precipitation has fallen on land higher than the sea. You find them where the irresistible force of flowing water meets immovable objects: mostly rock. In the long, long run, of course, the river always wins. The moving water grinds stone, as it grinds continents, into sand and carries the debris to the ocean floor in preparation for the next continental uplift.

But for a time the hard rock resists erosion. Unyielding, it turns the river into a writhing white snake of energy and motion. In oceans the water remains stationary; the waves move. The opposite occurs on rivers. The waves stand still as the water moves through them. So, instead of being carried along on the face of a wave like a surfer, the river runner goes up and down for the full roller-coaster ride. To get an idea of the scale involved, think of yourself as sitting in a boat on the floor of your living room. The waves in Big Drops can be as high as the ceiling—of a room on the second story! The biggest rapids have many of these giant "haystacks" lined up in a row.

If river waves were smooth and regular, whitewater boating would be like an amusement park attraction: fun, a little scary, yet essentially predictable and safe. But the tons of water in a wave can have a nasty way of rising up and exploding unexpectedly in your face. There are dark, churning holes between waves that can trap boats and bodies for anxious seconds or minutes—the "Maytag treatment," as boatmen say. Now imagine a generous assortment of exposed, boat-breaking rocks randomly sprinkled down the length of the whitewater slalom course, and the full dimensions of the challenge become clearer. The prospect of running such water ties the stomachs of even the best boatmen into knots. It also brings them back, time and again, to stand beside a wild river above a Big Drop.

Rapids have a relentlessness about them that attracts a special breed of people. There is no turning back, no slowing down. In contrast, a climber of rock or ice moves slowly. If one route will not "go," it is possible to retreat, regroup, and try something else. The mountain does not pull the climber upward at twenty-five miles per hour, demanding instant and irrevocable decisions. You can brake a sports car, check to the side of a ski slope, or luff a sailboat into the wind, but in a Big Drop you have only one shot. Commit a raft or dory or kayak to the power of the rapid and you must make the run—in the boat or in the water, in one piece or in several. What does it take to face this everything-on-the-line finality? Ernest Hemingway defined courage as grace under pressure, and that is essential. So is the capacity for being energized, not paralyzed, by fear. Boatmen know what Winston Churchill meant when he advised: "Play for more than you can afford to lose, and you will learn the game."

Time was, and not all that long ago in American history, when Big Drops were not run for fun. Nor, for that matter, were they run out of necessity. Following the custom—and the trails—of Indians, pioneers on the eastern and northern rivers routinely carried their boats around wild water. *Portage,* the French term for the laborious process, stuck. In more ways than one, portaging was a drag, but for nearly three centuries neither boats nor boatmanship in North America were adequate to meet the challenge of major rapids. Even a river explorer of the stature of John Wesley Powell, leader in 1869 of the first documented trip through the Grand Canyon, regularly carried his fragile wooden boats around whitewater, or "lined" them down on ropes from the shore. Some Big Drops were not run at all until the 1960s.

There is a new clientele in the cowboy bars of Stanley, Idaho, Flagstaff, Arizona, and Green River, Utah. The new kids in town usually wear shorts and tennis shoes, but nobody snickers. Boatmen tend to be young, strong, cool and tanned the color of the rocks among which they work and play. They carry knives and pliers in leather sheaths on their belts. When they talk it is more often than not about Big Drops.

Defining a Big Drop is almost as difficult as running one. One man's terror is another's "piece of cake." Estimation depends on experience. In the course of ten thousand miles of commercial and private river running during the past decade, we have challenged all the rapids discussed here, most of them many times. But in choosing the Big Drops, we tried to look beyond our own experience to the historical record. The reputation of a particular rapid was an important criterion. Through conversation, questionnaire, and library research, we gathered the opinions of river runners past and present. Their responses varied widely, and none of them had seen all the rapids we ultimately chose.

Knowing our list would be controversial, we agonized over the final nominees. There was a temptation to overemphasize the Grand Canyon of the Colorado River. We finally chose Lava Falls and Crystal, but what about House Rock and 24½ Mile Rapid, which have claimed more lives? And Hance, Horn, and Hermit? Granite, Upset, and 232 Mile? They all could qualify as Big Drops, but we decided to limit our discussion to two Grand Canyon rapids in order to include different but equally challenging ones elsewhere in the West.

The decision to go beyond the Grand Canyon only increased the problem of choice. First, we had to consider whitewater so difficult that it had seldom if ever been run successfully, and then only with extensive portaging, lining, and specialized shore-based rescue equipment. Cross Mountain, through which the Yampa River races in western Colorado, is a case in point. So are New Mexico's upper Rio Grande and the North Fork of the Payette in Idaho. Without question these rivers contain Big Drops, but we wanted rapids that could be run more or less regularly by experts in standard river boats. Niagara Falls, after all, has been "run" in a barrel. So awesome rapids like Dagger Falls on the Middle Fork of Idaho's Salmon River are left for bolder boatmen of the future whose equipment and technique may well surpass our own by a proportion equal to our distance from the nineteenth-century river explorers.

With river friends we whiled away many hours and not a few beers guessing and second-guessing the rapids to include here. Many were nominated. Snaggletooth on the Dolores River in Colorado had a number of advocates, as did Skull Rapid on the upper Colorado in Westwater Canyon. Wyoming river runners voted for Lunch Counter Rapid on the Snake River, and Californians cited the Bailey Falls–Staircase complex on the Stanislaus. Others felt there were several rapids on Idaho's Selway River below Moose Creek more deserving of mention than some of those we ultimately chose.

A complicating factor in the selection process was the constant variation of rivers. It is said, quite correctly, that you never run the same rapid twice. Rocks shift position. So do sand bars and logs. Holes appear and disappear from year to year and even week to week. And the amount of water coming down the river changes everything. At some flow rates one or another of our rapids might not qualify as a Big Drop. Big Mallard on Idaho's Salmon River is tough at lower flows and, historically, one of the most feared rapids on the river, but it virtually disappears when runoff flows are greater than 50,000 cubic feet per second. At this high-water stage, Ruby Rapid and Groundhog Bar are much tougher to run than Big Mallard. But high-water conditions occur on the Salmon for only a few weeks a year, and some years not at all.

We also puzzled over how to rank seemingly easy rapids that have nonetheless devastated river runners over the years. Steer Ridge Rapid on the Green River in Utah's Desolation Canyon is a case in point. Experienced boatmen laughed in our faces when we mentioned Steer Ridge as a potential Big Drop. Granted it presents no problem if you know where it is located and what you are doing in a boat, but you could not prove that by the several river runners who have drowned in Steer Ridge in recent years. John Wesley Powell also had trouble there in 1869.

While the present treatment is limited by design to the American West, we should at least acknowledge the existence of formidable whitewater in other parts of the nation and the world. The *Maid of the Mist* takes crowds of tourists on the Niagara River below the famous falls, but the gorge downstream from there has awesome whirlpools that have held boats and bodies for many days. The Chattooga River, shared by Georgia and South Carolina and made known by the film *Deliverance,* has claimed the lives of eighteen river runners in the last few years. Most of them were inadequately prepared and equipped, but the fact remains that the Chattooga is a bigger killer than the Colorado in Grand Canyon. West Virginia's New River has rapids such as Double Z and Greyhound Bus Stopper that are major league by anyone's standards. So are Pillow Rock, Lost Paddle, and Iron Ring on the Gauley River, also in West Virginia. Farther north, Pennsylvania's Youghiogheny River regularly flips boats in Cucumber, Railroad, and the Dimple. It is also the most heavily run river in the United States. It could be argued that the biggest eastern rapid of them all is the Great Falls of the Potomac, almost within the sight of the nation's capital. Running it is prohibited, but both the fast, rock-walled chutes of the Maryland side and the main falls, closer to Virginia, appear possible, given the best in boatmanship and equipment.

European kayakers and canoeists, practicing on the fast, small streams that drain the Alps, have become the world's best, but exploration of the largest whitewater rivers is led today by American boatmen schooled in the Big Drops of the West. You can find Grand Canyon veterans pushing back the frontier of river running in Alaska, Africa, and Asia. They have traveled north to run the Chilko, Stikine, and Alsek Rivers in British Columbia and the Susitna near Anchorage, Alaska. Tributaries of the Nile high on the Ethiopian plateau are starting to be explored, and a few western river runners have brought their boats to the main stem of the Zaire (formerly Congo) River below Kinshasa. The biggest runnable drops of all may well prove to be on those rivers that drain the great Himalayan massif in Central Asia. Fed by the snowpack and powered by the vertical drop of the world's high-est peaks, the upper reaches of the Ganges, Indus, and Yangtze prom-ise the ultimate in whitewater. It is good to know that a few Big Drops remain to be run.

We undertook this book because we sensed that whitewater boating in the American West has entered a new era. The people who made early whitewater history are gone. Regrettably, no historian will ever collect the experiences of such pioneers as Nat Galloway. The second generation of western boatmen, the men and women who followed the explorers and organized the first commercial operations, is also pass-ing from the scene. Their stories exist in perishable form—in the talk of boatmen around campfires and in the bars of small western towns. It was time, we thought, to gather and preserve this history before it, too, disappeared down the stream of time.

We also hoped to dramatize the fact that Big Drops, for all their might, are highly vulnerable. Dam builders characteristically eye whitewater with as much enthusiasm as boatmen. Stored behind con-crete, the energy that once propelled a boat can turn a turbine. In the West dams are both agent and classic symbol of the civilizing process. In reasonable numbers they enhance our lives, but the balance is hard to maintain. A major portion of the greatest whitewater in the West has gone the way of the Indian, the buffalo, and the redwood; we should think of the rapids that remain as a rare and endangered species. There are far fewer major rapids left in the West than there are wilderness areas or even grizzly bears. Big Drops, and the wild rivers that create them, are in fact the rarest outdoor recreational resource, and already dams have been seriously proposed that would inundate every Big Drop discussed in the following pages. They deserve instead our best preservation efforts. Without them wilderness whitewater boating will exist only as history.

We are grateful for our friends of many western river miles: Blaine and Penny Braniff, Rob Braniff, Keith and Becky Boman, Hugh and Lou Greer, Jim and Meredith McKittrick and Jim Jr., John Hartman, Rachael Hartman, Scott Hartman, C. Ray Varley, Rick Beguelin, Jim Joslyn, Gary and Diane Goodheart, Phil and Pam McLenden. Jan Collins and Sandy Nash have been with us through most of the Big Drops on the rivers and off, and Laura and Jennie Nash have bailed us out of trouble on more than one occasion.

From veteran river runners, whom we think of as the second generation following the explorers, we have drawn valuable assistance. These people made river history as well as interpreted it: Martin Litton, Fred and Maggie Eiseman, Georgie Clark (better known on the rivers as Georgie White), Jack Currey, Otis "Dock" Marston, Jack Reyonds, P. T. Reilly, Ted and Don Hatch, Bill Belknap, Bryce Whitmore, Walt Blackadar, and Ken Sleight.

Professionals in federal river and land management offices were generous with their help. We are especially grateful to Marvin Jensen, Carl Rust, Robert Yearout, Steve Martin, Sam Warren, Dave Ochsner, and Wilbur L. Rusho.

For sharing their experiences on western rivers with us, we thank J. Cort Conley, Verne Huser, Jim Campbell, Dick Barker, Bart Henderson, Tom Olson, Frank Ewing, Ron Hayes, A. C. Ekker, Pete Mills, Don Neff, Ron Smith, William McGinnis, John Dondero, John D. Hunt, Walter Rist, Art Woodworth, Regan and O'Connor Dale, Dee Holladay, Kim Crumbo, Don Harris, Joe Munroe, R. P. Helfrich, Art Gallenson, Vladimir Kovalik, Mike Ferguson, John Blaustein, Richard Bangs, and George Wendt.

Finally, we are grateful, both as boatmen and authors, to the rivers themselves for the physical and aesthetic challenges that go with the flow.

ROBERT O. COLLINS   RODERICK NASH

March 1978
Santa Barbara, California

One

Clavey Falls

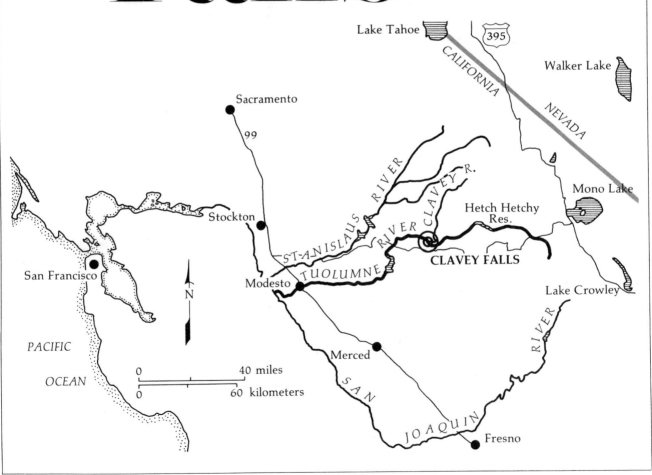

We said there warn't no home like a raft, after all. Other places do seem so cramped up and smothery, but a raft don't. You feel mighty free and easy and comfortable on a raft.

MARK TWAIN

Along with large rocks, gravel bars, and resistant bedrock formations, a river's rate of descent creates Big Drops. The slope of a stream is usually measured in feet per mile, and some comparisons are useful in putting the Tuolumne (pronounced to-OL-uh-mee) River and Clavey Falls into perspective.

A mature river like the Mississippi lumbers from St. Louis to New Orleans at a rate of descent of about two feet per mile—just enough to keep Old Man River rolling along. The Colorado is a much younger, hence steeper, watercourse. Through the Grand Canyon of Arizona it drops 2,167 feet in 279 miles, an average of just under eight feet per mile. Water flowing down this kind of slope produces an alternating pattern of major rapids followed by mile-long calm stretches. Oregon's Rogue River averages 12.4 feet per mile, and its rapids are steeper and more frequent than those of the Grand Canyon. A still sharper rate of descent is found on the Middle Fork of the Salmon River in Idaho, which races downstream at an average of 27 feet per mile. In high water conditions, a river like this, or the Selway, just to the north, seems like one continuous rapid.

Then there is the Tuolumne. Pounding down a deep canyon through the golden foothills of California's Sierra Nevada, this river's runnable section drops 54 feet per mile, or seven times the rate of the Colorado in the Grand Canyon and twice the rate of the Middle Fork. Particularly during high water, many boatmen regard the Tuolumne as the most challenging raftable river in the West. It is a relentless force, with rapids blending one into the other; only occasionally can a boatman escape the

Here and in the following two photos, Dennis Vitarelli is at the oars of a classic military surplus "ten-man" raft, on a left-side run of Clavey Falls. After slamming down the main falls, he regains control and looks anxiously downstream at the remainder of the rapid. By Art Vitarelli.

grip of the current to catch his breath and ease strained muscles. Then, as he looks back upstream, the Tuolumne appears to be a white staircase descending the Sierra.

The unusual name of this unusual river has its origins in the local Indian dialect. *Talmalamne* meant a cluster of stone wigwams. But given the multipurpose functions of most aboriginal words, *talmalamne* may well have referred to the circle of tepee-shaped granite peaks that form the main crest of the Sierra at the Tuolumne's source. Mount Lyell, 13,114 feet, is one such pointed landmark. The meltwater of two small glaciers clinging to its northwestern face starts the river.

In the next phase of its 158-mile length, the Tuolumne lives in high country, flowing through forested valleys that spread out at 8,600 feet into the largest upland meadow in the Sierra. A paved road brings thousands of visitors to Tuolumne Meadows every summer. Below this point, however, the river is seldom seen as it enters Muir Gorge and rages along the bed of a deep, precipitous canyon. A century ago John Muir scrambled through here, the din of falling water pounding in his ears. No one boats the Tuolumne at this elevation.

At 3,800 feet—still in Yosemite National Park—the river dies for a time. In 1913, after a protracted controversy, Congress authorized a dam at the lower end of Hetch Hetchy Valley. Completed ten years later, it created a granite-walled reservoir in a place once considered the aesthetic equal of Yosemite Valley, a few miles to the south. Many people today believe the Tuolumne ends in the Hetch Hetchy impoundment, its water diverted into aqueducts and destined for power plants, irrigation ditches, and the pipes and faucets of San Francisco. Some of the Tuolumne does, of course, go this route, but enough water remains in the river below Hetch Hetchy to make possible one of the West's most exciting whitewater rides. Indeed, to give the dam builders their due, the released water from hydroelectric operations has the beneficial effect of making the Tuolumne runnable in California's dry summer months.

Thirteen river below the Hetch Hetchy spillways, the Tuolumne can be run by experts in kayaks, decked whitewater canoes, and modified rafts. Eight miles farther, at Lumsden Camp, the increasing amount of water and decreasing rate of descent usually permit the use of standard inflatable rafts. Barring mishaps, it takes only two hours to run the five miles to Clavey Falls, but the Tuolumne can spoil the best laid plans. Regardless of their skill, first-time boatmen on the Tuolumne pay their initiation dues to the river in the form of broken oars, upsets, and torn boats. The United States Forest Service, which manages the river once it leaves Yosemite National Park, used to place its registration box not at the put-in, but after the first two rapids, on the theory that any boatman who reached the registration point in one piece was either good enough or lucky enough to have a reasonable chance of completing the run.

The Tuolumne moves so quickly and drops so precipitously around so many blind corners that boatmen require several runs to decipher its obstacle course. The rapids present several possible channels and the need for an instant decision in very fast water. The wrong choice is quickly rewarded, and the unfortunate boatman is left draped around a rock, pinned on a log, or overturned at the base of an eight-foot waterfall. It is, of course, possible to walk down and scout the whitewater ahead, but how much river can one memorize? The Tuolumne's rapids are so long and complex that keeping a planned route in mind is extremely difficult. Once on the racing water, chosen landmarks or "keys" blur into a pastiche of waves, rocks, and shoreline vegetation. Moreover, the Tuolumne is what boatmen call a "technical" river. It consistently demands a degree of precision in rowing and finesse in reading and running fast water, seldom required on the larger western rivers. Broken boats and bodies are commonplace on the Tuolumne. Those theoretical two hours to Clavey Falls can easily become two days, and Clavey can put a permanent end to a river journey.

Just above Clavey Falls the Tuolumne relents a bit, as if to anticipate its biggest drop. After threading slots only inches wider than the raft and setting up to ride down a succession of sudden, sharp ledges, it is a blessing to sit at the oars and look at the scenery. Then ahead on the right appears a flash of whitewater that first-timers mistake for Clavey Falls. It is, rather, the last few yards of the Clavey River, blasting through boulders to make a grand entrance into the Tuolumne.

The Clavey is a major tributary with branches reaching sixty river miles to the top of 9,000-foot ridges north of the Tuolumne's canyon. The name comes from an English immigrant, William Clavey, whose widow and son tried to run cattle from the 1890s to the 1940s in the chaparral-choked foothills between the Tuolumne and the river that bears their name. The Clavey funnels water and, during storms, large rocks, down a very steep gradient along the north side of Jawbone Ridge. Tumbling into the Tuolumne, these boulders make Clavey Falls. The Tuolumne powers through them and smashes into a sheer, two-

hundred-foot cliff opposite the mouth of the Clavey River. The cliff restrains the river, forcing it into the boulders. The result is a long, spectacular clash of an irresistible force against an immovable object that leaves even the most hardened boatmen stunned when they see it for the first time.

Clavey Falls is divided into two main channels by a large island of boulders that clogs the middle of the Tuolumne. The flow on the right side is larger, but leaps fifteen feet down a rock-studded chute into a maelstrom of green and white. The vertical drop of the left channel is only half that of the main falls on the right, but a left-side run brings boats dangerously close to the base of the cliff and its churning whirlpools. Below the boulder island, the right and left channels converge just in time to plunge through a formidable hole, and twenty feet farther on, the current splits savagely around a large rock. Below this obstacle come two sharp drops in low water or a series of large standing waves in high, and finally a tight, rocky bend to the left. From the top of the main falls to the bend is almost a third of a mile.

The challenge of running Clavey Falls begins with the landing to scout the rapid. Because of the cliff, scouting must be done from the right shoreline, which also features the Clavey River confluence. Usually the Clavey is too fast and too deep to ford safely, so the only alternative is to remain in the boats until its mouth is passed and then pull to the right bank. The maneuver sounds easier than it is since only thirty feet separate the Clavey confluence and the start of the fast water at the top of Clavey Falls; moreover, the Clavey enters the Tuolumne with a force sufficient to kick a boat into the main current and propel it straight for the falls. With everyone intensely aware of the Big Drop just ahead, there can be momentary panic as the boatman powerstrokes onto the little gravel beach just a few yards from the brink.

With bow lines tied and double-tied to brush or a boulder, it is time to go and look at Clavey Falls. Styles vary. Some boatmen dash down the shoreline, leaping rocks and splashing through small pools. They hurry to wait, unmoving, on the ledge below which the main falls thunder. Others try to play it cooler, perhaps lighting a smoke or joking with passengers; but soon they too stand silently on the ledge over the falls. By unspoken agreement boatmen at first say little in such situations. Their eyes move constantly, searching for routes. After a time someone will venture an opinion. It will be discussed, modified, and discussed again with much pointing and even stone-tossing in an effort to pinpoint a location in the rapid.

On a right-side run the first difficulty is the small rocks above the main falls. The boatman must pick his way through them carefully in order to reach the lip of the falls with his bow pointed straight down the only clear chute. Too far right and he will plunge into a churning white vortex that could hold an overturned boat and its former passengers indefinitely. If he misses the chute in the other direction, the boat will hurtle over the lip of the falls to smash on the jumble of sharp, black rocks in the center of the river. The least serious mistake is to slip into the main chute sideways; the boat will simply capsize and its occupants swim the rest of Clavey Falls. Entered correctly, boats in the chute tilt sharply downward at angles approaching sixty degrees. Standing almost vertically on his foot brace, the boatman anticipates the jolt at the bottom on the fall. Two water-covered ledges flash by underneath; then dagger-sharp rocks appear to the left and right. Oars are useless at this point. Even if a boat impelled by such force could be controlled, the amount of air beaten into the water by the fall makes it futile to dig and pull a blade; you cannot pull against bubbles and foam. Accurate prior positioning is the only key to a successful passage through the top of Clavey.

The alternate way to run the first part of these falls is down the left-hand channel, to the left of the boulder island and close to the cliff. In low water this run is mandatory. It begins with a row across the Tuolumne; there is a little room on the left bank before the cliff to land and read the water. At first glance it appears impossible to get a boat through the jumble of table-size rocks with which this route through the rapid begins. The lesser of many evils seems to be a narrow, twisting passage about fifteen feet out from the shore. The current is fast here, and the boatman must pivot repeatedly to keep from jamming his raft against a rock. There is little room to maneuver. Broken oars are a distinct possibility, and to lose control in this way would be disastrous since the twisting slot drops boats into a foaming pool just above the falls. There is only time for one, perhaps two, strokes, and they must accomplish two things: keep the boat off the cliff face and straighten it for the plunge over the fall. The frightening price of not making effective use of the moment in the pool is to have a boat pinned into a crevice in the cliff. Held as in a vise by the raging current, the boat fills with water and either capsizes or moves sluggishly sideways over the fall to a probable flip.

Once below this fall, the worst may seem to be over, but Clavey holds more surprises. One moment a boat is ten feet out from the cliff in five-foot waves and more or less in control, the next it is up against the rock wall. The explanation is the powerful current pouring down the right side of the rapid and intersecting the left-hand route at this point. Anything floating, such as a riverboat, goes along for an unwelcome ride headlong into the cliff. Only by anticipating the sideways blast, angling the boat, and rowing hard can boatmen avoid eating rock. It is no different for boats using the right channel. So great is their speed coming off the chute over the main falls that they are propelled straight across the Tuolumne and into the cliff.

Some boatmen try to fight the hydraulics and keep off the cliff. It is also possible to go with the flow and play the cliff as one would the side of a pool table, deliberately allowing the boat to ricochet and, according to the angle of rebound, making the necessary adjustments to ride through what is known as "the big hole in Clavey." A large rock, eight feet off the cliff, is the problem. In low water it is exposed, inviting boats to wrap around its upstream side; quick thinking and rowing are essential to dodge it on either side. Higher flows cover the rock, but create a monster hole. Most boatmen simply straighten out and slam into its center. They know their rubber boats will fold into a "V," but they count on the speed of the current to spit them out on the downstream side.

All that now remains of Clavey Falls is a long, dragon-shaped rock with a sharp upstream edge that can slice rubber like a razor, and another hundred yards of waves and ledges. Invariably a boat is so heavy with water at this point that control is difficult. With a final effort the boatman pulls to the right and attempts to land in the fast water along the steep right bank. Many fail in this endeavor and are obliged to run several hundred more yards through another, very rocky rapid before they can relax.

Within a half day's drive of fifteen million people, it is remarkable that the Tuolumne was not run until the 1960s. The first known attempt was that of a group of fishermen from Sacramento who thought it would be easier to float the river than walk along its banks. They were

in for a big surprise. By the time they reached Clavey Falls both boats and morale were in tatters, and they wisely portaged the Big Drop. Their report, and that of the few hikers who reached the bottom of the Tuolumne's canyon, discouraged river runners until 1965, when Knoel Debord, a Sierra Club member from Oakland, took a kayak down the river. Debord portaged Clavey, as did Gerald Meral and Richard Sunderland on November 4, 1968, when they took kayaks down the Tuolumne. Meral and Sunderland did, however, exercise the privilege of pioneers and name several pools and rapids. Excited by what they had seen in the canyon, the men returned the following May and, with Jim Morehouse, kayaked the river. Its flow was 4,800 cubic feet per second—ideal for an attempt at the right channel in Clavey Falls—but inexperience bred conservatism, and again they carried their boats around the rapid. The first known run of Clavey occurred on July 20, 1969, at a flow of 4,000 cubic feet per second. Sierra Club kayakers, including a fourteen-year-old girl named India Fleming, made the run without incident.

The summer of 1969 also marked the beginning of rafting on the Tuolumne. Bryce Whitmore, a veteran California river outfitter, had been searching for an alternative to the Stanislaus River for his commercial trips. He wanted a longer, more challenging journey on a less crowded river. Whitmore and a team of his best boatmen tested the Tuolumne for a week in late July and found the flat "Huck Finn" rafts they used quite capable of handling the river. At Clavey, however, they lined the rafts down the right shoreline. The next season Whitmore scheduled several trips on the Tuolumne, but his brochure carried the warning that the river "requires the best equipment, most skilled oarsmen, and lightly loaded rafts." The run, he added, was "not recommended for your first whitewater trip, or for the faint hearted." But, he concluded, the Tuolumne offered more thrills and more challenge than any eighteen river miles in the American West. Few who made the run with Whitmore disagreed, even though they continued to line their boats around Clavey Falls.

In May 1970 the authors became the first rafters to run Clavey Falls. Bryce Whitmore told us the Tuolumne run would take lots of time, and that was an understatement. We spent hours crashing through thickets of manzanita and poison oak along the river to study its rapids, but we still had trouble. One of our boats ripped open on a rock, lost air, and wallowed helplessly down a quarter mile of rock-strewn waves. Another wrapped around a rock, filled with several tons of water, and had to be extricated with fixed ropes from shore. Running scared by the time we reached Clavey Falls, we landed well above on the right and barely managed to stumble across the torrent coming down the Clavey River. The sight of the rapid left us limp; there seemed no way it could be run. We paced the right shoreline again and again, memorizing the rocks, waves, and currents.

Today's perspective is different, but since no one had yet put a raft down this Big Drop, we could not be sure if a boat would make it down the falls, between the rocks, and through the big hole. At length we decided to portage and walked back to where the boats were tied. But our minds continued to churn, and as we reached the boats we turned to look back downstream to where the Tuolumne vanished into the space above Clavey Falls. "Why not?" we thought simultaneously. After all, we had come to run, not walk, the Tuolumne, and it was precisely challenges like this that had brought us to wild rivers in the first place.

Once we were committed, the run went smoothly enough. It was unnerving above the falls, slaloming through random rocks, aiming for a chute we saw only in our memories. At what seemed like the last possible second, the chute opened ahead of us. For a moment we hung poised on the brink. Then, unbelievable speed. The rocks we had studied from shore for so long went past in a blur. Ahead was the cliff: we leaned on the ten-foot oars, not really rowing but straining, in a kind of isometric exercise, against a constant force. Even so, one boat glanced off the rock wall. The beauty of inflatables is that they bounce rather than shatter or dent, and this time we won the billiard game between rubber and rock. Rebounding off the cliff, the raft spun into perfect position for the big hole. It seemed much larger on the river than it had from the shore, but there was a thread of water moving through the reversing wave. We adjusted to hit it square on; then, with Grand Canyon instincts, we pushed with the oars to increase the raft's momentum going into the hole, thus giving it a better chance of popping through. It did, but knee-deep with water, and there was no time and no one to bail. We struggled to keep the unwieldy craft facing downstream as we plowed over and through the lower waves and ledges. In one sense the weight was a blessing—a boat carrying an extra ton of water has a low center of gravity and is very hard to flip. In landing such a heavy boat, however, you pay the price. Only after several abortive attempts could we make the raft stick into a semblance of an eddy along the right shore, leap out, take a turn with the bow line around a rock, and notice our hands shake as we tied up.

In time others came to try their hands at Clavey Falls. Some got through and some did not, but everyone learned this was a "boatman's" as opposed to an "equipment" rapid. The distinction is clear and important. On big water, such as the Grand Canyon's Lava Falls, the equipment brings you through. A big boat compensates for the boatman's mistakes; it may get pounded, but it will float out the downstream end right side up. It is almost (but not quite) impossible to flip one of the giant thirty-three-foot pontoons, or multiple pontoons. These big rigs are usually run straight down the middle of a rapid. They eat every hole, yet they flush out. Try the same technique on the Tuolumne, and your trip, if not your life, will end in the first mile. The Tuolumne is a "boatman's" river because expertise in reading whitewater and rowing it precisely is mandatory for a successful run. A mile on the Tuolumne calls for more maneuvering than a hundred miles on the Colorado. But with Sierra snowfields melting down the Tuolumne in May and June, it is sometimes the case that neither big boats nor skilled boatmen ensure a safe passage.

One June a few years ago a group of campers near the Tuolumne put-in were startled by the sudden appearance at their evening fire of a boatman who worked for a leading western river outfitter. He seemed shaken, but after several cups of coffee began the story of his day at Clavey Falls. Because of the high water his company had canceled its scheduled trip and bused the would-be passengers out of the canyon. The boatmen, however, decided to run for their own fun. There were two boats: a rowed raft carrying two men and a stripped-down boat which five persons attempted to steer with canoe paddles. With many of the Tuolumne's rocks covered by the high water, they shot down to Clavey Falls in an hour. No one had ever attempted the Big Drop with so much water in the river, but the crew was in a "go for it" mood. The raft with oars ran first, careening down the main falls and somehow negotiating the quarter mile of ten-foot waves beyond. The paddled raft ran second, with the boatman at the campfire among its crew. He was washed over the side below the main falls and recalled nothing but an occasional gasp for air until he was pulled from the river by the rowers at the end of the rapid. The three men waited and waited, peering upstream for a sight of the paddled raft and the four remaining members of the group. Nothing appeared, and, fearing the worst, they ran up the right shoreline. Still no raft. Then they saw it, pinned into an eddy against the cliff and trapped so securely that the four remaining paddlers were helpless in their efforts to work back into the downstream flow. The possibility of their swamping and drowning in that whirlpool was desperately evident. The cliff prevented any rescue from river level, so the three on the right shoreline ran back to their boat, crossed the Tuolumne in calmer water below Clavey, and climbed the back side of the cliff with a long rope and some rock-climbing hardware known as Jumar ascenders. Locating a big ponderosa pine on the top of the cliff directly over the beleaguered boat, the rescuers tied on and lowered their rope. One by one the people on the river climbed the line a hundred vertical feet to safety. The last task was to pull the empty raft up the cliff and carry it below Clavey Falls.

Whitewater boating had barely begun on the Tuolumne when it seemed destined to end. On December 4, 1968, the San Francisco Public Utilities Commission released a report proposing more intensive use of the river's "remaining power drop" for hydroelectric generation. A new dam below the one already restraining the river at Hetch Hetchy Valley was proposed, along with a series of tunnels and a generating plant right at Clavey Falls. Actually this was repetition, not innovation. In 1907 the Tuolumne Electric Company erected a hand-fitted stone powerhouse a mile below Clavey. It supplied electricity to rim communities until 1938, when a giant storm put 38,000 cubic feet per second in the Tuolumne and cleaned out all but the foundations of the bridge and building.

Initially San Francisco's 1968 proposal did not elicit much opposition. Few knew what was at stake, but the Sierra Club, remembering Hetch Hetchy like the Alamo, was instinctively suspicious of the city's plans for the river. Rather than build new dams, the Club argued that the existing ones on the Tuolumne should be removed. As Michael McCloskey explained, "We've already had the experience of reclaiming logged-over land for parks. We think it's time the same concept be applied to dams." By the early 1970s McCloskey, along with many environmentally conscious Americans, was asking quite seriously if dams added to or detracted from the quality of a society's life. In a state that had intensively utilized its flowing water and, in the case of the Stanislaus River, was about to eliminate its most popular whitewater run, a wild Tuolumne was an especially precious resource. The United States Congress, at least, held this view. On January 3, 1975, it designated the Tuolumne a "study" river for the National Wild and Scenic Rivers System. This action placed a moratorium on further development and mandated public hearings. Congress will ultimately decide the issue (probably not before 1980), and Clavey Falls has a fighting chance at a future of turning boats rather than turbines.

Meanwhile the rapid continues to generate improbable stories. One evening Bryce Whitmore camped several miles below Clavey on the big beach opposite Indian Creek. As the rafts were being unloaded, it became painfully clear that the box of cooking pots was missing. To his chagrin Whitmore remembered leaving it in his garage at home. Lacking the means even to boil water for coffee, the party scoured the bushes for rusted pots prospectors might have abandoned, or any container that would hold water. As dusk fell, Whitmore saw a box floating down the middle of the Tuolumne. Someone rowed out and brought it into camp. To the astonishment of the hungry campers, it contained a complete set of pots and pans. There was no explanation, except prayers, for its presence until several other packs and bags appeared in the river. Then an overturned raft floated past. Whitmore towed it to shore, but found no sign of its former occupants. By this time it was dark and dinner was simmering in the newly acquired pots; then out of the darkness came a shout from upstream, and into the circle of firelight staggered four disheveled river runners. They told how they had flipped in the big hole in Clavey that afternoon. Their boat had continued on downstream too fast to follow on foot through the Tuolumne's dense riparian vegetation, so there was no alternative but to walk on down the river in the hope of finding the boat caught in an eddy. Just as they were about to give up the search and climb out of the canyon, they saw the light of Whitmore's fire through the trees. Dinner, served from their own pots, never tasted better.

Two

Rainie Falls

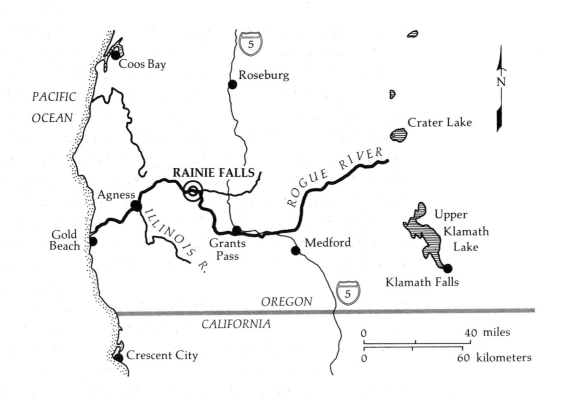

There exist in rapids oscillations beyond prediction, and your misfortune may be to hit that build-up at exactly the wrong time.

DOUG REINER

You are on your way to run the Rogue. Depending on where you started, you may be driving west through the hot, treeless Great Basin of the western states. As the open miles of Utah and Nevada slide by, and the temperature soars into the hundreds, it is tempting to fantasize about the green canyons of Oregon's premier river.

The Rogue is born at 5,200 feet in the Cascade Range near the ancient exploded volcano that now contains Crater Lake. It starts as a small mountain stream, then drops into the broad, fertile Rogue River Valley, where the farms and orchards around Medford and Grants Pass are usually clouded by haze from lumber mills. The Rogue moves on, searching for the Pacific. The Klamath and Siskiyou mountains stand in its way, and over the ages the river has cut a canyon. The best scenery and whitewater are here. There are no roads. People refer to this stretch of the river as the "wild Rogue."

Driving west across the desert, one thinks of the deep green forests and their towering trees: western red cedar, Douglas fir, Port Orford cedar, western hemlock, sugar pine. On the ocean side of the coast ranges, fog and rain create a lush vegetation and a junglelike understory—myrtle, rhododendron, azalea, dogwood, dense skeins of wild grape, and an astonishing variety of ferns. After three hundred searing miles of a Nevada summer, it seems impossible that such things exist.

To think of the Rogue is to think of wildlife. No one who has run the river forgets the sight of a great blue heron, poised in the shallows, still as stone. When the boats come too near, the bird vaults upward and cruises the spaces between the shoreline pines with slow, powerful wingbeats. Often there is ocean-born fog on the lower river. Through it deer move like wraiths. At night, on your ground cloth, you can hear their hooves as they graze within yards of your camp. The Roosevelt elk are more wary, preferring the high ridges. But black bears prowl the river banks; you see their tracks on Solitude Bar, and at night they crash through the brush, annoyed at the intruders who have displaced them. Float quietly, look carefully, and your chances are good for seeing the best river folk of them all—the otters. They are totally at home in water, and their frolicking always brings admiring smiles to less skillful river travelers. Mergansers streak up and down the river corridor; kingfishers dart across it to snatch a fly; and high overhead the osprey and the eagle circle imperiously, eyeing the blue thread set in green velvet as it moves to the sea. Such images make the desert miles seem shorter.

The Rogue has been called "the fishingest river in the West." In summer it is too warm for much action, but as the year wanes the salmon and steelhead runs begin. You can stand at a major rapid like Rainie Falls and watch one of the greatest shows in the West. At unpredictable intervals a great fish, fighting the current to return to the place of its birth, throws its twenty, thirty, or forty pounds into the air. Arching over the tumbling water, tail lashing for added momentum, the fish tries to climb a wall of water. Few make it up the main falls of Rainie; the rest fall back into the white cauldron at its base. Later they find easier going up side channels and continue on their ancient mission of self-perpetuation.

Rich in fish, game, and timber, the watershed of the Rogue inevitably became a bone of contention among those who lived there and those who came to the river later. The Indians were the first inhabitants along the canyons of the wild Rogue. They were Takelmas, but the Europeans who began to trickle into southwestern Oregon in the late 1830s called them simply the Rogues. Isolated in the canyon, they had little contact with the coastal Indians and none with the early explorers and fur traders. They hunted deer, elk, otter, and beaver, but most of all they derived their sustenance from the river. They would wait patiently on the ledge below Rainie Falls to spear the salmon and steelhead rising in the pool below. The Rogues had lived from time beyond memory in this lovely land of fish and animals and flowing water.

The trappers were the first white men to venture into the canyon of the Rogue. Peter Skene Ogden led a party of Hudson's Bay Company trappers into the valley of the Rogue in March 1827. Others followed. Michel La Framboise led a brigade of trappers into the Rogue River Valley in 1833. But the trapper presence was fragmentary, and in just over a decade settlers were following their footprints. But settlers wanted land for farms, not the rugged country of the wild Rogue, and for them the Rogue River Valley was a place to pass through. Langford W. Hastings, in his *Emigrants' Guide to Oregon and California*, described the Rogue of today's river runners: "Its current is very rapid, and it has numerous falls and rapids, which much obstruct its navigation, even for boats and canoes."

Relations between the Rogues and the newcomers were hostile from the beginning and remained so until the Rogues were finally forced from the river country. As early as 1834 the Rogues were attacking the settlers passing between the Willamette Valley and California. Every year thereafter they assaulted the wagon trains, provoking increasing hostility on the part of the Oregon settlers. The settlers, though, were going through to more fertile land and learned not to linger and re-taliate. Not so the miners who came out of California in 1851 and spilled over the Siskiyou Range and down into the Rogue River Valley. Unlike the farmers, the miners were a tough, brawling, barbarous lot, pre-pared to fight anyone for their claims, and quick to rally against any and all who might oppose them. Unhindered by law, order, or any author-ity, they killed indiscriminately and without remorse. They began with the Rogues.

From 1851 until June 1856 the Rogues and the miners, known as volunteer companies, fought for the land of the Rogue River. Harass-ment, pitched battles, and treachery, punctuated by a truce in 1853 euphemistically called a peace, characterized the relations between the miners and the Indians. Truces seldom last, and in the autumn of 1855 the volunteer companies, supported by federal troops, launched the final campaign against the Indians. The Rogues fought back against miners and troopers first at Galice, where today many river trips begin. The Indians retired to Grave Creek, a mile and a half above Rainie Falls. The volunteers and troops pursued; they were driven back on the high ridge above Grave, but rallied and followed the Indians into the depths of Whiskey Creek, a mile below Rainie Falls. Here they could not dislodge the Rogues, and the campaign was abandoned. The Rogues were left alone to winter by Rainie Falls, but their respite from fighting was only temporary. In the spring of 1856 the volunteers and federal troops again took the field, and at Big Meadows on the Big Bend of the Rogue, the Rogues fought their last battle. Defeated, they surrendered and on June 10, 1856, left for the Siletz Reservation at the headwaters of the Willamette.

Silence settled over the Rogue River Canyon. The human drama had reached its conclusion, and today, driving over the Nevada desert toward the river, one might think of those tragic days. But they were not without adventure, and adventure, after all, is still sought in our own turbulent times. And so, in the shimmering heat of the desert, the mind wanders to the Rogue's ultimate test—running Rainie Falls.

For boatmen the upper river poses few problems. Children from families camped in the roadside park dabble about the river on inner tubes and air mattresses. Where the road ends at Grave Creek, the river becomes more serious. The rapid below the bridge is the first major rapid; its deceptive boulders have broken many oars, punctured many tubes, and caused not a few river parties to question the wisdom of attempting the trip. It is always sad to see dreams die, but Grave Creek Rapids is a well-placed filter. Better to wipe out here, where cars are within walking distance, than to abort a trip deep in the roadless canyons ahead.

There are other memorable rapids on the Rogue. In low water Tyee Rapids demands a run that literally kisses the grassy right bank.

A "catacraft" designed by Bryce Whitmore about to enter the chaotic, reversing waves at the base of Rainie. By Bryce Whitmore.

Wildcat offers two routes around an island at the entrance, then options end as boaters must pick their way down a rock-studded chute. The pieces of broken boats decorating it are incentive enough to make the right moves. Black Bar Falls is a succession of sudden, six-foot drops—no problem for larger boats taking them bow first, but that position is easier to visualize than to attain in the complex currents of a narrow gorge.

Most boatmen who choose to portage or line around Rainie Falls regard Blossom Bar as the most demanding rapid on the river. The first problem is to locate the rapid. It is easy to float on calm water past the huge rocks at the entrance and suddenly find it necessary to row for your life. Wiser boatmen climb the cliff on the right and scout the river as it tears through a "rock garden" the length of a football field. A successful run involves at least three total reversals in direction: right, left, right, and sometimes left again. It is necessary to pull hard each time, stop the boat, spin it, and pull hard back again. Timing is the key, and only the very best oarsmen avoid a "billiard shot" off one of Blossom's many rocks. (There were more of them before the 1930s, when Glen Wooldridge used explosives to blast a wider channel for his boats.)

Mule Creek Canyon, perhaps even more than Blossom Bar, lingers in the mind after a run down the Rogue. It is more a tunnel than a rapid in the usual sense, and the adventure begins when the Rogue, normally 50 to 100 feet wide, cuts a narrow trench into bedrock. Narrow, in this case, means *narrow;* most of Mule Creek Canyon is only ten to fifteen feet wide. At the Coffee Pot, an aptly named, bubbling, circular chamber in the rock, the whole Rogue River moves through an eight-foot passageway in solid rock. Turn a seventeen-foot raft sideways in here, and you stay for a while. Hit a driftwood log jammed sideways, and you tear a boat in half. Fortunately there are no ledges or midstream rocks in Mule Creek Canyon, but it is always a sobering experience to enter the mouth of the longest, narrowest passage of any major river in the West. Near the end of the chasm there is a reward. Look quickly to the left and spot a graceful waterfall, bordered by ferns, dropping in several stages over the canyon wall into the Rogue.

And then there is Rainie Falls, the unforgettable Big Drop of the Rogue. Even the name is difficult. It originated as a memorial of sorts to a nineteenth-century prospector named Reamy or Ramey, who was killed by Indians in the vicinity of the falls. But Reamy soon became Rainy or, as the United States Forest Service standardized it, Rainie. The mist that perpetually hangs over the drop may well have inspired the change.

Rainie is more of a pure waterfall than any of the other Big Drops. There are no rocks to dodge, no intricate route to follow. In one clean, quick leap the Rogue plunges fifteen vertical feet over a ledge. At the bottom is a frightening spectacle: a chaos of white, churning water that on first glance appears destined to swallow and hold any boat exposed to it. And that's all there is to Rainie. Below the drop the Rogue quickly regains its composure. Rainie is both the shortest and, potentially, the most dangerous of the Big Drops.

The river above the falls is as calm as the river below. There is plenty of time to hear the booming thunder, note the misty rain rising in the air, and see the Rogue drop out of sight. Boatmen land on the left, tying to small trees whose bark has been worn smooth over the years by the bow lines of river travelers. A long ledge of rock running parallel to the river affords an excellent vantage. Rainie is also the Big Drop to which you can get the closest; the falls drops away virtually beneath your feet.

At Rainie Falls you understand the situation as soon as you walk up to inspect the run, for it lacks the sophistication of other Big Drops. The river plummets smoothly over the lip and down the face of the ledge. So far, so good. But then the Rogue goes crazy. Technically, what happens is a reversal. The water dropping over the falls plunges to the bottom of the river channel, and, deflected upward out of this hole, mounds into a back-curling wave six to eight feet high. So strong is this down-up-and-around motion of the water that the topmost levels of the river actually flow upstream. A boat, log, or body going over the falls is first driven down almost vertically near the bottom of the riverbed. The next motion is sharply up on the curler wave and on downstream—perhaps. The alternative—and always a very real possibility in Rainie—is to remain in the hole between the falls itself and the reversing wave. A boat would eventually be spit out, but nothing that breathes oxygen could be expected to survive more than a minute or two.

The prospect of being trapped by the current at the base of the falls is uppermost in the mind of the boatman standing on the rocks at the lip of Rainie. He studies the water, repeatedly allowing his eyes to follow a single patch of water over the falls and into the hole. His hope is to find a pattern, a highway of water that consistently moves through the reversal and might therefore carry his boat along with it. But the complex hydraulics below a drop like Rainie are difficult to follow. At a given moment there is an order of sorts to the shape and direction of the boiling waves, and the same order will reappear in an irregular cycle. In between, other things are happening. The inescapable conclusion is that a successful run, even survival, in a drop like this depends in good part on chance. There is no way of calculating what the moving water will be doing the moment your boat is passing over, through, and under it. Catch the cycle at one phase, and you can pop through with astonishing ease. A second or two later, in exactly the same place, you may be going against the grain with the river hammering and tearing at your boat and body. It is that element of unpredictability that causes boatmen to stand and stare at Rainie Falls.

There are several approaches to the curved lip of the falls. The far left has the advantage of a secondary buffer wave reflecting off a rock. Riding it down lessens the jolt at the bottom but exposes boats to the danger of a sideways or quartering attitude. The big reversal makes quick work of boats that do not hit it square, bow to stern. The right side offers a better chance of taking the reversal directly on the bow, but the drop is very steep. A boatman running the right discovers that instead of sitting down he is standing, feet braced against the rowing frame in front of him. The crunching jolt at the bottom folds the rubber boat around him. Should he fail to brace solidly, knees slightly bent like a skier absorbing the shock of a mogul, he will almost surely be pitched over the bow of the boat into the raging water at the base of the falls.

These realities give Rainie its reputation. They explain why it has a rating of VI on the international scale of whitewater difficulty: "Very dangerous. Limits of possibility. Many who inadvertently or unwittingly try this level do not survive. Experts generally leave it alone!"

In truth, many choose not to run Rainie. There are several narrow channels skirting the main falls on the right. Salmon use these partly man-built fish ladders to avoid the big ledge, and river runners can walk their boats down a series of pools. Or, closer to the falls, they can use ropes and brute strength to hold empty boats as they bump and grind over a succession of lesser ledges.

Until recently almost every river traveler on the Rogue bypassed Rainie Falls in this way. The wooden "drift boats" that Glen Wooldridge began using on the Rogue in 1915 had excellent maneuverability, but were not really designed for big waves and extreme turbulence. Wooden boats, moreover, usually came out second best in collisions with rocks such as those that line the channel immediately below Rainie Falls. So a tradition of *not* running Rainie developed among the local Oregon guides. It was said (and printed on the official river map) that a portage around Rainie was "mandatory." Some even implied it was illegal to run the falls.

This state of affairs existed with regard to the biggest rapid on the Rogue when Zane Grey arrived in Grants Pass, Oregon, on September 3, 1925. Grey was a fishing fanatic, and his best-selling westerns financed his passion. The Rogue soon became his favorite trout and salmon stream. He built a substantial cabin at Winkle Bar and visited it regularly for the fall fish runs until his death in 1939. Grey had much to say about the early attitude toward Rainie Falls. On his initial 1925 trip down the river he used four eighteen-foot skiffs, canoe-shaped craft with a narrow, blunt stern, sharp bow, and high gunwales. Each had two seats and watertight compartments at either end. Zane Grey did things in the grand manner. There were also four twenty-three-foot dories in his party. Heavier than the skiffs, they had raised bows and sterns and flared gunwales.

The Zane Grey party put in below the hamlet of Galice and experienced their first problems at Grave Creek Rapids, where jagged rocks tore open one of the skiffs. It sank immediately, a lesson not lost on later designers of multichambered inflatable rafts. Undaunted, Grey's party pressed on to Rainie Falls. None of his guides even considered running the rapid. They landed on the right on rocks that, according to Grey's journal, were "almost impossible to stand upon." Grey also recorded that all the luggage in the seven remaining boats had to be carried 300 yards around Rainie Falls. The group toiled for hours. Then it was time to bring the boats around. Grey described the process:

My boat was the fifth in line to go down the chute. I waded down the rocky channel, holding hard. There was no one to help at the moment, and I imagined that I could do it alone. When my heavy boat turned into that pitway it shot down like a flash. I could not hold the rope. My feet were jerked from under me and went aloft, while the back of my neck, my shoulder and right elbow crashed down on the rock. I was almost knocked out. Fortunately, the boat lodged below and soon the men got to it. I had all I could do for the time being to drag myself out of the water to a safe place. I thought my arm was broken but, fortunately, I had sustained only severe bruises. My heavy shoes were studded with hobnails, yet were as slippery on those infernal rocks as if they had been ice.

Looking back at Rainie from below, an idea occurred to Grey. "It'd be a good idea for the government to put their criminals in boats and send them down the Rogue to shoot the falls. If any of them got to Gold Beach (where the river enters the Pacific Ocean) alive, they'd deserve to be set free."

At extreme high water, to be sure, Rainie "fills in," becoming just a succession of rolling waves. Veteran Oregon guide Bob Pruitt ran it under such conditions in the 1950s in a wooden drift boat. People were stranded by the flood downstream, and Pruitt went to the rescue. He left Hellsgate at the improbable time of 2:00 A.M. and reached Agness, forty miles downstream, in seven hours. With the Rogue racing along at twenty miles per hour, Pruitt had little choice but to run Rainie Falls. There was virtually no chance to get to shore once his wild trip began.

In the 1960s a new generation of boatmen with new kinds of boats came to the canyons of the Rogue. Schooled in the heavy water of the Colorado and the sharp drops of the foothill streams of California's Sierra, the newcomers looked at Rainie less as an impossibility than as a supreme challenge. Their inflatable boats bent rather than shattered on impact and bounced back for more. In the event of a flip, an inflatable could serve as a giant life preserver to which people could cling. The state of the art in whitewater boating was also improving, and river runners were trying and achieving feats that left old-timers incredulous. It was tempting, standing above Rainie Falls, to "go for it," as boatmen would say. The rocky portage, as Zane Grey had reported, was laborious, time-consuming, and, in terms of injury to legs and ankles, probably just as dangerous as the main falls. But the compelling consideration for river runners, as for climbers of ice and rock walls, was the challenge. Like Everest, Rainie Falls was there. Could it be run?

Obviously there was risk involved, but river runners, like climbers, live with risk; it is what brings them to the sport in the first place. "Will I be safe on your trip?" customers frequently ask whitewater guides. "Absolutely not," one invariably replies. "The only thing I will guarantee you is that you might be killed." Then, with a twinkle in his eye, he adds, "If you want to be totally safe, never leave your bed."

Thus it came to pass that what was insanity for one generation of boatmen became a reasonable risk for another. Rainie Falls began to be run. Usually most of the passengers and essential equipment are unloaded first. Life preservers have a special value in such situations, and they are carefully adjusted and tightened. The run is scouted; the "keys" for the entry memorized. Back in the raft, inevitably, second thoughts arise: Should I go for it? Is it crazy to jeopardize boat, gear, and the success of the river trip for a possible moment of exhilarating conquest?

Exerting the usual damming effect of a Big Drop, Rainie slows the Rogue; boats move at a snail's pace as they approach the lip of the falls. The boatmen stand on their seats and look ahead, though there is not much to see except space and spray and the river moving on into the distance. Finally it is too late for reconsideration. The boat gathers speed, tilts down and farther down. On good runs it is over in a flash:

the shuddering jolts, the darkness of the big hole, the bow straining to climb the reversal wave, the tailwaves below. Ten seconds at most have elapsed.

Then there are the other kinds of runs. The boat slams down and does not climb up. Caught between the falls and the reversal, the boat veers sideways. It is very dark, very wet. The boat overturns, leaving its passengers to the mercy of the river. One involuntary swimmer at the base of Rainie traveled underwater down the Rogue for three hundred feet before surfacing unconscious but alive. He was wearing a good life preserver, too. A large dog without a preserver also dumped below the falls and was never seen again, despite hours spent pacing both shorelines. Still, many sane, successful runs of Rainie Falls have been made. The water level, the quality of the equipment, and the skill of the boatman are all determining factors. Given adequate assurance on these counts, the run is within the limits of possibility.

With so many Big Drops in the American West either drowned in reservoirs or threatened with inundation, it is encouraging to know that in October 1968 Congress placed an 84-mile section of the Rogue in the National Wild and Scenic Rivers System. With a history of recreational boating as long as that of any other western river, the Rogue was an obvious nominee for the first group of eight rivers to be protected under the new legislation.

The National Wild and Scenic Rivers Act established three categories of protection, depending on the degree of development of the river corridor. The system applies nicely to the Rogue. From the Applegate River's confluence with the Rogue to the bridge at Grave Creek, the Rogue is a "recreational river." This means that there is abundant road access and considerable shoreline development. The objective of management (in this case the Bureau of Land Management and the United States Forest Service) is to control further development and maintain the river in a free-flowing condition—no dams or irrigation works. The thirty-three miles of river below Grave Creek, including Rainie Falls, are in the category of "wild river." Here management is instructed by the act to maintain wilderness conditions (no roads or further development) and to encourage primitive types of recreation. Unfortunately, from some perspectives, several lodges and the use of powerboats continue on parts of the "wild river" section of the Rogue, permitted because they existed prior to 1968. Below the roadless canyon, the Rogue again becomes a "recreational river" and, for a few miles, a "scenic river," which means that some road access and construction exist.

Management of the Rogue has recognized that this river has exceptional appeal to noncommercial or private boating parties, many of them just beginning to master whitewater skills. With the exception of Rainie Falls, which all beginners would do well to portage, there is no reason why a serious and well-prepared group of novices cannot float the river safely. Given the existing roads and backcountry lodges, assistance is never more than a few hours away. Consequently, nonguided, do-it-yourself use constitutes a third to a half of total river traffic. Acting in the face of opposition from some guides and commercial river running companies, Rogue management has defended a fair opportunity for the private party on the river.

Big Drops like Rainie Falls make for great camps. The tension of the run mellows into satisfaction. Only the egocentric or the very young babble about conquests. Zane Grey caught the mood of the Rogue after Rainie. He had camped, as today's runners do, on the big beach at Whiskey Creek. And his party, like today's, drank up the beauty before them:

Idyllic days they were, verily the dream days of an angler. October brought out the intense golds and reds of the forest; cool, clear, silent nights with myriads of white stars; crisp dawns with the purple mist veils changing to silver; and warm drowsy days in which it seemed always afternoon.

Three

Hell's Half Mile

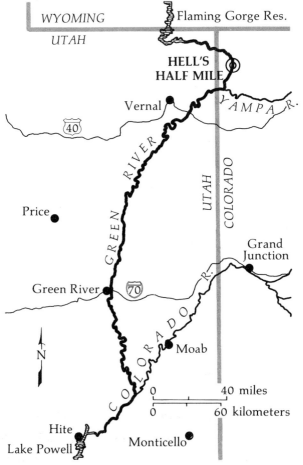

At one place as we were being hurled along at a tremendous speed we suddenly perceived immediately ahead of us in such a position that we could not avoid dashing into it, a fearful commotion of the waters, indicating many large rocks near the surface. The Major stood on the middle deck, his life-preserver in place . . . and peered into the approaching maelstrom. It looked to him like the end for us and he exclaimed calmly, "By God, boys, we're gone!"

FREDERICK S. DELLENBAUGH

The sun of the Colorado–Utah borderland is bright at noon, and the sky between the rock walls of the Canyon of Lodore is a dazzling, rich blue. The boatmen pull their rafts slowly out of the current and slip quietly to shore. They hear all the sounds of the river—the gurgle of eddies swirling around the rocks along the shore, the call of a canyon wren, the swish of air among the water reeds and box elders, and behind these intermittent sounds a continuous thunder from where the river disappears downstream in a flurry of spray. The boatmen hear this sound deep in their guts. They know what it means. With deliberation they weave through the rocks and disappear into the trees toward the portage trail. Here, trudging along a path worn dusty by a century of river travelers, the sunshine broken by pine and juniper, it seems unnaturally quiet. The boatmen top a low and rocky ridge and the roar is in their ears again. They begin the descent, pausing occasionally to squint through the trees at the section of the Green River known as Hell's Half Mile.

The Canyon of Lodore was named by Andrew Hall, a Scotsman who made his way West and at only nineteen became a crewman on John Wesley Powell's great expedition down the Colorado River in 1869. Hall was shot down in 1882 while guarding a stagecoach and is now forgotten and unknown except for that moment when he looked at the dramatic portals of the Canyon of Lodore and remembered the nursery rhyme "The Cataract of Lodore," written in 1820 by the English romantic poet Robert Southey. The poem is a rhythmic series of alliterative and rhyming phrases.

> Its caverns and rocks among:
> Rising and leaping,
> Sinking and creeping,
> Swelling and sweeping,
> Flying and flinging,
> Writhing and ringing,
> Eddying and whisking,
> Spouting and frisking,
> Turning and twisting,
> Around and around
> With endless rebound!
> Smiting and fighting,
> A sight to delight in;
> Confounding, astounding,
> Dizzying and deafening the ear—with its sound.

Andy Hall remembered the last line of the poem, "And this way the water comes down at Lodore." So Lodore the canyon was called, despite the protestations of the Americans with Powell who disputed using a European import. It is, in fact, one of many European names that today are scattered across the maps of the Colorado Basin.

No one forgets the entrance to Lodore Canyon. Powell called it "the very gates of Lodore." In fact, the Uinta Mountains of northeastern Utah begin there. The Uintas are one of the few major mountain ranges in North America that extend east to west, rising as a great dam through which the Green River has cut its path. Some twenty-five million years ago the upper Green River drained eastward into the North Platte and ultimately to the great basins of the Missouri and Mississippi, cutting along the way the valley now called Brown's Park.

The water-level view of a "triple rig" in action. By Ralph Gray.

From the crest of the Uintas the lower Green drained south and west into the basin of the Colorado. Then twelve to fifteen million years ago the eastern end of the Uinta Mountains dropped 4,000 feet, forming a large trough. At the same time the present Continental Divide rose in the east. Blocked from flowing eastward to the Platte, the Green River formed a chain of lakes in Brown's Park and penetrated southward through the Uintas. Twelve million years ago the Uintas began to rise, and simultaneously a warmer, postglacial climate released large amounts of water. The two parts of the ancestral Green River joined. One major stream now flowed southward out of Wyoming to gouge Lodore and the deeper canyons to the south and west.

Brown's Park, just upstream from the Gates of Lodore, is a place to pass through. The Indians and the mountain men came to Brown's Park and moved on. Today the campers arrive in their recreational vehicles only to depart. Even the boatmen do not linger, but pull downriver to the hard rock of Lodore. The ominous Gates of Lodore dominate Brown's Park with cliffs rising two thousand feet, dwarfing the scrub and cottonwoods of the park. In Brown's Park there are mosquitoes, saw grass, and mud; in Lodore, rock and moving water. All of the early known adventurers entered the Gates with foreboding—and rightly so. On Friday, May 8, 1825, the famous entrepreneur of the fur trade, William Henry Ashley, passed through the Gates of Lodore to Hell's Half Mile with deep premonitions of disaster.

As we passed along between these massy walls, which in a great degree exclude from us the rays of heaven and presented a surface as impassable as their body was impregnable, I was forcibly struck with the gloom which spread over the countenances of my men; they seemed to anticipate (and not far distant, too) a dreadful termination of our voyage, and I must confess that I partook in some degree of what I supposed to be their feelings, for things around us had truly an awful appearance.

Ashley lost no boats in the Canyon of Lodore, but over forty years later John Wesley Powell was not so fortunate. The first major rapid in Lodore, Disaster Falls, destroyed *No Name*, a twenty-one-foot craft made of oak planking with watertight compartments. Its boatman, O. G. Howland, carried Seneca Howland, his younger brother, and Frank Goodman, an Englishman, along for the ride. Powell described the misfortune of June 9, 1869:

I walk along the bank to examine the ground, leaving one of my men with a flag to guide the other boats to the landing place, I soon see one of the boats make shore all right and feel no more concern; but a minute after I hear a shout. Looking around I see one of the boats shooting down the center of the sag. It is the *No Name* with Captain Howland, his brother, and Goodman. I feel that its going over is inevitable and run to save the third boat. A minute more and she turns the point and heads for shore. Then I turn downstream again and scramble along to look for the boat that has gone over. The first fall was not great, only 10 or 12 feet, and we often run such. Below the river tumbles down again for 40 or 50 feet in a channel filled with dangerous rocks that break the waves into whirlpools or beat them into foam. I pass around a great crag just in time to see the boat strike a rock and rebounding from the shock careen and fill the open compartment with water. Two of the men lost their oars, she swings around, and is carried down at a rapid rate broadside on for a few yards and strikes amidships on another rock with great force, is broken quite in two, and the men are thrown into the river, the larger part of the boat floating buoyantly. They soon seize it and down the river they drift past the rocks for a few hundred yards to a second rapid filled with huge boulders where the boat strikes again and is dashed to pieces and the men and fragments are soon carried beyond my sight. Running along I turn a bend and see a man's head above the water and washed about in a whirlpool below a great rock.

Powell lost the *No Name* but no men in Disaster Falls. Today boatmen look beyond Upper and Lower Disaster Falls to Triplett Falls and to the Big Drop of Lodore—Hell's Half Mile. The boatmen hit the slots in Disaster and snake through the rocks of Triplett to squat in the dirt of the portage trail, surveying the currents and rocks of Hell's Half Mile. A golden rabbit bush is in the full bloom of summer, but few notice it. All eyes—tired, experienced, fearful, and sometimes wise—read the water as it drops thirty feet through Hell's Half Mile. The tumultuous water and jutting boulders make this rapid one of the most difficult on the rivers of the American West.

The boatmen move down through the cedars and pines to the rocks below. Here they do not find the grandeur of the Grand Canyon, the lush greenery of the Salmon, or the bright quartzite of Cataract Canyon. Their gaze is held by a maze of huge boulders cleft from the canyon walls, through which they must find a way. No stream has deposited these house-size rocks. Between the rocks and among them and over them and around them the Green River swirls through the

Uintas. The water erodes the rocks of Lodore, transporting them grain by grain a thousand miles to the sea. What does the boatman see? What does he feel as the sun beats down on the dusty trail by the raging rapid? This rock is exposed; that one is covered. It is easier on the right. Certain trouble down the left. Usually they are somber and serious, but sometimes cavalier. The thunder from water and rock continues. When faced with the river in all its power, boatmen sometimes concentrate on the insignificant and the trivial; they turn away from the river to examine an evening primrose. As if by signal the boatmen suddenly stand erect and trudge back along the portage trail, slosh through a shallow stream, and work their way down through a stand of juniper to the start of Hell's Half Mile.

The early river runners—John Wesley Powell, Ellsworth and Emery Kolb, Julius Stone—portaged around Hell's Half Mile along the trail Powell's men constructed in 1869, laboriously carrying their gear over the rocks and roots to the base of the rapid and then returning to line their boats by rope and muscle through the side channels and eddies. On June 15, 1869, Powell looked at Hell's Half Mile for the first time in dismay, and later set down this description.

During the afternoon, Dunn and Howland, having returned from their climb, we run down, three-quarters of a mile, on quiet water, and land at the head of another fall. On examination, we find that there is an abrupt plunge of a few feet, and then the river tumbles, for half a mile, with a descent of a hundred feet, in a channel beset with great numbers of huge boulders. This stretch of the river is named Hell's Half Mile.

The remaining portion of the day is occupied in making a trail among the rocks to the foot of the rapid.

June 16.

Our first work this morning is to carry our cargoes to the foot of the falls. Then we commence letting down the boats. We take two of them down in safety, but not without great difficulty; for, where such a vast body of water, rolling down an inclined plane, is broken into eddies and cross currents by rocks projecting from the cliffs and piles of boulders in the channel, it requires excessive labor and much care to prevent their being dashed against the rocks or breaking away. Sometimes we are compelled to hold the boat against a rock, above a chute, until a second line, attached to the stern, is carried to some point below, and when all is ready, the first line is detached, and the boat given to the current, when she shoots down, and the men below swing her into some eddy.

At such a place, we are letting down the last boat, and, as she is set free, a wave turns her broadside down the stream . . . . They haul on the line to bring the boat in, but the power of the current, striking obliquely against her, shoots her into the middle of the river. The men have their hands burned with the friction of the passing line; the boat breaks away, and speeds, with great velocity, down the stream.

The *Maid of the Canyon* is lost, so it seems; but she drifts some distance, and swings into an eddy, in which she spins about until we arrive with the small boat and rescue her.

Hell's Half Mile was actually named by John F. Steward on Powell's second expedition down the Colorado in 1871. Frederick S. Dellenbaugh's record of this adventure and scientific exploration is the most accurate and readable account of running the Colorado. He was only seventeen when he left Green River, Wyoming, with Powell on May 22, 1871. Dellenbaugh secured his place through a relative, Almon H. Thompson, who was Powell's brother-in-law and second-in-command of the expedition. Fortunately, Dellenbaugh had talent as well as connections. He painted the first pictures of the canyon country, and in later years tramped all over the world, recorded his travels, and helped to found the Explorers Club.

On June 23, 1871, Dellenbaugh recounted in his journal the rigors of Hell's Half Mile.

The entire river for more than half a mile was one sheet of white foam. There was not a quiet spot in the whole distance, and the water plunged and pounded in its fierce descent and sent up a deafening roar. The only way one could be heard was to yell with full lung power. Landing at the head of it easily we there unloaded the *Dean* and let her down by line for some distance. In the worst place she capsized but was not damaged. Then the water, near the shore we were on, though turbulent in the extreme became so shallow on account of the great width of the rapid here that when we had again loaded the *Dean* there were places where we were forced to walk alongside and lift her over rocks, but several men at the same time always had a strong hold on the shore end of the line. In this way we got her down as far as was practicable by that method. At this point the river changed. The water became more concentrated and consequently deeper. It was necessary to unload the boat again and work her on down with a couple of men in her and the rest holding the line on shore as we had done above. When the roughest part was past in this manner, we made her fast and proceeded to carry her cargo down to this spot which took some time. It was there put on board again and the hatches firmly secured. The boat was held firmly behind a huge sheltering rock and when all was ready her crew took their places. With the Major clinging to the middle cabin, as his chair had been left above and would be carried down later, we shoved out into the swift current, here free from rocks. She literally bounded over the waves that formed the end of the descent, to clear water where we landed on a snug little beach and made the boat secure for the night. Picking our way along shore back to the head of the rapid, camp was made there as the darkness was falling and nothing could be done that night.

It was next to impossible to converse, but everyone being very tired it was not long after supper before we took to the blankets and not a man was kept awake by the noise. It seemed only a few moments before it was time to go at it again. All hands were up early and the other two boats were taken laboriously down in the same manner as the *Dean* had been engineered, but though we toiled steadily it was one o'clock by the time we succeeded in placing them alongside that boat. Anticipating this, Andy's utensils were taken down on the *Nell,* and while we were working with the *Cañonita,* our good chef prepared the dinner and we stopped long enough to fortify ourselves with it. Having to build a trail in some places in order to carry the goods across ridges and boulders, it was not alone the work on lowering the boats which delayed us. While we were absorbed in these operations the campfire of the morning in some way spread unperceived into the thick sage-brush and cedars which covered the point, and we vacated the place none too soon, for the flames were leaping high, and by the time we had finished our dinner at the foot of the rapid, the point we had so recently left was a horrible furnace. The fire was jumping and playing amidst dense smoke which rolled a mighty column, a thousand feet it seemed to me above the top of the canyon; that is over 3000 feet into the tranquil air.

Powell's expedition was not the first to face Hell's Half Mile. William Henry Ashley was there in 1825, when the West was the land of the Indian peoples and the mountain men. Ashley was born in Virginia in 1778. Looking to the west like his fellow Virginians Lewis and Clark, he went to the Missouri Territory when he was thirty years old. There he prospered, mining saltpeter, and met Andrew Henry, who mined lead near Potosi in southwest Missouri. As the demand for lead and saltpeter declined after the war of 1812 they looked for new financial opportunities. Ashley was an extraordinary man. Active in the territorial militia, he advanced from captain in 1813 to general in 1822; the following year he was elected lieutenant governor of the new state of Missouri.

Politics prospered no more than mining, however. In 1824 Ashley was defeated in the election for governor of Missouri and, like many losers, went West. As early as 1822 he and Andrew Henry sought their fortunes in the reviving fur trade. They dramatically altered the conduct of the business: instead of trading with the Indians for pelts, Ashley brought men west to trap the beaver. Trapping demanded different talents than trading, and Ashley found men who combined these skills. They were a new breed—the "mountain men." Spreading out through the rivers and canyons of the West, the mountain men trapped so well that the beaver nearly became extinct. At the end of summer they gathered at a rendezvous to sell their pelts. This institution, too, was Ashley's doing. Instead of establishing a series of fixed trading posts similar to those constructed throughout the West by Hudson's Bay

Company; Ashley held rendezvous in crossroads like Brown's Park where the trappers could bring the pelts to trade for the goods of eastern America.

On April 21, 1825, Ashley launched his bullboat on the Green River, known then by the Crow Indian name of Seeds-ke-Dee. Floating through Red Gorge to leave his mark and his name at Ashley Falls, he emerged on Tuesday, May 5, 1825, into Brown's Park.

After descending six miles, the mountains gradually recede from the water's edge, and the river expands to the width of two hundred and fifty yards, leaving the river bottoms on each side from one to three hundred yards wide interspersed with clusters of small willows. We remained at our encampment of this day until the morning of the 7th, when we descended ten miles lower down and encamped on a spot of ground where several thousand Indians had wintered during the past season. Their camp had been judiciously selected for defence, and the remains of their work around it accorded with the judgment exercised in the selection. Many of their lodges remained as perfect as when occupied. They were made of poles two or three inches in diameter, set up in circular form, and covered with cedar bark.

Until the 1840s Brown's Park was a popular site for the annual rendezvous. It was a French Canadian, Baptiste Brown, who wandered into the basin, built himself a cabin, managed the rendezvous, and put another name on the map of the West. Brown's Park was a land of big sky where in the late summer the trappers and Indians bartered their pelts, drank whiskey, fought, fornicated, and prepared for the coming winter in the lonely canyons which stretch through the forests of the Uintas to the Colorado Plateau. Ashley brought the men to the mountains, but he was not one of them—a Jim Bridger or a Jedidiah Smith or a Jim Beckwourth. He returned west only once, in 1826. In that summer he sold out to a company of young men who were later famous in the lore of the West—Jedidiah Smith, David E. Jackson, and William L. Sublette. Ashley himself returned to Missouri, was elected to Congress, and continued a successful political career in Washington. What re-

When water buries the raft, passengers appear to be surfing. By Ray Varley.

mained of Ashley's voyage was a message carved into the rocks of Flaming Gorge—"Ashley 1825"—and his journal, which describes how he and his men portaged around the rapids of Lodore to make their way down to the confluence with the Yampa, Whirlpool, and Split Mountain canyons.

After Ashley came William Manly, one of the hardy young men who started west as a twenty-nine-year-old roustabout, got the gold fever, and headed for California. When the leader of Manly's wagon train announced they would spend the winter of 1849 in Salt Lake City, he and six companions went down the Green on two twenty-five-foot canoes hewn from pine trees and lashed together. They went through

Lodore, portaging around some rapids, lining others, and running a few. They left the river in Gray Canyon and made their way with great agony through Death Valley to the Pacific.

Others came after Manly. They are still known to river people, who speak of them around the campfires. In 1891 a man named Snyder upset in Lodore, borrowed a horse and rode over the mountains. We know nothing more. George F. Flavell ran a flat-bottomed skiff through Lodore in 1896 with Ramon Montos, but, like Powell, he lined Hell's Half Mile. There were probably others. Man's curiosity is unquenchable, and a flowing river irresistible. But river men tend not to be very literary, and these early pioneers, probably not even literate, left few records but their footprints.

After John Wesley Powell the next recorded descent through the Canyon of Lodore was accomplished by Julius F. Stone in 1909. An industrialist from Columbus, Ohio, Stone had met the remarkable Nathaniel T. Galloway in the Henry Mountains of Utah in the early 1890s. Nat Galloway was a hunter and trapper from Vernal, Utah, whose reputation was one of the best in the upper Colorado Basin. In his quiet and unassuming way Galloway was a genius. For years he had wandered through the deep canyon country, trapping and hunting. Julius Stone employed him as a guide on the 1909 expedition, and later recounted that Galloway had the most astonishing knowledge of animals and their ways of any man he had ever known.

But Galloway's genius went beyond trapping beaver and shooting deer. Before him, boatmen rowed down the river as they would on a placid lake. The bow of the boat was pointed downstream, and one or more oarsmen would pull hard with their backs to the waves and holes and rocks. With their backs to the rapid the boatmen theoretically had the strength and power to move the boat faster than the river, so that the speed would be sufficient to control the boat by a rudder guided by another man. Dellenbaugh graphically described this way to run rapids, rightly pointing out, however, that it was unnerving to the oarsmen to enter a dangerous rapid with their backs to the rocks and waves, not knowing where they were going. In order to maintain any maneuverability the boat would, of course, have to keep a speed greater than the current, proportionately increasing the danger of striking rocks and waves.

Nat Galloway changed all this. Instead of rowing blindly backwards into a rapid, Galloway turned his boats around, faced downstream, and rowed against the current. This simple but astounding difference marked the beginning of modern river running, and to this day the technique is used by every boatman on the river. Not only can a boatman enter the rapid looking downstream to see where he must maneuver to avoid the rocks and holes, but he dramatically increases his maneuverability by pulling backward and across the current, moving from one side of the river to the other, picking his way downstream. Moreover, by pulling upstream against the current there was no need to have a separate steersman in the stern, for the oarsman could now slalom through the rocks and holes and eddies. Orders no longer had to be shouted back and forth above the roar of the torrent.

Galloway had worked out this method during many years in the canyon country. His first extended river trip was in 1895 when he traveled alone from Green River, Wyoming, and then up the Colorado to Moab. His first successful trip made him bold. Beginning at Henry's Fork in September 1896, Galloway started down the Green River, coming upon Frank Leland and William Chesley Richmond at Little Hole. Intrigued by the prospect of adventure in the deep canyons to the south, Richmond agreed to accompany Galloway, and in February 1897 they completed the river run to Needles, California. We do not know around which rapids, if any, Galloway lined his boats.

By this time rivers were in Galloway's blood, and he was making profits from trapping the beaver which inhabited them. Later in 1897 he trapped and hunted down the Green River from Vernal, Utah, to Lee's Ferry, where he packed out westward through the pines of the Kaibab Plateau. From then on, each year found Galloway on the rivers. Always inquisitive, he experimented with new boats and in 1908 invented a steel boat which made the run from Green River, Wyoming, to Green River, Utah, through the Canyon of Lodore and Hell's Half Mile. Perhaps by then his experience was sufficient to run the rapids of Lodore, for Nat Galloway liked to run, and by temperament was not disposed to line his boats. On a cold evening many years before, in November 1898 in the depths of Glen Canyon, Galloway again met Stone and inspired him to follow the river flowing southward through the great walls of time. In the autumn of 1909 he led Stone and his party southward through the canyons.

This was the first whitewater trip in the West that could be termed "commercial," in the sense that a sportsman seeking recreation hired a guide. Stone was an avid outdoorsman and had considerable experience on Canadian rivers. He had his boat built to Galloway's design. With Galloway he was responsible for the next major breakthrough in the technology of river running in the American West—construction of lighter boats for greater maneuverability, complementing the revolutionary rowing techniques Galloway had perfected. The boats, made of five-eighths-inch Michigan white pine, were sixteen feet four inches long, four feet wide, and sixteen inches deep. They were flat-bottomed, weighed 243 pounds, and were intended for only one man. There were watertight compartments in each boat and a canvas shield to keep the cockpit dry from splashing water.

With Galloway in the lead, the Stone party negotiated Ashley Falls and in four days passed through the Canyon of Lodore. Much to Stone's dismay, Galloway insisted on running the dangerous rapids himself after the equipment had been unloaded and portaged around the rocks. Thus he snaked through Hell's Half Mile while the others walked, stumbling over the boulders and slipping in the slime, along the remains of the portage path which Powell and his men had built many years before.

Two years later, in 1911, Ellsworth and Emery Kolb used Galloway-designed boats to travel downriver from Green River, Wyoming, to the Gulf of Mexico. Like Powell and Stone before them, the Kolb brothers carried their equipment around Hell's Half Mile; floundering over the limestone boulders, they tumbled down through gullies where scraggly cedars tore their clothing. The Kolbs spent the whole day carrying their loads three-quarters of a mile around Hell's Half Mile and then slowly lined their boats down through the lower rocks.

With a short rope fastened to the iron bar or handhold on the stern, this end was lifted on to the crosspiece, the bow sticking into the water at a sharp angle. The short rope was tied to the stump so we would not lose what we had gained. The longer rope from the bow was thrown over the roots of the tree above and we both pulled on the rope until finally the bow was on a level with the stern. She was pulled forward, the ropes were loosened, and the boat rested on the crosspieces. The motion picture camera was transferred so as to command a view of the lower side of the barrier. Then the boat was carefully towed and slid forward a little at a time until she finally gained headway, nearly jerking the rope from our hands and shot into the pool below.

The Kolb brothers emerged from Lodore Canyon on October 2, with Galloway not far behind. Putting in at Green River, Wyoming, in September, a few days after the Kolb brothers had started, Galloway was using an experimental canvas boat which he had tested earlier in Desolation and Gray canyons. He ran Disaster and Triplett, then shot down through Hell's Half Mile, ultimately emerging at Green River, Utah, on October 27, 1911. The journeys of the Kolb brothers and Galloway in 1911 mark the end of the pioneer river running through Lodore Canyon and Hell's Half Mile. Nearly ninety years after William Ashley, Nat Galloway demonstrated that Hell's Half Mile could be run.

Other men followed the pioneers, but they were men of different nature and designs. They came to measure the power of the river and to seek ways to harness it. Survey parties from Utah Power and Light Company scoured Lodore to identify favorable dam sites for the development of hydroelectric power. Behind the potential dam builders came the surveyors of the United States Geological Survey. All through

the 1920s the USGS mapped the Canyon of Lodore. There were un-
doubtedly other adventurers besides the survey parties, but they left no
mark and are unrecorded or unrecalled. Perhaps they portaged Hell's
Half Mile rather than dare its boulders. Men do not like to recount their
inadequacies.

After the early runs, Lodore remained forgotten. Perhaps the adventure seemed diminished after the pioneering years, for nearly a quarter
of a century passed before a new challenger reached Hell's Half Mile.
On October 4, 1937, Haldane "Buzz" Holmstrom left Green River,
Wyoming, to become the first man to run alone from Wyoming to
Hoover Dam. He faced hundreds of miles and hundreds of rapids on
his epic journey. He lined only five rapids—Hell's Half Mile was not
one of them. In the account of his run Holstrom quaintly refers to
himself and his boat as "we."

When you understand that the speed of the current here is better than
twenty-five miles an hour—it seems much faster, but that's how the Government experts measured it—and that the full force of the river rolls down at
that speed, you can imagine how fast the rocks seem to be leaping toward you
and how exact must be your control on the oars to dodge in and out.

Halfway down the boiling chute, we struck a submerged boulder. You can't
see such things in advance in such water. Had we been going head-on, the
boat would have been done for, right there, but at retarded speed the rein-
forced stern held. We hung for a split second, head-on in the current, then
swung into the full grip of the heaped-up channel, out of control and speeding down upon the big rocks that must be avoided.

I gave the oars all I had, whirled the boat and pulled for my life. The instant
we were in the clear we struck again, and this time the river seized my left oar
and tore it from its socket. We hurtled sideways toward a huge boulder, and it
was there that the boat itself did the trick. It slid upon the rock instead of
crashing—I was thankful then for the rake I'd given her bow—spun, and slid
off. By now I had the oar in place, and we eased between the remaining rocks
to a safe landing below. It seemed like the boat almost chuckled out loud at me
there, when we were in the clear. "Happy to oblige. But next time don't
depend so much on me."

The principal problems with Hell's Half Mile are its length and its boulders. In most rapids a boatman can mark a rock or a tree on shore to designate the spot where the proper maneuver will deliver him safely down the rapid, but this is difficult in Hell's Half Mile. It is so long that one despairs of trying to keep an accurate memory of where to go and what to do. One of the great oarsmen of the American West, Fred B. Eiseman, Jr., compares studying Hell's Half Mile to memorizing the complete score and all of the singing roles of *Parsifal.*

As the torrent crashes down, over, and around the boulders, boatmen memorize the first slots and the currents swirling through the rocks. They talk little and think much, their eyes moving over and over the sequence of rocks and currents and eddies. Occasionally they look too long at the whitewater and lose their nerve; others look too fleetingly and do not read the water accurately. Some throw pieces of driftwood into the channels to see where they descend, but a boatman never really knows where his boat will go if he cannot read the water itself.

Hell's Half Mile drops thirty feet in less than half a mile. The rapid is dominated by great blocks of red quartzite that have fallen from the cliff into the river to create the confusion and chaos at the top of the rapid known as Boulder Falls. That is where the trouble starts: in this brief section of not more than a hundred yards, where the blocks from the canyon walls have almost dammed the river. From up on the portage trail the boulders look small, but once the boatmen have made their way to shore and leaped on some of them to search the current, they appear enormous and threatening—ominous, reddish presences obstructing passage down to the quieter waters below the rapid. They block the right bank so thoroughly that even the most skillful boatman could not pass, and force the river between the left bank and a huge boulder in the middle. This rock, which Gaylord Staveley has called "The Big Boulder," must be avoided or the boats will plunge into the hole and the standing waves beyond. In low water the rock protrudes, creating even greater difficulty and often stopping large pontoons. On the left a whole coastline of large boulders thrusts the current back into the center, which is now reduced to less than fifty feet. Racing and forcing through this narrow purgatory, the river pours over the huge boulder into a gaping hole and then spreads out around two great islands in a litter of rocks, chutes, and holes. These shallow, rock-strewn channels have ripped boats and can stall one in mid-course, but they can be run. The fear of Hell's Half Mile is that awesome rock over which the river plunges in the middle of Boulder Falls.

The question of how to maneuver past purgatory point in Hell's Half Mile depends on the water level; the run can be to either side or over the rock. On Memorial Day in 1969 Gaylord Staveley and Fred Eiseman made an epic run in heavy wooden cataract boats to commemorate John Wesley Powell's first trip down the Green and Colorado Rivers a century before. In Hell's Half Mile Stavely slid adroitly past a large rock at the top and began to move to the right, but a little too quickly. Slightly misjudging the thrust of the water coming off the rocks on the left bank, he slipped over the great rock in the center and directly through the hole with his six-hundred-pound cataract boat, *Norm*. Eiseman, directly behind, had the advantage of seeing the force of the current and, falling farther to the left, shot down the left-hand chute, thereafter to zigzag through the boulder-littered shallows to the beach below.

Today in lighter rubber rafts one can maneuver more deftly than in heavy cataract boats, and can even dodge around the right side of the big boulder in the middle—or, as Stavely and others have done, simply go over the rock and hit the hole below. The hole is big and powerful, and smaller boats have plunged into it with enough force to throw out their passengers, but inflatable rafts will take the pounding better than Gaylord Staveley's cataract boats.

On that Memorial Day people, not boats, dominated the scene. When Staveley and his party ran Hell's Half Mile, a large gathering of outfitters and passengers had arrived there, the advance guard of the many who have since overwhelmed the great rivers of the West. This evidence in 1969 of the large numbers of people who were prepared to run western rivers was a revelation.

As Gaylord Staveley and his party studied and read the waters of Hell's Half Mile, others came to do the same. Only the big pontoons did not bother to look, but with thirty-three feet of heavy rubberized nylon and a dozen or more people they simply "slithered down over the falls." No matter how many attempt Hell's Half Mile, however, they will all be haunted by the big boulder, barely covered by the river and peering out like a face from behind the "thin gray, green mantilla of falling water." From what point does the water start down the falls—to the right of the big rock or to the left? That is the essential problem of Hell's Half Mile.

And so you sit in the July sunshine watching the river move down through the canyon. The boatmen have made their calculations—where to pull, how to pull, into which current to slide, where to square off to make the run. Some boatmen are paid to understand this, others do it for the exhilaration and the challenge. The boatmen look at one another, nod, and slowly make their way back through the snake grass and juniper trees to the boats. Before a Big Drop no one talks much. There is little to say at that moment, and the boatmen themselves are particularly cool, trying not to betray the fear that sticks in their bellies. They have memorized the currents; they have oriented themselves to the rocks, which are so demonstrably different when looking downstream, not up. The gear is secured. Life jackets are buttoned down. The boats move into midstream and catch the current. The box elders near the river sway in the wind, and the last boatman watches the leaves rustle as the lead boats disappear into Boulder Falls.

Though the last oarsman is not the pathfinder, his position is psychologically the most difficult. He must watch the others press on ahead of him, and the wait is trying. At times he can benefit by watching the runs of those ahead, otherwise he simply must sit above the roar of the rapid, waiting his turn while others are exorcising their fears below. He may be misled by those who have preceded him and make the same mistakes if he is not skillful in reading the water. Moreover, he bears a special responsibility. The last oarsman carries the safety lines to pull his comrades off the rocks if necessary and he sweeps the river clean to see that all the pieces and people are appropriately rescued and carried down. But this responsibility does not weigh as heavily as the knowledge that when the others have run, whether there is difficulty or not, he must then take his turn and strain to run the rapid far behind those who have gone before, only to land exhausted at the bottom just as the others have bailed their boats and are ready to continue. In 1969 Staveley, running the first boat, succinctly summed up the plight of the rear boatman: "The last oarsman is subject to the most mistranslation of course and maneuvering, if there is any, by each succeeding oarsman of the columm. He's the troubleshooter, charged with seeing that all other boats are finding safe passage down the river ahead of him."

There is always that forbidding silence in the boat at the top of a rapid. The boatman sees the spray below as the Green River tears at the rocks of Boulder Falls, and looks again at the box elders and the junipers down below. Then he must concentrate, pulling away hard into the center of the river, moving his oars carefully in order to strike at the right moment. And then from the top he sees the rocks which he has studied down below. The boat moves forward ever so slowly, creeping, and suddenly the river catches the raft. He pulls hard to the right to see the ledge where he has planned to go, squares off and hits it, and goes over into the trough below with water cascading down over boat and boatman. He moves on knowing that he has run Boulder Falls. And then the rapid begins again, for the river stretches out across the rock shoals where there is a constant darting, dashing, moving from side to side, pulling hard, making his way down the river until he has passed through Hell's Half Mile.

And so the rapid is run. Hell's Half Mile is not a killer, but it is nasty, brutish, and long. Like most rapids it is unique, incomparable. It does not have the gushing force of Clavey Falls on the Tuolumne or the massive waves of Lava Falls on the Colorado. It is much longer than Rainie Falls on the Rogue and lacks the deceptive subtleties of Big Mallard on the Salmon.

At the end of Hell's Half Mile is a small beach on the left where John Wesley Powell and Frederick Dellenbaugh camped on the second Powell expedition down the Green and Colorado. Here the boatmen pull in for congratulations or consolations. They look back at the water tumbling down through the boulders. The boats are unloaded, the cooking fire lit, and later, as the smell of coffee floats through the camp at the end of another river meal, a brisk wind comes up the canyon, fanning the embers and lifting away a new song inspired by the day.

I was ninety miles out of Denver
in the wild and drifting snow.
Three days across the mountains
Seemed a lifetime to go.

Green River was a-callin'
Brown's Park layin' low.
The ghosts of Butch and the Sundance Kid
are the only friends I know.

Hell's Half Mile . . .
Hell's Half Mile . . .
I'll see you in a while.

Four

Warm Springs

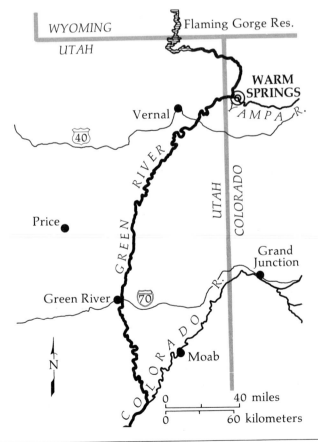

WYOMING

UTAH

Flaming Gorge Res.

**WARM
SPRINGS**

Vernal

YAMPA R.

40

GREEN RIVER

UTAH

COLORADO

Price

Grand
Junction

Green River

70

COLORADO R.

Moab

N

0   40 miles

0   60 kilometers

*It was 20 degrees down with the most gigantic waves and foam and holes on all
sides of me. Very narrow—like trying to run down a coiled rattler's back, the
rattler striking at me from all sides. I was shoved to the left bank about an inch
from the cliff where a foot-wide eddy existed. For perhaps a mile I skidded and
swirled and turned down this narrow line. I kept telling myself, "You can roll
in this," but all the time I knew I couldn't. I expected to get jammed into the
cliff but never touched it. Eventually I squirted out into a pool right side up and
safe only to flip in another whirlpool before reaching shore.*

WALT BLACKADAR

Before the night of June 10, 1965, there was only a minor riffle
where Warm Springs Draw meets the canyon of the Yampa River in the
extreme northwest corner of Colorado. The low water of midsummer
did expose two rocks, but even a child could, and sometimes did, float a
boat through the wide slot between them. The few waves below the
rocks were purely roller-coaster fun.

Then the big rain began. In May and June 1965 heavy rains fell on the
Warm Springs watershed seventeen out of twenty-one days. The
ground on the steep slopes that rise several thousand feet above the
draw became supersaturated and in spots turned to the consistency of
jelly. On June 10 the earth started to move. Lubricated by the heavy
runoff in Warm Springs Draw, a slurry of soil, stones, uprooted trees,
and drowned animals responded to the pull of gravity. As it passed the
springs that gave the place its name, the thick brown soup still moved
slowly and sporadically. Thereafter it picked up both speed and size,
building into a wall of semisolid debris about fifteen feet high.

Warm Springs Draw widens into a sizeable delta just before its confluence with the Yampa, but such was the momentum of the flash flood
that it hardly paused. Crashing into the Yampa, the mass of rock and
gravel filled the river bed and rolled up against the cliff on the opposite
bank.

For a few hours the Yampa was completely dammed. Campers downstream at Echo Park watched with astonishment, especially in view of the heavy rains, as the level of the river dropped quickly to a trickle. The condition was temporary, however; pooling up behind the debris dam at Warm Springs, the Yampa's force became irresistible. Sometime in the early morning hours of June 11, 1965, the river breached the natural dam and, with a guttural roar, resumed its accustomed task of carrying the continent toward the Pacific. After several hours of rapid erosion there was a ragged S-shaped channel dropping steeply through the remains of the landslide. Enormous waves and holes studded its half-mile length. A Big Drop had been born.

Daylight on June 11 found several river parties moving down the Yampa toward Warm Springs, completely unaware of the changes ahead. The first boats belonged to Hatch River Expeditions, one of the oldest companies in the river-outfitting business. Hatch's twenty-seven-foot pontoons, powered by oars, were usually more than adequate to negotiate the relatively mild whitewater in the meandering sandstone canyons of the Yampa. The Hatch party, consisting of a troop of boy scouts from Denver, two adult leaders, and two experienced boatmen, had put in at Deerlodge Park, about fifty river miles above Warm Springs. For several days they marveled at the Yampa's sculpture. At one point the river doubled back on itself so sharply that a float of seven miles was required to reach a point less than a linear mile away—a bowknot bend. Some of the scouts scrambled over the low divide on foot and waited for the boats to come around. Another highlight was where the Yampa undercut its bordering cliffs so deeply as to produce massive overhangs. Manganese oxide left black stripes on the tawny rock. Sliding close to the base of these "tiger walls," the river runners felt as if they were in a cave. At the Grand Overhang, a stone dropped straight down from the top of the thousand-foot cliff would land on the Yampa's *opposite* bank.

The heavy rains soaked the camping gear of the Hatch party, but the boatmen were professionals who knew how to cope with such conditions. The new rapid at Warm Springs was something else.

Al Holland rowed one of the Hatch boats, Les Oldham the other. About a half mile above Warm Springs Draw, Holland and Oldham drifted together to discuss the fact that the river seemed strange to them compared with previous trips. They had no way of knowing that it had risen and slowed behind the new rapid. Rounding the last bend above the draw, their confusion turned to anxiety. A roar that, in Holland's words, "sounded like a locomotive" echoed up the canyon. Still uncertain what had happened, the boatmen continued to drift downstream along the left-hand shore, peering ahead through the spitting rain. They made no attempt to row to the right, land, and scout ahead. It may have been that the initial drop of the new rapid was so sharp that the boatmen's river-level perspective revealed only space and distant tailwaves. Or perhaps they were unable to act against their knowledge that there just was no major rapid at Warm Springs. In any event they continued past the point at which they might have pulled their heavy rigs out of the current.

Les Oldham entered the tongue first and accelerated down it directly toward an enormous hole. Recognizing the danger, he pulled frantically on his left oar in an effort to direct the pontoon right of the hole. He succeeded, but the force of his pull broke the pin holding the oar to the frame, and Oldham's own power catapulted him backward into the river. Miraculously, the boat wallowed through right side up.

In the second pontoon Al Holland watched Oldham being snapped from his boat, then turned his attention to waves he remembered as over twenty feet high. It must have been a riverman's nightmare: floating on what was supposed to be quiet water, he was suddenly fighting the Yampa for his life. Holland won; Oldham did not.

After successfully running Warm Springs, Holland pulled to shore, organized the passengers on both boats, and began to search for Oldham. After several hours it became apparent that their search was for a corpse. Moving on in rain and silence to Echo Park, the party reported the fatality. Someone recalled that at the time he entered the rapid,

Oldham was sitting on his life preserver. Seventeen days later Oldham's body washed ashore at Island Park.

Following the report of the drowning, National Park Service rangers dispatched a plane to warn other boats on the Yampa above Warm Springs. Flying low over the startled river parties, the pilot dropped a sealed container into the river. The note inside told of the new Big Drop and the way it had claimed its first life. Shaken, Dee Holladay and other boatmen approached Warm Springs with extreme caution. Hugging the right bank, they landed on the upper edge of the debris fan extending from the draw and walked down through the jumble of logs and rocks to read the whitewater ahead.

Warm Springs is one of the longest and technically most difficult rapids in the Colorado drainage; its most frightening aspect is its ability to flip even the largest river boats in at least eight different holes. This is in marked contrast to many Big Drops (Hell's Half Mile and Big Mallard are examples), where the problem is concentrated in one rock–hole combination. At the top of Warm Springs a short, fast tongue ends in very large but still regularly shaped waves. Holland described them as "twenty-footers," but objectively seen they are only about half that height. The entrance waves lead directly into a maelstrom of whitewater on the left at the foot of Warm Springs Cliff. The holes here are formidable, virtual waterfalls behind the nearly exposed boulders. Rocks washed into the Yampa by the 1965 landslide are one cause of the chaos. Another is the slabs and cornices fallen from Warm Springs Cliff.

There is no ambiguity about how the upper part of Warm Springs must be run. Since no boat can count on surviving the left side, it is imperative to pull off the tongue to the right and skirt the edge of the cliffside holes. The maneuver sounds easier than it is. The Yampa thrusts boats left, toward the cliff, and to overcome this force it is necessary to row powerfully in large waves. This means the boat must be angled to the right. As a result, it strikes the waves in a dangerous

A headstand or "endo." Some kayakers do it on purpose as a stunt; others have it done to them by the power of the river. By Bart Henderson.

sideways attitude. Hundreds of pounds of water slosh in, making control more difficult. Moreover, the big waves prevent oars or sweeps from obtaining a good grip on the water. At the top of a wave a boat sits on a pinnacle, and oars cannot reach the water. In the troughs the walls of water are so close together that it is almost impossible to stroke and recover an oar. Only the most careful timing permits a boatman to row at all. To panic and flail wildly is to remain in the grip of the main flow and headed directly for trouble.

If Warm Springs Rapid ended with the initial big waves and the holes along the cliff, it would be imposing enough to warrant Big Drop consideration. In fact, two-thirds of the rapid and several major obstacles are still to come. The first of these are several midstream rocks that force boatmen to pull far right, almost against the right bank. This puts them in the line of a long, sharp boulder bar extending into the river from the same right bank. Particularly with boats heavy from water shipped in the upper part of the rapid, the rocky bar is hard to avoid. Ungainly pontoons repeatedly strike it sideways, and some roll over with astonishing ease almost within touching distance of spectators on shore. A smaller rowed boat can miss this hole, but only if the boatman accurately calculates his position in the rapid, anticipates far enough upstream, and leans into his pull with every ounce of strength.

The price of missing the right-side boulder bar is to enter once again the main current left of the center of the river. Ahead are two enormous rock barriers, just awash in high water. Below them are still other huge, barely submerged rocks, most of which have tumbled from Warm Springs Cliff in the last decade. The left side of the river is again disaster. So once more the boatmen force tired muscles to spin their rigs and pull out of the main flow to the right. The boats that reach this point in the rapid with broken or lost oars or minus a boatman (who may have been tossed from his seat like Les Oldham) or too heavy with water to maneuver will almost certainly upset behind or, in low water, wrap around these rocks. What all this means is that a perfect run of Warm Springs is a right–left–right slalom. Each move must be made against the main force of the river and in waves of formidable size.

Just as he had been the first white man to look with a scientist's eye at Hell's Half Mile, Satan's Gut, and Lava Falls, John Wesley Powell also led the way into the lower canyon of the Yampa. Of course, Warm Springs Rapid did not then exist as a Big Drop, but Powell formed an accurate conception of the geography and geology of the region. On June 20, 1869, Powell and his men rowed up the Yampa from its confluence with the Green River in Echo Park. Taking full advantage of eddies and backwaters, their boats rounded several mile-long bends. Near Warm Springs Draw they abandoned the effort and landed on a sandbar below a break in the golden cliffs which Powell used to gain access to the rim of the Yampa's canyon.

According to his journal for June 20, Powell walked "over long stretches of naked sandstone, crossing gulches now and then." It was a crisp, sparkling day in the mountains. "The air is singularly clear to-day," Powell reported. "Mountains and buttes stand in sharp outline, valleys stretch out in perspective, and I can look down into the deep canyon gorges and see gleaming waters."

Looking northeast from this vantage Powell could see the snow-capped Wind River range as it defined the Continental Divide in central Wyoming. Only a hundred linear miles distant, the Wind Rivers were actually beyond the starting point of Powell's river journey three weeks earlier. Farther away and more to the east, he noted the highlands in the vicinity of Rabbit Ears Pass, Colorado. The Yampa rises in the high meadows and pine forests of this section of the Divide. But the view west was the most imposing. Beyond the sagebrush-dotted benchlands and yellow cliffs of the Yampa's inner gorge, Powell faced the Uinta Range. Trending east–west across Utah and into western Colorado, the Uinta uplift runs squarely across the courses of the Green and Yampa rivers.

The few whites who had seen this landscape before Powell could not understand why the rivers had cut canyons through the Uintas rather than veering around them. The wilderness priests of Spain, Escalante and Domínguez, remarked on the way the combined Yampa and Green came directly out of a "split" mountain. A half century later, in 1825, William Ashley and his company of trappers, scouring the Yampa and the Green for fur, understood no better the seemingly illogical geography of rivers that ran directly into, rather than around, mountain ranges.

Powell came next, and standing above Warm Springs Draw on that clear day in June 1869 he found the explanation: the rivers came first. The mountains rose later, after the Yampa and the Green had already established their courses off the Continental Divide. As the great Uinta uplift occurred, the rivers cut deeper and deeper through the rising skin of the earth. What Powell saw below him were the entrenched meanders of a formerly lazy valley river. The ancestral Yampa's loops were now incised in Weber sandstone a thousand feet deep. Powell scrambled back down to his boats with the essential thesis later scientists would use to interpret the region's geology.

After Powell's short venture up the Yampa in 1869, the river was not run again until 1909, when Nat Galloway and his son Parley floated the entire Yampa Canyon. Characteristically river wise, Galloway chose the high water of June to make the trip. He wanted to run the Yampa before the decreasing flow of summer transformed it into an unfloatable rock garden. Moreover, Galloway had a date with Julius Stone to run the Green and Colorado from Wyoming to California in the early fall.

The shy Galloway did not care to surround his remarkable river-running feats with fanfare. This was not true of a team sponsored by the *Denver Post* in 1928 for the second descent of the Yampa. Headlines screamed about how the four-man party made one harrowing escape after another. One story detailed the "tragic" loss of a boat and equipment. There was no mention that the real tragedy was the *Post's* choice of a time to run the Yampa. In August the river was predictably low and rock-choked. The four men struggled along, often dragging their boats. The final article about their trip appeared under the headline "Glad to Get Home Alive!" Nat Galloway would have been amused.

Few who run Warm Springs Rapid today are aware how close the 1965 flash flood came to pouring its debris into a man-made lake rather than a living river. In the early 1950s the United States Bureau of Reclamation almost built a dam—Echo Park—on the Green River two miles below the Yampa confluence. The resulting reservoir would have inundated the canyons of both the Green and the Yampa, and the site of Warm Springs Rapid would have been several hundred feet under the water of a lake. Another Big Drop, Hell's Half Mile, would also have been lost.

At the outset it seemed that the canyons of the Yampa and the Green would be safe, protected as part of Dinosaur National Monument,

The long and rocky course of Warm Springs in low water. By Michael Gill, from *Whitewater Rafting* by William McGinnis.

which is administered by the National Park Service. The unusual name of this reserve came from the discovery in 1909 by the Carnegie Museum's Earl Douglas of a remarkable deposit of dinosaur bones on the northeastern slope of the Uinta Basin. Geologists believe that 140 million years ago the area was a sandbar in an ancient stream. The bodies of dinosaurs, some as long as eighty-four feet, came to rest on the bar and were covered by muds and sands that, over the eons, totaled five thousand feet. During this time, fossilization occurred as silica replaced the organic materials in the bones. Then, in another chapter of earth history, erosion peeled off the five thousand feet of sedimentary rock. Douglas arrived at the precise tick of geologic time that found the bones exposed on the surface of the earth just as they were 140 million years before.

Excited by what turned out to be one of the world's greatest collections of dinosaur remains, Douglas and other scientists urged their preservation. President Woodrow Wilson responded in 1915 by designating an 80-acre Dinosaur National Monument around the deposit. No rivers were involved at all. But in 1938 President Franklin D. Roosevelt enlarged the reserve to 200,000 acres. Now about one hundred miles of the Green and Yampa canyons were included as well as the surrounding benchland and peaks reaching nine thousand feet. The Colorado–Utah state line almost bisects the monument.

In the 1940s the Bureau of Reclamation began plans for a ten-dam, billion-dollar Colorado River Storage Project. One of the key structures was slated for the lower end of Echo Park, a few miles below the confluence of the Green and the Yampa. By the early 1950s the controversy over Echo Park Dam had reached nationwide proportions, involving Americans in a debate over protected wilderness very similar to the 1913 one concerning Hetch Hetchy Valley and the Tuolumne River. In both cases the principal issue was whether development should be permitted in an area (Dinosaur National Monument, Yosemite National Park) specifically dedicated to preserve the natural environment.

On a deeper level, the Echo Park controversy brought the American people face to face with perplexing questions about the meaning of progress and of happiness. In many eyes Echo Park was a showdown between priorities. "Let's open this to its ultimate and inevitable extent," one dam opponent urged, "and let's settle . . . once and for all time . . . whether we may have . . . wilderness areas . . . in these United States." Everyone realized that as Dinosaur went so would go a number of pending applications for economic exploitation of national parks. "Perhaps the stage is set," another preservationist remarked, "for a full dress performance by all those . . . who are protecting the West's recreational and wilderness values."

One of the first salvos in the Echo Park fight came from the facile pen of Bernard DeVoto. Writing in the *Saturday Evening Post* for July 22, 1950, DeVoto opened with a question: "Shall we let them ruin our national parks?" He argued that if the integrity of Dinosaur were compromised in the interest of economic development, no unit of the national park system would ever again be safe. In weighing the value of wild canyons and their rivers, DeVoto urged his countrymen to take their uniqueness into account. Flatwater impoundments were plentiful. You could, DeVoto pointed out, sail or waterski on dozens of them in the West. Wild rivers large enough for whitewater boating were rare, and the Yampa and the Green were two of the best. DeVoto noted that people traveled across the continent to run the Dinosaur rivers, then asked rhetorically, "Would you drive 2,000 miles to sail a dinghy there?" In DeVoto's eyes the whole nation was the loser in an exchange of a spectacular and rare recreational opportunity for a commonplace one. He rejected totally the Bureau of Reclamation's contention that Echo Park Dam would improve the recreational value of Dinosaur National Monument.

The bureau quickly rose in response. Its elaborate color brochure argued that the reservoir would improve the accessibility and even the beauty of the canyons. "Echo Park Dam," the developers asserted, "will create a playground for millions." The statement ignored the fact that for those who love wilderness, "play" and "millions" are contradictory. The Sierra Club and the Wilderness Society followed this line of reasoning in contending that in the interests of diversity and of fairness there should be opportunities for those who coveted solitude, danger, and wildness. It was a mistake to reduce national parks and monuments to amusement parks on the basis of some twisted definition of democracy. As in the case of great art or music, only a minority might appreciate wild rivers, but that minority surely had a right to a small fraction of the American landscape.

Such arguments received wide distribution in the film *Wilderness River Trail*, produced by Charles Eggert and veteran whitewater boatman Martin Litton in February 1954. Shown to thousands, including some members of Congress, it dramatized what was at stake in the canyons of the Yampa and the Green. Another broadside in the Echo Park battle was a book edited by novelist and historian Wallace Stegner,

This Is Dinosaur: Echo Park Country and Its Magic Rivers. Like the film, this book was a potent weapon in the defense of the American wilderness. Preservationists of the 1950s were determined not to lose Dinosaur as they had lost Hetch Hetchy in the 1910s by failing to state their case effectively.

Wilderness defenders also showed that since Hetch Hetchy they had learned how to play the game of politics more skillfully. The leading conservation organizations pooled their efforts in several lobbying agencies and prepared for congressional hearings with great care. Besides making a case for wild rivers, the preservationists schooled themselves in the techniques of power politics. By the end of 1955 the entire issue boiled down to the fact that the friends of Dinosaur had the support of enough congressmen to stalemate the *entire* Colorado River Storage Project indefinitely. It then became a case of simple political horse-trading. The price of passing the project was the deletion of the dam. Realizing they were trapped, the advocates of western water development grudgingly settled for less than the full loaf. When the Colorado River Storage Project became a reality on April 11, 1956, the act of authorization contained the stipulation that "no dam or reservoir constructed under the authorization of the Act shall be within any National Park or Monument."

In many ways the 1956 defeat of Echo Park Dam marked the finest hour in the history of the American wilderness movement to that date. The loss of Hetch Hetchy had in some measure been avenged, the national park idea reaffirmed. Moreover, success in defending Dinosaur encouraged preservationists to press for still more positive protection of wilderness. In the same year as the Echo Park victory Congress began consideration of the National Wilderness Preservation Act. After eight years of complex and often bitter negotiation, America constructed the world's first legally authorized system designed to protect, specifically, wilderness. The Yampa Canyon, as part of the roadless backcountry of a national monument, will ultimately be included in the National Wilderness Preservation System. Whether it will actually re-

The boatman's perspective at the start of Warm Springs. By Ray Varley.

main wilderness, country capable of giving visitors a wilderness experience, is not as certain.

The problem, as on many other whitewater rivers in the West, is people. The wilderness qualities of the Yampa are very close to being loved to death. The Yampa is exceptionally vulnerable to overcrowding. It is relatively accessible; a day's drive brings river runners from the metropolitan areas of Salt Lake City and Denver. Except for Warm Springs Rapid, which can be portaged, the Yampa is relatively easy to run. A novice can muddle through leaving only a little paint on an occasional rock to testify to his troubles. But the biggest factor in the crowding of this undammed river is the way that the boating season is confined to the runoff months of May and June. Even with a permit system in effect, the Yampa is heavily used during the prime time. Campsites are scheduled in advance of river trips, and two or more parties often share the same site. It is rare when boats of other parties are not in sight most of the day.

Despite all this, a 1973 Utah State University study revealed that almost 50 percent of river runners believed the Yampa had "about the right level of use." This finding may be the most disturbing as far as the future of the Yampa as a wilderness river is concerned. What seems to be occurring on the Yampa is a tendency sociologists call displacement. People who like wilderness are being displaced by people who simply like to have fun outdoors. The change parallels the evolving nature of river running everywhere from a solitary, risky, expeditionary kind of activity to a form of mass recreation comparable to downhill skiing. River running continues to grow, but lovers of *wild* rivers who have the time and money now travel to Ethiopia, Nepal, New Zealand, Alaska, and Peru. There the sport is still young, the local people uninterested, and the rivers empty and wild.

As the displacement process continues, those running the Yampa are increasingly people-tolerant. They do not care if their river trip is not a wilderness trip. Utah State University found that 56.6 percent of the sample of Yampa boaters interviewed indicated that they made the trip for "fun and games, adventure, excitement." Only 43.4 percent defined their goal as "wilderness, solitude, back to nature." The conclusion is that more than half of the river runners on the Yampa are not disturbed by the presence of large numbers of people any more than they would be at a football game.

Amidst all of this new controversy over the inundation of wilderness by people rather than reservoirs, Warm Springs Rapid preserves an element of honesty. A ski resort may be crowded, with lift lines two hours long, but the expert trails with their six-foot moguls still exist. Each season Warm Springs wipes out a surprisingly high percentage of the boats that start down its tongue and gives a considerable number of river runners the unnerving experience of swimming a Big Drop. The regular action of the big waves below the tongue seems to mesmerize oarsmen, and they forget about the holes waiting downstream. Frozen to the oars, they ride on to certain upsets. On many trips Warm Springs claims half the boats in a party. A few years ago seven rafts entered the rapid in a neat formation and seven rafts floated out at the bottom upside down—still in formation. There was a lot of swimming that day. Even the professionals continue to have trouble in Warm Springs. The big pontoons some of them use lack the quickness in changing direction that success in this drop demands. Recently an experienced commercial boatman, a Green Beret veteran from Vietnam, rolled his rig at the top of the rapid. In the next three hundred yards Warm Springs picked his boat clean: oars, frame, packs, and people ended up scattered along several miles of shoreline.

Regulations and crowds are part of the Yampa today, but so is Warm Springs. It provides, after all, the opportunity to be challenged, and perhaps overwhelmed, by nature. For many this remains the essential part of a wilderness experience.

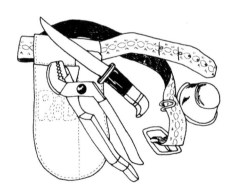

Five

Satan's Gut

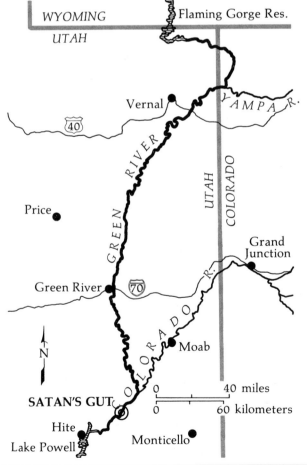

WYOMING
UTAH
Flaming Gorge Res.

YAMPA R.

Vernal

40

GREEN RIVER

UTAH
COLORADO

Price

Grand
Junction

Green River

70

COLORADO R.

N

Moab

COLORADO

0   40 miles

0   60 kilometers

SATAN'S GUT

Hite
Lake Powell

Monticello

This is a day when life and the world seem to be standing still — only time and the river flowing past the mesas.

EDITH WHARTON

Men marveled at the Grand Canyon but feared Cataract. In the labyrinth of canyons lacing the basin of the Colorado River, Cataract Canyon is the most deceptive and devious. Above are the placid waters of the Green and Colorado rivers, whose serenity lures the boatmen into unwarranted confidence and belies the turbulence ahead. Below Cataract the blue waters of Lake Powell shimmer in the sun, having drowned the spectacular rapid at Dark Canyon and the scenic wonders of Narrow and Glen canyons. Cataract Canyon is unique. The biggest cumulative drop along any comparable stretch of the Colorado River, it embraces some of the wildest, most challenging, and violent whitewater on western rivers. Here, in the short space of forty-one miles, the Colorado drops 415 feet, or ten feet per mile. Cataract is the deepest canyon in Utah, its walls towering 2,000 feet above the river. They are steep walls, precipitous, moving upward in hostile ledges which characterize the violence of the rapids they have created. There are few tributaries in Cataract Canyon, but during the thunderstorms on the dry plateau above, the rain, reddened by the desert soil, will plunge over the cliffs in dramatic vermillion waterfalls. They swell the river as it moves inexorably between the canyon walls to the three continuous rapids known collectively as the Big Drop. The third and biggest is Satan's Gut.

In high water, during the spring runoff, the three become one. At the beginning is a broad beach piled high with driftwood where many parties have camped before challenging the rapid. The first part of the Big Drop consists of rolling waves down a staircase of violent water. Here the current sweeps the boats into the second and more dangerous phase. A gigantic rock has fallen from the walls above and lodged in a slot in the right center of the rapid. Once beyond the rock, several hundred yards of large, rolling tailwaves suck bodies, boats, debris, and water toward one of the greatest holes on all the Colorado: Satan's Gut.

Cataract Canyon is still known as "the Graveyard of the Colorado" because so many have died in its rapids. Even those who survived being capsized or wrecked then faced the grim prospect of walking out of the canyon. Unlike the Grand Canyon, in which there are many trails to the rim, support, and safety, Cataract Canyon has few routes to the top of the gorge, and beyond is harsh desert surrounded by mountainous country made formidable by the scarcity of water and the heat from the implacable sun. There are those who have died on the plateau after surviving the rapids in Cataract Canyon.

The frontiersmen came west in search of minerals, beaver, and livestock, but even tough mountain men who penetrated into the canyon country in the 1830s shied away from Cataract Canyon. They left a few marks, but did not return. Those who came after the mountain men made their way into Glen Canyon to mine for gold, sought ranches in the canyon of the San Juan for cattle, and even went down into Narrow Canyon searching for minerals. But Cataract Canyon had little to offer except the excitement of whitewater.

Cataract Canyon begins just below the meeting of the waters of the Green River flowing southward from Wyoming and Utah and the Colorado flowing westward out of the Rocky Mountains. Originally called the Grand River, the mocha-colored Colorado merges with the clearer waters of the Green at the head of Cataract Canyon. Here at the confluence, on the sand of the west bank, John Wesley Powell and his men camped for several days in July 1869. They caulked the boats, dried their food, which had been diminished by two months' supply in the rapids of Lodore, and gazed upward to the bizarre formations on the canyon rim called by the Indians *Toom'-pin wu-near' Tu-weap,* the Land of Standing Rocks. This was "a whole land of naked rocks, with giant forms carved on it: cathedral-shaped buttes, towering hundreds or thousands of feet; cliffs that cannot be scaled, and canyon walls that shrink the river into insignificance, with vast, hollow domes, and tall pinnacles, and shafts set on the verge overhead, and all highly colored—buff, gray, red, brown, and chocolate; never lichened; never moss-covered; but bare and often polished."

On July 19 Powell and George Y. Bradley climbed out on the east side of the canyon across the river from camp. To the west rose the Land of Standing Rocks, and beyond stood mighty "cliffs where the soaring eagle is lost to view ere he reaches the summit." To the northeast were the towering peaks of the Manti La Sal, green with pine and capped by snow. In all directions there is "but a wilderness of rocks; deep gorges, where the rivers are lost below cliffs and towers and pinnacles; and ten thousand strangely carved forms in every direction; and beyond them mountains blending with the clouds."

Two years later Powell came back to the confluence on his second expedition down the Grand Canyon and lingered another five days on the same bank. Frederick S. Dellenbaugh thought it a dreary place, "with no footing but a few sand-banks that are being constantly cut away and reformed by the whirling current." Today the tamarisk form an impenetrable wall beyond the sand of the beach where Powell and his men camped amidst scrawny hackberry trees and weeds. Few people camp there today, but those who believe in history will sometimes stop to watch the meeting of the waters.

Those who have been through Cataract Canyon can understand why Powell spent five days at the confluence in 1871. He had been there before and knew what lay ahead down the narrow confines of the canyon. On his first expedition, in 1869, not knowing the dangers that lay beyond, Powell had sensed there was something ominous and elemental about the meeting of two great rivers. The rocks told him. Even to a novice the confluence signifies a beginning of new adventure, and to gaze downstream into constricting and rising walls, one instinctively knows that the days of quiet water are now behind. History and geology shrink before the force of these rapids which have killed more men than any other river in the West. The greatest of these is the Big Drop and the worst of the Big Drop is Satan's Gut.

Powell and his men left the confluence on July 21, 1869, and were in trouble from the start. "The river is rough, and bad rapids, in close succession, are found." After Powell's boat, the *Emma Dean*, was swamped and oars were lost, they became more cautious. Resin was collected to caulk the boats whose seams had been opened by the power of the water crashing over rocks and rising into standing waves. The oars were replaced by shaping cottonwood logs taken from piles of driftwood. On July 24 Powell reached the depth of Cataract Canyon at the top of Mile Long Rapid, where huge boulders choked the channel. Painfully they portaged the supplies across the boulder-strewn shore and then lined the boats down over the angular rocks that even today intimidate boatmen.

The following day Powell's party reached the top of the Big Drop. They attempted to run this, the most difficult rapid in the canyon, and at the outset the *Emma Dean* was caught in a whirlpool and more oars were lost. Putting ashore, all the boats were lined safely down through Satan's Gut. Powell was more fortunate than those who followed.

In 1875 Powell produced his report, "Explorations of the Colorado River of the West and Its Tributaries." It was in fact a composite of the journals of his first expedition in 1869 and his second expedition in 1871–1872, intermixed with his magazine articles in *Scribners Monthly*. Scholars have criticized Powell for taking liberties with history, but his purpose was to attract the attention of the public and particularly the Congress of the United States to convince them to grant additional funds for geological research. He was astoundingly successful: his report created a sensation in the Congress, which ultimately rewarded him with the directorship of the United States Geological Survey. The public was also delighted that a government report could be filled with such adventure and excitement.

Powell's report was widely read, and among its readers was a college student at Miami University in Ohio, Robert Brewster Stanton. Like so many after him, Stanton dreamed of the beauties of the Colorado and its great canyon with vertical walls a mile deep into the earth. He talked with his fellow students about grandiose schemes of building bridges across the chasm, and these dreams inspired him to a career in civil engineering. His subsequent work, which included a reconnaissance for the Southwest and Atlantic and Pacific railroads, brought him recognition for his talents as an engineer.

This was the great age of railroad building in the West, and Americans left their covered wagons to press westward on iron rails. The golden spike was driven at Promontory Point, Utah, on May 10, 1869, to link the Pacific Ocean with the Atlantic. It was twelve days later that John Wesley Powell set out from the town of Green River, Wyoming, to explore the canyons of the Colorado. The railway builders were insatiable: The Southern Pacific reached Yuma in 1877. Between the Rio Grande and Needles, California, came the forerunners of the Santa Fe. To the north the Rio Grande and Western cut across the Gunnison Valley to the Green River and beyond.

In the 1880s a prospector, S. S. Harper, made his way across southern Colorado and central and northern Arizona to follow the line of the Atlantic and Pacific railway survey which Robert Stanton had previously carried out. Under the bright moon and stars of those crystalline nights on the great plateau country of the Four Corners, Harper conceived of a railroad by the waters of the Colorado River, a route more level and practical than the mountain ranges he had so painfully overcome. He made his way back to Denver to sell his scheme. These were bonanza years in which men made and lost vast sums of money. Speculators from all over the world were investing in the magic rails which took the course of empire westward beyond the hundredth meridian to the Pacific Ocean. The West was a land of adventurers, hardy outdoorsmen, scouts, and surveyors plumbing their way to the Pacific shore. It was a land of businessmen and investors, too, smart men in swank suits who congregated in Denver to put together the schemes that would make their fortunes.

One of these men was Frank M. Brown, a State-of-Mainer by birth who grew up in Washington, D.C., and went west to work in Alaska for the Hudson's Bay Company. An entrepreneur, he heard of the great boom in Leadville, Colorado, and arrived there to be put in charge of the Farwell group of mines at Independence. He established a reputation for integrity, and his charisma attracted a wide friendship which the Denver *Republican* described as more precious than gold. He was known as "a man of force, with daring and enterprise." Brown made his money in the West and was determined to make more by taking the way westward through the canyons of the Colorado. After all, he thought, the waters of thousands of years had done the work of grading the perfect railroad bed. His acquaintance with Harper gave him the idea, and Frank Brown set out to turn the vague scheme of a prospector into a profitable enterprise.

Brown's ideas spawned more than just a railway to the Pacific. He was also after coal, to feed the furnaces of the iron horses rolling westward. There was none in California, but it was well known that large coal deposits were scattered all through western Colorado and Utah. What better way to carry the coal to the Pacific than down the water-level route along the Colorado River? Here was Yankee ingenuity utilizing the work of tens of thousands of years of cutting by water to create a route to the Golden State.

On March 25, 1889, Frank Brown formed the Denver, Colorado Canyon, and Pacific Railroad Company with S. S. Harper and set out to survey the route and to find financing to build it. Three days later the survey team, under the direction of Frank C. Kendrick, began the journey from Grand Junction down the Colorado past the Mormon community of Moab to the confluence with the Green River. Reaching the confluence Kendrick's party made their way up to the railroad town then called Blake, but now known as Green River, Utah. Here they were met by Brown and his expedition of sixteen men who were prepared to go all the way to the Pacific. Brown had advertised for a chief engineer to conduct the survey to the coast, and in the middle of April hired Robert Brewster Stanton. Stanton brought an engineer's realism to match Brown's enthusiasm.

Frank M. Brown never appreciated the power of moving water. He had talked with John Wesley Powell, who described with his customary eloquence the danger of river running down the Colorado, but Brown was not impressed. His boats were small, narrow, and lightweight compared to those of Powell. They looked superb, sleek, and fast, but they were hardly able to take the buffeting Brown and his men would soon experience in Cataract Canyon. Like most beginners on the river, his men brought too much personal equipment, too much luggage packed in cumbersome zinc-lined boxes, and not enough food and supplies. When loaded, the six boats were so heavy that Brown had to lash three together in order to carry all the unnecessary gear. This awkward raft was difficult to control and unmanageable in turbulent water.

The expedition left Green River, Utah, on May 25, 1889, and in four days floated down to the confluence with the Colorado. On May 30 they drifted two miles along the left bank below the confluence to the brink of Cataract Canyon. Of entering the Canyon, Stanton, the realist and engineer, later wrote, "It would be a great relief, if it were possible, for me to blot out all remembrance of the two weeks following this evening of May 31st." Stanton's forebodings were deepened by his engineer's calculation of the impact between Brown's light cedar boats and the hard rocks of Cataract Canyon. The boats may have been delightfully suited to maneuvering on the quiet waters above Cataract Canyon; not in heavy rapids. But the light construction of the boats was not Brown's greatest mistake: he had brought no life preservers, and this omission cost him his life.

Like Powell and many who have followed, Brown and his men were in trouble from the beginning of Cataract Canyon. At the top of the first rapid, known today as Brown Betty, after Brown's kitchen boat, Brown's cumbersome raft loaded with provisions and the boat towing it were swept away. To save themselves the men cut the rope to the raft

The camera angle makes this light raft appear to be in serious trouble near the top of Satan's Gut. By Ray Varley.

and watched it plunge over the falls and career down the river to be destroyed on the rocks below. This disaster was followed by others. Brown's boat capsized and he and two other men were swept down for more than a mile and a half before they were able to make their way to shore. Thereafter, they worked their way down through the canyon, portaging most of the rapids, sometimes losing the boats only to catch them below in the eddies, filled to the gunwales with water.

On June 7 the kitchen boat, the *Brown Betty*, was again upset, this time losing the remaining cooking gear. One boat was so badly battered that it was good only to be broken up to provide wood to repair the others. From one day to the next the expedition struggled down the canyon, portaging the supplies and lining the boats over the rocks along the shore with hands burned by the lines pulled by the force of the river. On June 11 their last ration of beans disappeared into the river and on June 12 the last coffee pot sank. The next day, June 13, they faced the Big Drop at its most dangerous time, mid-June. The full flood of the Colorado was hitting the most precipitous fall on the river, the third part of the Big Drop, Satan's Gut.

It took Brown and his men two days to line the boats and portage the supplies down through the Big Drop, and by June 15 all that was left were four boats and little food. Stanton took charge. He had the remaining supplies prepared and divided into sixteen portions, enough to last a week. The party, discouraged at the prospect, continued down the remaining rapids of Cataract Canyon to the quiet waters of Narrow Canyon where they were resupplied by provisions brought up from Dandy Crossing, where the prospector Cass Hite had settled in 1883 to mine for gold. Regrouped and newly supplied with food, Brown's expedition continued through Glen Canyon to Lee's Ferry. By July 9 Brown had gone overland to Kanab and returned with three boats and supplies sufficient to allow him to continue on his quest for a water-level route to the Pacific. Below Lee's Ferry was Marble Canyon, where they portaged Badger and Soap Creek rapids, camping at the foot of Soap Creek. The following day Brown's boat capsized a half mile below Soap. Having no life preserver, Brown was drowned in whirlpools, leaving only his notebook floating on the river. Stunned, the party spent the remaining daylight vainly seeking the body, which never was found. Three days later a second boat capsized, and two other members of the expedition, Peter Hansborough and the black steward, H. R. Richards, were drowned. The deaths completely destroyed the sagging morale of the Brown expedition, and Stanton decided to leave the river at the first available point, just north of Vasey's Paradise. To his credit, he did return in 1890 to complete the railroad survey that no one ever used.

After the railway builders came the miners. In 1891 James S. Best led a party of nine men in two boats: prospectors setting out to make their way down the Colorado seeking minerals and wealth. They drifted past the confluence and then, like Brown and Stanton, they too were in trouble at the beginning of Cataract Canyon. At the top of Mile Long

Rapid opposite Range Canyon one of their boats smashed into a large rock in mid-river and broke into pieces. Though the men were able to save themselves, they lost valuable supplies and the boat. Nine men were now left in the remaining boat, the *Hattie*, and their reaction to Cataract Canyon and its rapids was dramatically recorded in their own inscription at the head of Mile Long Rapid: "Camp #No. 7. Hell to pay. No. #1 sunk and down." With only one boat for the whole party, they proceeded cautiously and like those before them lined through the Big Drop.

Best was not the only one to lose boats in Cataract Canyon. In September 1907, Bert Loper with Charles Russell and Edmund Monnette lost his steel boat in the Big Drop and, like Best, had to continue in a single boat to Dandy Crossing, which is now known on the river as Hite. The following year W. J. Law lost his boat in the Big Drop, and two years later Pat Malone saw his partner drown in Satan's Gut. In 1910 Satan's Gut claimed two men and a boy. The next year two unidentified men left Green River, only to wreck their boat and perish at the bottom of the Big Drop. Between 1909 and 1912 at least seven men lost their lives in the Big Drop, most at Satan's Gut.

The challenge of the river and the lure of riches have drawn men to Cataract Canyon. Some are known; most are not. But there were some who came and lived to write of their adventures, leaving behind a vivid picture of the Big Drop. On September 12, 1909 Julius F. Stone left Green River, Wyoming with four boats and the redoubtable river guide Nathaniel T. Galloway. Stone was a serious man with an eye for profit from the fire engines he manufactured in Columbus, Ohio, and the puritan values of mid-America. Unlike the mountain men, the railway builders, or the prospectors, Julius Stone came to Cataract Canyon for adventure. And, like most who venture into the wilderness for pleasure, he came superbly equipped with four boats built to his specifications and the finest boatman of his day—Nat Galloway.

In September the water is low in Cataract Canyon, and Stone found that the rocks were exposed and plentiful. One member of the party, S.

S. Dubendorff, from Richfield, Utah, careened off the large rock at the top of Mile Long Rapid, lost most of his supplies, and thought he would have drowned were it not for his life jacket. Still, unlike Brown and Stanton, who had lined their boats down the Big Drop in high water, Stone and Galloway were prepared to run. So impressive were the falls that Stone attempted to take a photograph of the Big Drop.

Wishing the picture of a boat in turbulent water, I purposely went through the largest waves of Rapid No. 23 [Satan's Gut] with the result that the boat failed to rise over the second wave; also the third one. Both of these broke entirely over the boat, the first one carrying away the fender and everything else moveable in the boat except myself. The print shows indistinctly the boat just before it disappeared under the second wave, and you see by the result that our experiment was practically barren of the object sought.

In 1901 Ellsworth and Emery Kolb gazed across the rim of the Grand Canyon and instantly knew they had found their home. The canyon worked its magic, and the Kolb brothers stayed to build a house where they could see in every direction the grandeur of the mesas, buttes, and the chasm plunging to the river. In the next forty years the Kolb brothers ranged through the canyon country, carrying out their profession of photography. They explored the depths of the Grand to the Colorado and hiked the side canyons which lead to the river, they read the report of John Wesley Powell's expedition, and over the years met and talked with Stanton, Stone, Galloway, Russell, and Monnette. Year after year they saw the river flowing to the sea and reflected on its many moods, from placid water to turbulent and plunging rapids, visible even from a thousand feet on the Tonto Plateau, and in their thoughts was born a plan to follow Powell and make the first motion picture of the rapids and the walls that rise above them.

On September 8, 1911, Ellsworth and Emery Kolb left Green River, Wyoming, in two boats, the *Edith* and the *Defiance.* They passed through Red Canyon and Lodore, gaining sufficient experience in Ashley Falls, Disaster Falls, and Triplett to know they should portage

Hell's Half Mile. The Kolbs were men of common sense and enormous courage, with a deep love of the canyons and the river. They pressed on to the confluence of the Green and Colorado and on to the top of Cataract Canyon—by now well known as the Graveyard of the Colorado. Here in Cataract Canyon the Kolb brothers began to feel for the first time the force of water moving through big rapids.

We always thought we needed a certain amount of thrills to make life sufficiently interesting for us. In a few hours time in the central portion of Cataract Canyon we experienced nearly enough thrills to last us a lifetime. In one or two of the upper canyons we thought we were running rapids, now we were learning what rapids really were.

The Kolb brothers found more in Cataract Canyon than rapids. Their first night in the canyon they came upon a lone man in an old leaky boat. He called himself Smith. He was dressed in a neat suit and tie, cleanly shaven, and if not for the Kolbs would be forgotten. Charles Smith was a trapper who had made his way down the Green River, and although the Kolbs invited him to join them he was determined to go alone despite his rotting boat and his inexperience. He survived, clinging to his capsized boat as it plunged through Satan's Gut.

The next day the Kolbs set out again, running Mile Long and coming to the top of the Big Drop. They studied the first part of the Big Drop, watching logs and debris float through. Then they followed, Emery ending on a rock and Ellsworth moving too far to the left only to be pulled back into the main channel by the vagaries of the river, which left him and his boat filled with water. They camped that night at the bottom of the second part of the Big Drop, rested, and spent the following day reconnoitering Satan's Gut. Above Satan's Gut is that large pool in which even the most powerful boatmen find it difficult to maneuver. But in low water the Kolbs hit the channel just to the left of center and disappeared three times in the mountains of water that swamped their boats.

The Kolbs had run the Big Drop, and, although at low water, it was recorded on film that displayed their skill at maneuvering the heavy

Early morning sun reflected in the Colorado River.

A mere few feet of error in positioning can mean the difference between success and failure in a Big Drop. Lava Falls, the left side.

Running the "slot" in Lava, to the right of the falls.

A thirty-foot pontoon raft bends in the hole at the bottom of Lava Falls.

Running the "V" wave in Lava at high water.

Boat meets standing wave at the bottom of Lava.

Facing page: Overcast afternoon on the Rogue River, Orego

Kayakers may flip and roll back up
several times in a Big Drop. Lava Falls.

Small inflatable rafts such as this one
rely on bouyancy and maneuverability. Lava Falls.

The big hole in Crystal at high water.

cataract boats. They had learned to read the water and sucessfully pressed down the river to reach Needles, California, on January 18, 1912. They were on the river 101 days.

Others came after the Kolb brothers. Charles Smith, the trapper, and Galloway passed through the Big Drop in 1912. Bert Loper and Charles Russell followed in July 1914. From the beginning Loper, a veteran river man, knew they would be in trouble in the Big Drop. Russell's steel boats were only twelve inches deep, and Loper knew they would be sunk in the heavy water of Cataract Canyon. "The big drop in Cataract Canyon . . . was beyond description. It was a foam, a fury that drowned out even thought. It finished us. My friend lost his nerve and his mind completely. He dropped his oars. His boat swamped."

They lost both boats but saved their lives to hike out through the blazing heat, which blistered Loper and drove Russell insane. Reaching Hite and safety, Russell later died in a mental hospital, and Loper stayed on at Hite to marry an eighteen-year-old beauty, Rachel Jamison. This last disaster in the Big Drop marked the end of an era in the running of Cataract Canyon. Gone were the trappers, the prospectors, and the railway men. What seemed left for the Big Drop was to complete the geological survey which Powell had begun in 1869. Indeed, so thorough had been his explorations from 1869 to 1872 that half a century passed before scientists again took an interest in Cataract Canyon.

After the First World War greater wealth grew out of the West than was ever dreamed of by the forty-niners. Wealth sprang from power and irrigation; power for the burgeoning cities of California and water to make the desert bloom. Both of these needs, which John Wesley Powell had predicted fifty years before, the Colorado could provide. In order to produce electricity and channel water, science and technology were called upon. As early as 1889 the United States Geological Survey had begun stream measurements throughout the basin of the Colorado; now, in 1921, Cataract Canyon was carefully surveyed for its potential as a source of power and irrigation. Under the direction of W. E. Chenoweth a party of engineers and scientists was guided by the Kolb

Facing page: Afternoon thunderstorm in Grand Canyon, downstream from Nankoweap Creek.

brothers down Cataract Canyon. Ellsworth and Emery Kolb rediscovered the same thrill in running the Big Drop.

I ran three boats and had some trouble with each one. Boat one hit a rock, whirled bow first, submarined, and an extra oar was washed off and gave me a chase to the head of the next rapid before it was recovered. Run two an oar lock separated and I used an extra paddle to recover it. *Static* also hit a rock but no harm was done and we muddled through.

Try as it might, Satan's Gut could not claim the Kolbs or their boats.

After the geological survey of 1921 Americans had no practical use for Cataract Canyon. The beaver were gone, there was no gold, and the railway could not be built. Geological curiosity was satisfied by the final mapping. Indeed, Americans appeared to have lost interest in Cataract Canyon, which after all had claimed the lives of a third of those who had attempted to run it. Most of the drowned and dead had been the unknown and forgotten men of the disappearing frontier. America came of age in the 1920s with new amusements such as radio and motion pictures to keep the people at home. When they traveled it was by car or rail, both of which bypassed the formidable canyon country on the way west to the Pacific shore. Common sense showed that an honest man could not make a living out of the rock and sand of canyonlands. So the canyon rivers were left alone and remained much less traveled than during the decades of discovery before the First World War. River running had been exploration. Now it was to become adventure. The challenge and dangers of the Colorado were well known; in fact, danger was the principal attraction to the new era of river runners.

All of the river parties after the geological survey were characterized by an element of the absurd—hence their delight. There was Clyde Eddy and his party of nine college students, a dog, a tramp, and a bear, who left Green River in 1927. He was followed several months later by the Pathe–Bray party of professional motion picture photographers. The next year, 1928, Cataract Canyon witnessed the strange saga of

Glen R. Hyde and his bride Bessie, who set out alone from Green River, Utah, to pass successfully through Cataract Canyon only to drown somewhere below Lava Falls in the Grand Canyon. Years passed before men were seen again in Cataract Canyon. Satan's Gut claimed the kayak of Harold H. Leich in 1933, forcing him to swim to Hite and walk out to Hanksville. Five years later another party, including two remarkable women, Dr. Elzada U. Clover and Lois Jotter, capsized in Satan's Gut, but struggled on to Lee's Ferry. The pleasure trips were few, however, for Americans on the whole were not yet ready for mass outdoor recreation. The exception was Clyde Eddy.

Clyde Eddy grew up in Utah and Colorado and in 1919 had hiked down the Hermit Trail in the Grand Canyon to see the river. Like so many before him he became obsessed by the waters flowing to the sea and spent the subsequent years developing equipment and supplies and talking with those who had run the Colorado. In the spring of 1927 he placed an advertisement in university newspapers calling for volunteers to accompany him on an expedition. Where, he did not say. Eddy knew of the Pathe–Bray party and was determined to keep his intentions secret from the collegians who responded to his invitation: "Volunteers are wanted for important geological–geographical expedition scheduled to leave New York City about June 10 to be gone about six or eight weeks." Clyde Eddy had a deep belief in the adaptability and resourcefulness of college men which he had learned in the trenches of France in the First World War. He felt that a "pink-wristed" college boy will stand up as well in the face of long and continued danger as the average "hard boiled Army sergeant." And so the collegians came to the Colorado. Nine in all, they came from Harvard, Notre Dame, Northwestern, and Coe College. They were incongruously joined by a bum who happened to be in Green River, Utah, making his way west.

Eddy may have longed for daring adventure, but he planned his 1927 expedition with great care. He had three specially designed boats: the *Coronado*, the *Powell*, and the *Dellenbaugh*. They were twenty-two feet long, had a five-foot beam, and were built of Mexican mahogany with oak ribs. He recruited Parley Galloway as boatman. Forty years old and the son of the famous Nat Galloway, Parley had been on the rivers since he was fifteen years old, but had never been below the confluence of the Green and the Colorado. To complete the party, there was an Airedale dog named Rags and a bear cub christened Cataract by the collegians. And off they went from Green River, Utah, thirteen in all, with great exuberance and confidence until suddenly confronted by Cataract Canyon.

Under Galloway's tutelage Eddy and his collegians had begun to understand the secrets of running rivers. Eddy wrote eloquently of the qualities required of boatmen. "Successful rapids running calls for intimate knowledge of the river, cool judgment, courage, willingness to take appalling but unavoidable chances, and fine skill in handling boats."

As they worked their way down Cataract Canyon they ran a few rapids but lined most, carrying the equipment, stumbling over the boulders and driftwood along the shore. Like most inexperienced river runners they had more equipment than they required; it was soon left behind. They lined their boats through Mile Long Rapid, nearly losing one at the top, and here Eddy described the fury of the great holes that strike fear in the hearts of boatmen.

The muddy water sweeping down stream pours over a great boulder in the channel. There is a "hump" in the river where the boulder rests and that hump, called a "pour", is all there is to warn the navigator of the terrible menace in his way. Then, with a roar, the water plunges down into the "hole" and woe betide the man whose boat is caught in its frightful vortex. One navigator on the river, swept toward a "hole" and unable to pull away from it, turned his boat stern first and resigned himself to his fate. The stern of his eighteen-foot boat swept over the "pour", dropped into the "hole" and the boat turned over from end to end on the unfortunate explorer. A "hole" is a miniature waterfall and a man caught under its drop is trapped and held there, battered to pieces, smothered by the cruel, muddy river . . . "Holes" to me were the most dreadful of the many dangers on the river. Rocks can be seen and they strike you clean and honest blows. Whirlpools are quiet and their dangers lie hidden below the swirling surface of the turbid stream. The possibility of being struck by falling rocks is remote. A "hole" may be hidden anywhere below an innocent looking "hump" in the surface of the water and the churning fury of its vortex—the eddying turmoil of its roaring, foaming water—brings swift death to any man thrown into it. His puny effort is hopeless, struggling vainly against the current which inevitably sweeps him under the "pour", battering him against the rocks until he is dead.

Lining the first part of the Big Drop, they lost control of one of the boats, which was swept into a large hole and immediately capsized, breaking open the hatches and losing all the food and equipment. Thereafter, they portaged all the supplies around the first part of the Big Drop in a pouring rain, tripping, sliding, and falling over the slippery rocks. The heavy rain continued, and the Colorado was rising rapidly as they landed at the top of the second part of the Big Drop. Here Eddy compared the water level with pictures taken by Emery Kolb in 1911. At the top of the second part of the Big Drop is a huge rock where boatmen today slice to the left and drop behind in the dead water to give pause to line up the run down the slot. In 1927 the rock was completely covered, forming an enormous hole as the water cascaded over it. Eddy capitulated to the river, and once again they hauled the supplies around the fall and lined the boats down through the second part of the Big Drop to the head of Satan's Gut.

That night, July 5, they were awakened by a rumble like thunder. In fact, the sky was bright with stars. The rumble was not the rain but the river. Desperately in the dark they hauled their equipment up the talus slope as the river rose swiftly. The flow was later gauged at 119,000 cubic feet per second, the highest water in many years. In Green River, Harry Howland tried to warn them by placing messages in bottles and tossing them into the river. It did little good as the collegians watched Cataract Canyon in full fury. The following day they waited for the torrent to subside, then hauled the boats around Satan's Gut. The Big Drop had been passed again, not run, but safely portaged.

Bruised and battered, the Eddy expedition finally reached Lee's Ferry, from which four of the original collegians, Rags, and Cataract continued down the Colorado to Needles, California, which they reached on August 8, 1927. They wrecked one boat in Dubendorf Rapid and nearly left the dog behind on a stretch of beach. In the end the one who made it through with the most equanimity was the bear. Perhaps it was his nature, but Cataract seemed to accept the perils as something that every bear should experience.

Rivers attract extraordinary people, and Cataract Canyon more than its share. Powell, Brown, and Stone were all unusual men; Eddy was certainly equal to them, as were Norman Nevills and Amos Burg. Nevills had run on the San Juan in 1933, 1934, and 1936 in cataract boats and pioneered commercial trips down the Grand Canyon in the thirties and forties, but he never liked Cataract Canyon. His first trip was in 1938, when he led an expedition that included Dr. Elzada Clover and Lois Jotter, the first two women to go down the Colorado. Their boat, with Wayne McComkie at the oars, turned over in Satan's Gut and inspired the inscription chiseled into stone "Turned over #2." Nevills ran Cataract Canyon and Satan's Gut again in 1940 with Barry Goldwater, the future U. S. Senator from Arizona.

More significant, although not recognized as such at the time, was Amos Burg's run down Cataract in an inflatable raft in 1939. Burg, who was a photographer of international reputation, presaged the new age of recreational river running by using a rubber raft. During World War II the inflatable assault craft was developed to attack the island bastions of the new Japanese Empire, and huge quantities were manufactured. Surplus military inflatables began to appear on western rivers shortly after the war, and the same technology has gone on to produce the inflatable rubber rafts in which tens of thousands of people have since run rivers. Compared to previous equipment, the inflatable was relatively inexpensive, so its widespread availability represented a key development in the growth of river running as a sport. Dick Griffith and Kenny Ross were among the first to use inflatable craft after the war, but the application of this technology to large recreational river trips owes most to the extraordinary talent of a remarkable woman, Georgie White.

The average person could probably not imagine an individual such as Georgie White. She created a second revolution in river running in the American West. The first revolution had been inaugurated when Nat Galloway ran his cataract boats stern first. Every boatman since Galloway has followed this technique, which gives greater control and maneuverability in rapids. The second revolution was precipitated by Georgie White's use of military surplus inflatable rubber rafts. These neoprene rafts built by the United States Navy were fifteen feet long and seven feet wide, and could support ten men and 3,600 pounds of equipment. Known as "ten-mans," they were manufactured by the thousands and sold cheaply at the end of the war as surplus. In 1946 Harry Aleson of Richfield, Utah bought a smaller "seven-man" inflatable raft, in which he and Georgie White ran Cataract Canyon and Satan's Gut. On that trip they upset in some rapids and portaged around others. From 1947 to 1954 Georgie made many runs through Grand Canyon in a ten-man, often alone. Otherwise, only the odd person or the stray outdoorsman ventured into the canyons during those years. There was Norman Nevills with his cataract boats, but his trips were expensive and only for the few. Georgie White changed all that. She opened the river for the many.

It was in 1954, halfway through a trip down the Grand Canyon, that Georgie took the first step in the "inflatable revolution." She lashed together three of her ten-man rafts side-by-side, thereby obtaining greater capacity, stability, and safety than any craft previously had offered in the big water of the Colorado. One innovation of the "triple rig," as it soon became known, was that it was run perpendicular to the current by two oarsmen manning sweeps in the front and back. But of greater consequence, the triple rig permitted more people to run the river with fewer boatmen, and in greater safety, than the cataract boats of Galloway or Nevills. Along with Bus Hatch, Rod Sanderson, and Moki-Mac Ellington, Georgie and her triple rigs led the way through Cataract for later boatmen like Dee Holladay, who has run Satan's Gut more than any other riverman. To this day a properly lashed and loaded triple rig is still the safest and most stable rowed boat on big western rivers.

The triple rig was only the beginning. In the winter of 1954 Georgie purchased three neoprene bridge pontoons, thirty-seven feet long and shaped like big sausages. When lashed together and steered by a 10 h.p. outboard motor, these pontoons formed a raft twenty-seven feet wide that could carry many people and surge through the biggest rapids on the Colorado. Georgie wanted to introduce her passion for the river country to more people at less cost, and the pontoon raft, with subsequent refinements by commercial outfitters, made it possible for thousands to experience canyon country. But ironically, this product of her ingenuity has been the single most important factor in transforming river running on her beloved Colorado from a wilderness experience to mass outdoor recreation. She succeeded beyond her wildest dreams. With the best of intentions, she initiated the myriad of problems created when many people descend upon a fragile environment.

Georgie's greatest run in Cataract Canyon came in 1957, when she encountered the highest water stage since that seen in 1927 by Clyde Eddy, his collegians, and the bear. The Big Drop was enormous on June 14, 1957. The head boatman was Fred Eiseman, who had run through the Grand Canyon on two occasions but knew little of Cataract. He had even less experience with the enormous amount of water pouring through the canyon. Immediately upon entering Cataract in June of that year, however, he was aware that they were all in trouble.

As every honest boatman knows, there are moments when the equipment compensates for human error or helplessness. The stability of the triple rig did it for Fred Eiseman in Cataract Canyon that day. The Big Drop was a maelstrom at 110,000 cubic feet per second, and it left an

With Sandy Nash holding down the bow, Rod Nash threads through the irregular waves of Satan's Gut. By Ray Varley.

indelible impression upon him and his passengers. A passenger, Joel Sayre, wrote:

Well, Cataract may be absolutely lousy with rocks, but I can't remember seeing a single one sticking above the surface. I remember nothing but waves and waves. They were gathered in conventions and these conventions seemed to stretch from cliff wall to cliff wall, the biggest waves heaped up in the middle, and the smaller ones curling in from the sides to join them, gathering force on the way. And the conventions got larger and tougher to deal with as the run went on.

Twenty years later Fred Eiseman remembers that extraordinary run:

My recollections are of total helplessness. The water was so high and so powerful and fast that there was no doubt whatsoever who was in charge—

the river. I had no feeling of being able to affect the course of the boat, except when in an eddy. There were almost no rocks in the river to avoid. If there had been, I wouldn't have been able to avoid them anyway. As soon as one shoved the boat off from shore, it was caught in a powerful grip of the current, and the enormous energy of the water made any attempt at rowing seem ridiculous. It was about all we could do to hang on, try to avoid the biggest waves, and marvel at how fast the scenery was going by, and hope we'd make it to shore before Boulder Dam.

Georgie warned of the Big Drop and Satan's Gut. But Cataract's rapids vary enormously in proportion to the stream flow. All rapids do, of course, but Cataract rapids change more than most, I think. In 1957 it was virtually impossible to distinguish one rapid from another. I think it would have been impossible even with a map and guidebook. The danger resulted from huge waves—laterals and tail or convergence waves—not from rocks and holes. There was little shoreline. It was largely submerged. Trees, partly under water, lined the banks and one was as likely to get snagged or ripped up by them as by mid-river rocks. If one jumped ashore to a rock with the bowline, it was extremely difficult to hold on to the boat. In fact, we left one passenger behind, temporarily, for this very reason.

I couldn't possibly tell which was the Big Drop. There was no clear-cut separation between rapids at all—just enormous waves, tapering into huge waves, tapering into colossal waves, and then way back to just enormous. Perhaps it was the rapids in which one of our passengers got thrown out, as Joel describes. I managed to haul her back in. It wasn't really very heroic. I didn't have anything else to do—or at least couldn't do anything else. More likely, the Big Drop was the one in which the super colossal waves pancaked the front boat [of the triple rig] back on to the rear one.

Today around the campfires in Cataract Canyon the boatmen talk of that great run of Georgie White and Fred Eiseman in 1957. In her own quaint way Georgie summed it up the best: "I never saw worsen than Cataract. The average can't imagine."

Twelve years later, in 1969, Gaylord Staveley and Fred Eiseman ran the Green and the Colorado Rivers a hundred years after John Wesley

Powell. Having run Lodore and Hell's Half Mile, they left Green River, Utah with six cataract boats constructed of oak framing and marine plywood, to camp at the confluence where Powell had slept a century before. On July 19, the Staveley expedition left the confluence and floated down to the beginning of Cataract Canyon, running with precision: Staveley first in the *Norm* and Doug Reiner bringing up the rear in the *Joan.* Unlike those who had gone before, the seven boatmen and passengers ran smoothly down the beginning of Cataract Canyon. As they dropped through Brown Betty their thoughts were on the Big Drop that lay below. They ploughed through Mile Long Rapid, digging their oars into the crests of great waves and riding out the troughs.

On the left-hand side of the river opposite Teapot Canyon there is a long sand beach behind which are mountains of driftwood. Below the beach is the top of the Big Drop. To the boatmen the Drop is a staircase of huge waves and rocks and deep holes. In low water the boatmen can pull into the eddies on either side, but in high water there is no respite. Staveley and his crew hit the big rollers at the top of the Big Drop, trying to avoid the rocks jutting out from the right. The *Sandra* was holed by one of the hidden rocks and nearly sank before making shore. The holes in the *Sandra* were so large that at first it appeared that the Big Drop had claimed yet another victim. All day they worked: cutting, sawing, and patching with planking, resin, and fiberglass. By evening the *Sandra* was ready for Satan's Gut.

The river above was nearly brought to a standstill by [the rocks'] close-set, steeply coursed arrangement from bank to bank. Then, when it finally pitched over the edge, the waiting rocks instantly tore it to shreds. Some remaining declivity below, mild when seen as part of the same structure, caught it still fizzing from its stupendous aeration, started it moving downstream again, and narrowed it into another rapid, a mild one, not far beyond.

All rapids have rocks, but the third part of the Big Drop has huge boulders which have broken in chunks from the left wall of the canyon and fallen into the river to create the great hole known as Satan's Gut. Like others before and after him, Gaylord Staveley looked at Satan's Gut with awe, respect, and fear.

A strand of water emerges taut and glistening from a chink somewhere up near the brim of the harsh, bouldered face and stretches down to disappear into the featureless turbulence below. It is narrow and it shines and its slippery-smooth appearance sets it visually apart from everything else in the rapid. Looking down on it is almost like looking into an immense surgical incision. The name of the rapid is apt; its most prominent feature looks visceral. Down that glossy filament of water that was no wider than our boats we'd have to run to make it. Entered right it would amount to perhaps three boat-lengths run between bottomless, thrashing abysses, then safe water below. Entered wrong . . .

Some boatmen miss the slot, some of the best. Gaylord Staveley looked back from the bottom of Satan's Gut to see the *Bonnie Anne* move too far to the left, hang on the brink, and drop into the enormous hole which has devoured so many other boats. The *Bonnie Anne* rose up and turned over. There was recovery—there always is on a good expedition—but Satan's Gut had once again demonstrated its power.

Boatmen fear Satan's Gut not only because its force can destroy them and their boats, but because of the large pool above it. The powerful currents and eddies of this pool make it exceedingly difficult for the boatmen to find the slot between the Gut on the left and the huge wave that explodes in the middle of the river. And much of the fear, if not mystery, of Satan's Gut is due to confusion as to its precise location.

The name Satan's Gut was coined on a trip led by Kenny Ross when he hit the third part of the Big Drop in August 1952. After successfully shooting the slot between the rocks and the explosion wave in the middle of the third part of the Big Drop, a passenger exclaimed it was like passing through "Satan's Gut," and Kenny Ross perpetuated the name. Ironically, in river lore the Gut became more awesome and terrifying as the boatmen talked of it, while they themselves became increasingly confused as to what exactly constituted Satan's Gut; and each of the early runners, Bud Hatch, Rod Sanderson, Moki-Mac Ellington, and Georgie White, had a different interpretation. Above 35,000 cubic feet per second, the river rises to pour over the great blocks of limestone on the left, creating one of the largest holes on the length of the Colorado River. To those who came after Kenny Ross and to those who will come in the future, Satan's Gut is that hole. It is this high water plunging over those rocks which creates Satan's Gut. Yet rivermen speak with such respect for Satan's Gut that it has become the name for the entire third part of the Big Drop, whether referring to the slot between the rocks and the explosion wave when the river is low or the deadly hole created by the river plunging over those blocks of limestone in high water.

The trick to Satan's Gut is entry. So precipitous is the fall in high water that boatmen cannot see the slot to the center. Rather, they have to locate their position with reference to the features on shore and in the river. Boatmen call these "keys." In low water a small curler wave, insignificant and no more than six inches in height, leads to the slot. To find that key wave is all the more difficult because of the large pool and eddies at the top, which frequently defy the strongest boatman to keep control when the precision of his entry is crucial. Thus that little curler wave becomes all important—a little, but vital, ripple at the top of this huge rapid. It is the key which boatmen seek as they meander in the eddy above, poised to avoid veering left into the rocks at low water or into the Gut in high flood. The boatmen float and look, then see the curler wave and hopefully hit the slot. It is the ultimate performance in Cataract Canyon.

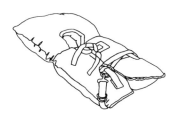

Redside

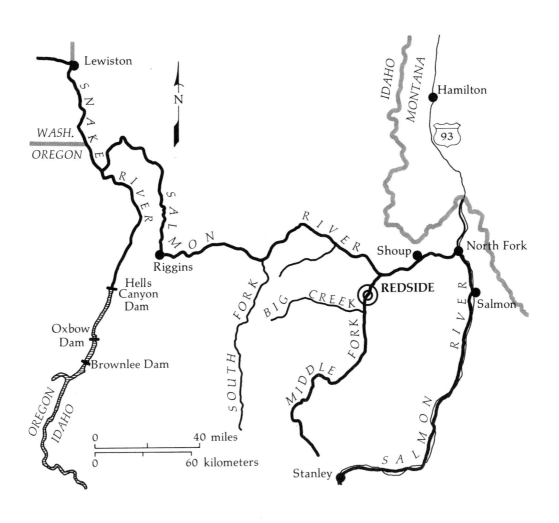

If there is magic on this planet, it is contained in water.

LOREN EISELEY

The great canyon of the Middle Fork of the Salmon River lies deep in the high country of Idaho, west of the Continental Divide. Central Idaho remains today the largest wilderness area, outside Alaska, in the United States. Isolated and remote, the Middle Fork nestles in the heart of the Salmon River Mountains, a chaotic jumble of peaks and ridges north of the tumultuous crags of the Sawtooth Mountains. So formidable are the approaches that pioneers long avoided the canyon of the Middle Fork. Yet this isolation is now its attraction. Here in the golden summers are brilliant wild flowers scattered through high meadows that disappear into precipitous ravines and deep gorges the sides of which are covered with tall pines. The peaks and battlements that defend the Middle Fork of the Salmon are crusted with snow throughout the year, but in the heart of the canyon, where elk winter, there is little snowfall. In its upper reaches the canyon of the Middle Fork is the home of the lodgepole pine, Douglas fir, and the Engelmann spruce; farther down the canyon appear the western yellow pines, especially along Big Creek, which flows eastward into the Middle Fork from the vast Idaho Primitive Area. Downstream, in Impassable Canyon, are ponderosa pine, mountain mahogany, and the bitterbush higher up on the slopes.

Below the passes of the mountains that defend this wilderness are lakes filled with the crystal water of melted snow. Men came to the uplands of the Middle Fork in search of gold, but found only trees and water, ice and snow. Occasionally, they discovered a bubbling hot spring, an unexpected contrast to the icy waters of the lakes and the creeks that plunge down to meet the river. Through this high country are trails as old as the Indians and the animals they hunted.

There are over forty major rapids from the launch area below Dagger Falls to the confluence with the main Salmon ninety-seven miles downstream. But in the high water of the spring runoff the Middle Fork, with its descent rate of twenty-six feet per mile, becomes one continuous rapid. In June 1974 the United States Forest Service described any attempt to run the river as "suicidal." Even in lesser years the upper river is so swift that boatmen have no time to rest on the oars and drift with the flow. The Middle Fork is a millrace punctuated by major rapids. There is Velvet Falls, so named because you cannot hear its roar until you are on the brink, and Powerhouse Rapids, with its boulders and a cliff at the bottom. Some boatmen have persistent trouble in Pistol Creek with its tight S-turn in a narrow channel; there the waves lash powerfully and chaotically back from the perpendicular walls. Farther downriver, Tappan Falls has claimed more than its share of boats. It requires skill and sensitivity to hit the right-hand slot at the top of the falls. Rubber Rapid also demands precise placement at the entrance. But the rapid held in awe by boatmen around the campfires on the rivers of Idaho is Redside.

A Big Drop is unmistakable when you are on the river, but the names people pin on places cause confusion. The Forest Service, the U.S. Geological Survey, local river guides, and out-of-state boatmen all have taken the liberty of applying different names to the same rapid on the Middle Fork. The rapid at Golden Creek that we call Redside is also known as "Porcupine," "Eagle Rock," and "Sevy's Rock." The rapid just below that we call Weber is also called "Redside," "Little Porcupine," "Loin of Pork," and "Corkscrew."

Redside takes its name from the colorful cutthroat trout that live in the cold, clear waters of the Middle Fork. The rapid has none of the trout's subtlety, but much of its power and guile. It lies on a right-hand curve of the river, its entrance guarded by two huge midstream rocks and the holes below them. At normal water levels the obvious run is between the two rocks, but the drop is sharp and the surging eddies below can spin a boat unpredictably. Most boatmen swing close to the right-hand rock to take the drop. Then a hard choice confronts them:

downstream one hundred feet is the worst rock on the Middle Fork. In appearance it looks friendly—round, smooth, and symmetrical. But the current from both the right- and left-hand slots slams directly against it. Boatmen have the option of trying to pull left of this gumdrop-shaped rock in heavy current or trying for a right-side run. The latter involves precise maneuvering at the top of the rapid. If a boat barely skims the right entrance rock, and if it has enough lateral momentum on the tongue, it is possible to catch the big eddy behind the rock and come almost to a stop. From this position making the pull right of the lower rock is no problem. But in the accelerating current at the top of the rapid such a course is much easier plotted than rowed. For the heavier boats with the ungainly sweeprigs favored by Idaho guides it is almost impossible. The consequence of missing the eddy is ramming the lower rock. The lucky boats spin around it, one side or the other; the unfortunate are pinned against the rock for minutes, hours, or days.

In high water, it is possible and necessary to hug the right or inside bank all the way around the curve at Redside. A giant hole spans the center of the river, but the rocks that normally block the far-right chute are sufficiently covered to create a washboard down which a boat can bump. The lower rock, which in high water becomes submerged and causes a gigantic, churning hole, is kept safely to the left. However, under runoff conditions the water below Redside is the fastest water on the Middle Fork. In a matter of seconds boats that have passed through Redside face the vicious, angled waves of Weber Rapid. Indeed, in the minds of many Middle Fork boatmen "Redside" signifies a full half-mile of whitewater beginning at Golden Creek and continuing past Mist Falls. Historically it has proven the toughest stretch on the river.

Weber is also on a right curve of the Middle Fork. An enormous rock extending from the right bank forces boats down a gauntlet of waves and holes. These increase in size until, at the center of the curve, a vicious hole extends almost the full width of the constricted river. No one really misses this hole. A good run clips its right corner and the jolt is terrific. Less fortunate boats enter farther left, toward the hole's greatest depth. Often boats hit this hole sideways—the result of frantic efforts by the boatmen to pull right. A flip is more than likely in low water and probable in high.

The character of the Middle Fork has been determined more by those who bypassed its wilderness than by the Indians, trappers, miners, and ranchers who penetrated into the canyon. In the 1830s the mountain men of William Ashley were roaming through the Snake River country to the south looking for beaver. Others, like John Work of the Hudson's Bay Company, had been there before the mountain men, but they all stayed far from the great crags which protect the Middle Fork. With few exceptions, the great issues of the American West were decided far from the Middle Fork of the Salmon. The mountain men had adapted to and identified with the Indians, but they moved on when the beaver were gone. The miners were different. They claimed the land and disputed its patronage with the original inhabitants, the American Indians. Gold was discovered on the Clearwater in 1860, and rich strikes followed on the Salmon River, in the Boise Basin, Coeur d'Alene, and elsewhere in western Idaho. In 1863 a party of miners under the leadership of John Stanley wandered into the source of the Middle Fork, where they found bear in profusion fishing for the spawning salmon. And here in Bear Valley, as they named it, the Middle Fork of the Salmon starts on its way to the sea. To the west, in the basin of the Salmon River, mining towns flourished, then died when the gold was exhausted. After the miners came the sheepherders and potato farmers, supported by the railroads which penetrated into the valleys of lower Idaho. In 1863 Idaho itself became a territory. The frontier days were over, but the Middle Fork remained remote.

The Middle Fork country is a land of overwhelming rock sculptures produced by wind and water. Sharp peaks thrust skyward while sheer walls plunge into deep river canyons. The region is a great garden of granite monuments guarding access to the rivers. As described in a contemporary source:

Here is the largest solid expanse of blue peaks and nebulous mountainous distance in the United States. In any direction, for a hundred miles, and in some directions for much greater distances than that there is only an ocean of a thousand zeniths, each high and imperturbable, in a misty blue integrity of its own; the thousands of lakes, each cool and fragrant and perfect; the tens of thousands of wild animals hiding below among the millions of trees. From peak to peak, from backbone to backbone, the landscape lifts and falls until it shimmers in mist and distance and it withdraws to the far purple horizons, which look like neither fountains nor cloud. In the far southeast are the Sawtooth spires; in the far northwest is the tumbled blue cloud bowl of the Seven Devils.

This is the wilderness of the Middle Fork, where despite the influx of man, the valleys and peaks are still ruled by elk, deer, mountain goats, and sheep. Here is the land of the horned owl, the deer slipping quietly to the river in the evening, the stately mountain goats silhouetted on high crags, the bighorn sheep picking their way down some precipitous slope. There is wonder in all directions.

Around the campfires the boatmen talk about the history and lore of the Middle Fork, so isolated and yet so desired now for this very quality. In their tales is envy of the first men who dropped down from the high meadows into the canyon of the Middle Fork. Refugees themselves from an industrialized and increasingly urbanized society, the gold miners, hermits, trappers, and homesteaders have become legendary heroes to the boatmen who also love the wilderness and read the poetry of Robert Service.

Like any frontier, the Middle Fork attracted men who were either uncomfortable at home or disdained it. These were men with charisma and the capacity to adapt to any environment: men like "Trapper" Johnson who, at the end of the nineteenth century, had cabins scattered throughout the mountain country, and others, like Johnny Levine and Ed Chamberlain, who trapped through the canyon for beaver and otter at the turn of the century. Others followed these early trappers.

Cougar Dave was famous throughout Idaho as a mountain lion hunter. He was a remarkable man, not so much because of his accomplishments but because of his eccentricities. His real name was

The rock-choked Middle Fork of the Salmon, near Redside. By Ray Varley.

David Lewis, and the remote wilderness around Big Creek was like his personal fief, where he roamed with his dogs, hunting and killing, until his death in 1956 at the age of ninety-three. "His eyes were as cold as the back of a lizard and his skin was as leather thrice tanned, and his walk had the stealth of the cougar itself." Others came to the canyon to homestead on the flat deltas of the major tributaries. There were not many: Jim Bollard and his partner McNerney mined and raised hay and cattle at Thomas Creek; Jim Hash and his wife gardened at Little Creek, downriver; Ray Mahoney cultivated a large orchard at Mahoney Creek; and Bob Ramey and Jack McGivney ranched at Loon Creek. Many failed, some died, but those who came to ranch on the Middle Fork were the kind of people who could confront nature, challenge it, and survive.

The recorded history of the Middle Fork begins with warfare. The American Indians had long wandered up from the valleys east and west of the central Idaho wilderness through the canyons and creeks of the Salmon River watershed. Living in isolation, their world of forest and stream was suddenly challenged from the outside by newcomers, the Americans, including trappers, miners, homesteaders, even the United States Cavalry. Many came to seek their own gain, to live off the land and to profit from it. The cultures clashed, and there were heroes and villains on both sides, those who sought to understand and those who did not wish to. The newcomers bypassed the great primitive area of the Middle Fork. They encroached into Indian territory in eastern Washington and Oregon, and in 1878 the Bannock Indian war raged throughout southern Idaho and eastern Oregon. Defeated and in flight, many of the Bannocks drifted up into the wilderness area of the Middle Fork, seeking safety in the mountain fastness of the Sheepeater Indians.

The Sheepeater Indians were actually Shoshone, but were known as Tukuarika, or eaters of sheep. They had settled in the high uplands at the headwaters of the South and Middle forks of the Salmon River. Living in isolation, these mountain people, numbering about 150, had learned to survive in this demanding land by hunting the mountain sheep from which they were given their English name by the Army that subdued them. Many Bannocks, after their defeat in the war of 1878, chose the hardy but free life of the Sheepeaters rather than the alien existence of the reservation.

No one, least of all the United States Army, had shown any interest in the Sheepeaters until 1879, when they were blamed for ambushing four men in Long Valley and killing four Chinese laborers mining for gold near Oro Grande. Many attributed these attacks to agitation by the defeated Bannocks who had joined the Sheepeaters. The result was one of the most ill-conceived and unnecessary campaigns in the history of the Indian wars. When news of the killings reached Boise, Captain Reuben S. Bernard was directed to lead a detachment of seventy men of the First Cavalry to determine if the murderers were indeed Indians and, if so, to capture them. At the same time a second detachment of mounted riflemen of the Second Infantry left Camp Howard, now Grangeville, Idaho, under First Lieutenant Henry Catley. The two units were to move up into the high country and trap the Sheepeaters in a pincer movement. Brilliantly conceived in theory, this strategy had no place in the land of the Middle Fork and its tributaries, described by a contemporary as "the wildest and most impenetrable region of indescribable ruggedness and grandeur where lofty mountain summits alternate with abysmal canyons." From the outset everything went wrong for the cavalry. Deep snow blocked the valleys; the supply columns could not keep up with the advancing troops, who starved in their camps; and, of course, there were no Indians. The horses perished, the men faltered, and some died of spotted fever. In fact, Captain Bernard's company was so severely debilitated that he suggested recruiting the Umatilla Indians as guides to find the Sheepeaters, which the First Cavalry had not seen.

Catley's troop made better progress through the snow drifts, the raging torrents of the side streams, and, in the high country, fallen timber, which blocked the trails and obstructed the passage of mounted troops. Moving slowly down Big Creek toward the Middle Fork, Lieutenant Catley and his mounted infantry encountered terrain which was so precipitous that the troopers had to move in single file, leaving their supply column in the rear. They also encountered a small force of the Sheepeaters and stumbled into a position well prepared by the Indians. From behind every rock and knoll the Indians directed their fire on the exposed troops, precipitating confusion and retreat. The site of this battle still bears the name Soldier Bar, in remembrance of Private

Harry Eagan, Company C, Second Infantry, who was killed by Sheepeater gunfire.

Wanting only to be left alone, the Sheepeaters did not press their tactical advantage against the confused troopers. Lieutenant Catley ordered his men up to the crest of the ridge away from the rocks and trees of Big Creek. This, of course, was the reaction the Sheepeaters wanted. Once on top of the ridge the column was exposed to persistent rifle fire from the Indians along the slopes below the crest. Here, on the top of the ridge overlooking Big Creek, the troops found themselves trapped. Desperate for water, they opened a keg of vinegar—the name Vinegar Hill is still found on maps—and finally slipped away in darkness to the safety of Camp Howard. Lieutenant Catley informed his superiors that his command was too small to face the Sheepeaters, who in fact amounted to little more than twenty warriors, as the main body of Sheepeaters had moved down Big Creek toward the Middle Fork.

This ignominious retreat cost Lieutenant Catley his command, and Captain Bernard, a veteran of many wars on the American frontier, was appointed to lead the combined military expedition against the Sheepeaters. On August 13 he set out to find and capture these elusive Indians who, encouraged by the defeat of Catley's command, had attacked ranches west of the upland country of the Middle Fork. Bernard's column made its way slowly down Big Creek, led this time by Umatilla Indian scouts who had been specifically recruited to find the Sheepeaters. And find them they did. As the troops moved down Big Creek there was a continuous exchange of rifle fire between the Sheepeaters and the advancing scouts and cavalry. On August 20 the Sheepeaters attacked, were driven back, and hastily dispersed on foot into the high country above Big Creek and the Middle Fork. Persistent and aggressive, Captain Bernard pressed on after the Sheepeaters, leaving the Umatilla scouts to round up the abandoned horses. It was a futile chase. The heavily armed cavalry could not hope to catch the fast-moving Sheepeaters in their mountain homeland. Horses and pack mules went lame, and the cavalrymen, their clothes in tatters, were exhausted. The pursuit was abandoned. By the time they returned to Boise, Bernard's troop had covered 1,200 miles and had lost over 60 animals trying to catch 150 Indians. They had failed to find the Sheepeaters in the rugged terrain of the Middle Fork below Big Creek which Bernard named Impassable Canyon.

The only force now left in the field against the Sheepeaters was a small detachment under the command of Lieutenant Edward S. Farrow, who had retraced Catley's original route. On September 21 Farrow stumbled upon the main Sheepeater encampment and followed them from one camp to another until October 1, when the Sheepeaters, worn, hungry, and decimated, surrendered. The First Cavalry returned in triumph to Boise with fifty-one captives, who were promptly sent off to the Fort Hall Indian reservation. It was not one of the great campaigns of the First Cavalry.

Among the old-timers who tell stories of the Sheepeater War, there are still those who believe the campaign was instigated by merchants who were concerned about the movement of their merchandise in the summer season. Of course, there were also businessmen who profited from Indian campaigns by contracting for supplies for the Army. In 1878 the Bannock war brought thousands of dollars into southern Idaho at a time when money was in short supply. Perhaps a war against the Sheepeaters could sustain the flow of supplies and cash the following year; many also felt that the Sheepeaters could have no use for the gold the Chinese that they killed may have possessed. In any event, the only winner was the rugged country of the Middle Fork, which remained inviolate to all but the hardy and the adventuresome, whether homesteading by the river or running its rapids.

River running on the Middle Fork developed much later than exploration and river running on the Colorado. The Sheepeater War occurred ten years after John Wesley Powell's first expedition down the Green and the Colorado rivers in 1869. By comparison with the Colorado, the wilderness of Idaho was not easily accessible. Isolated by the mountains, the Middle Fork was left to the trout and the salmon and the steelhead coming home from the Pacific. No one knows who first

Rod Nash hits a slot on the Middle Fork. By Ray Varley.

ran the Middle Fork, but according to a Middle Fork boatman of today, Cort Conley, Edith Kimball of Salmon, Idaho, remembered that Captain Harry Guleke, the redoubtable and famous river man of the Salmon River, made the run on a raft, probably in the 1920s. Guleke told her, "I knew I wouldn't get into a place I couldn't get out of. Sometimes I was on the raft and sometimes I was under it. But I was never afraid. And until a man is afraid, he'll be all right."

Precisely when Guleke made this trip and why remain unknown, but now men were coming to the Middle Fork neither to look for gold nor to homestead, but to run rivers, and the Middle Fork was a supreme challenge. In the mid-1930s when Nevills and the Hatch brothers were beginning to run commercial trips on the Colorado, Dr. Russell G. "Big Joe" Frazier and Frank "Limber" Swain sought to conquer the Middle Fork of the Salmon.

Big Joe Frazier was the doctor for the Kennicott Copper Company in Bingham, Utah, and had learned of the Middle Fork from a hunting guide, Austin Lightfoot. Frank Swain was a deputy sheriff in Vernal, Utah, and caught the river fever from Parley Galloway. With Bus Hatch, Swain built two heavy cataract boats under Parley Galloway's instruction and subsequently tested them on trips down the Green River and the Colorado through the Grand Canyon. By then they were ready for the Middle Fork. They arrived at Bear Valley in July 1935. Unfortunately, the Middle Fork of the Salmon was not the Colorado in either Cataract or Grand Canyon. There were rocks and fast water rather than big waves and huge holes. Frazier's attempt was perhaps one of the most heroic in river-running history in the West, but he failed. Long on courage and short on technology, this run of the Middle Fork ended in the first few miles in broken boats but not broken wills. Big Joe Frazier was not a man to be deterred by failure or by the rocks of the Middle Fork.

He returned the next year, 1936, and, with Frank Swain and Bus Hatch as boatmen, successfully ran 125 miles from Bear Valley down to the confluence with the main Salmon. The river was in his blood, and he returned in 1938 to the rapids of the Middle Fork—Velvet Falls, Pistol Creek, Tappan, and Redside—on an expedition sponsored by the *Deseret News* of Salt Lake City. It was not the trout or the history of the region, but the rapids and rocks and the river that brought him back. That year the heaviest snows in a generation covered the Sawtooth Mountains. There was not another runoff like 1938 until the disastrous year of 1970. As in 1970, the flow of melted snow was swollen by heavy rains that turned even the most peaceful creeks into torrents. Undaunted, Dr. Frazier and Frank Swain put in on July 4 at Bear Valley in their wooden cataract boats. Hurtling down through fast water, they looked in disbelief at the mounds of debris piled along the banks and across the river by the force of fast-moving water. Within two miles, two of the four boats were destroyed on the rocks, and the expedition itself ended in an hour and a half, with the members walking out of Bear Valley for help. At the time, Frazier thought the failure was caused by faulty design and construction of the cataract boats. Perhaps this was so, but the upper Middle Fork in flood with a large melt and heavy rains can destroy in moments even the most sophisticated boat, wooden or rubber.

After their failure in 1938, Frazier and Swain returned to Utah determined to construct better boats for an expedition down the Middle Fork the following year. Amos Burg accompanied the expedition, which in 1939 had to pack the boats and supplies into the confluence of Marsh and Bear creeks now reached by truck and air-conditioned automobiles. Dr. Frazier's boat was the *Stefansson,* named for the famed Arctic explorer. Frank Swain's was the *Rimrock,* named in honor of Julius F. Stone, who had run the Colorado in 1909 and whom Frazier admired. Like Stone, Frazier was a financial sponsor of early river trips. Hack Miller ran the *Polly V,* christened for a famous lady of the Salmon River during the roaring days of fighting, mining, and ranching.

As in 1938, two of the heavy cataract boats with their plywood construction proved almost impossible in the rocks and high water of the river. They were holed by rocks and patched time and again, only to be holed again in the rapids downriver. Even in July it was cold, and the water was melted ice. By the time they reached Pistol Creek Rapid, they still had two serviceable boats and were running fast. Ahead was Redside, which, with Weber below, would later prove to be the biggest killer on the river. But in 1939 Frazier and Swain ran Redside successfully and continued on to the confluence with the main Salmon. Twice beaten, twice successful, they had established that man could run down the Middle Fork and through its biggest rapids.

For years after Frazier and Swain conquered the Middle Fork, only fishermen came down to the river for the Chinook salmon, the cutthroat, Dolly Varden, and rainbow trout. To them the river was fish, not rocks and holes and waves. The thrill of running the Middle Fork of the Salmon was for the future.

In the late 1950s and early 1960s there arose a sudden interest in America's vanishing wilderness. The backcountry was rapidly disappearing before an expanding and motorized population. There emerged an increasing sense of urgency that portions of the country must be set aside to preserve a wilderness environment for the future. These deep feelings and love for the wilderness, combined with the love of free-flowing water uninhibited by dams and unpolluted by the residues of an industrial society, produced legislation to protect the vanishing wilderness. There were few completely wild watersheds left in the United States. One of them was the Middle Fork.

On October 2, 1968, the Wild and Scenic Rivers Act designated the Middle Fork of the Salmon one of the eight wild rivers initially to be included in the National Wild and Scenic Rivers System. The act defined wild rivers as "those rivers or sections of rivers that are free of impoundments and generally inaccessible, except by trail, with watersheds or shorelines essentially primitive and water unpolluted. These represent vestiges of primitive America." The inclusion of the Middle Fork in the Wild and Scenic Rivers Act brought the river under the total management of the Forest Service in an effort to preserve the natural condition of the river and the quality of its uncontaminated water and to protect its environment from those who would wish to change it. Although heavily fished, the trout remain and the salmon still spawn. History still pervades the canyon, from the remnants of the Sheepeater campaign at Soldier Bar to the cabins of prospectors and homesteaders who sought the isolation and sanctity of the rugged cliffs. In fact, if it were not for the way down the river, Impassable Canyon below Big Creek would be impassable still, except for the few bold enough or foolish enough to follow Captain Bernard's cavalrymen.

The trips of Big Joe Frazier and Frank Swain were expeditions, but by the latter part of the 1960s, particularly after the designation of the

Middle Fork as a wilderness river in 1968, river trips down the Middle Fork became first a business and then an industry. Today nearly five thousand people run the river every summer. Unlike the Colorado River, the Middle Fork is a truly primitive river, wild, uncontrolled by dams, transformed only by the whims of nature. A free-flowing river like the Middle Fork can change dramatically from one year to the next, depending on the snows and the rains of early summer. When the river is high, it rushes from Dagger Falls to Indian Creek as one long chute. Below Indian Creek are Tappan Falls and the Big Drop at Redside.

Even the best boatmen fear the Middle Fork in full flood, and even their judgment can be confounded by the force and power of moving water. Such was the case in 1970. Late snows had fallen on the mountains surrounding the basin of the Middle Fork that year. When the snows began to melt, heavy rains poured down the streams and tributaries, flooding their banks and turning the Middle Fork into a raging torrent. On Sunday, June 21, 1970, three parties set out from Dagger Falls to run the river. Before they reached the first bend below Dagger, they all knew they had problems. Everett Spaulding, a veteran boatman from Lewiston, Idaho, had two wooden MacKenzie River boats and a sixteen-foot, ten-man raft. Gene Teague rowed one Mac-Kenzie, and Ken Smith the raft. They were to rendezvous at Indian Creek, thirty miles below Dagger Falls, to complete the party of six, including the newscaster Tom Brokaw and his friends from the world of business and banking. A few hours later a second party, led by Alfred E. Couture, an engineer in the Denver office of the United States Bureau of Reclamation, and twelve others, mostly from Denver, left Dagger Falls in two twenty-two-foot rubber pontoon rafts. A short time later a third group, led by Stanford University professor Donald Wilson, departed from Dagger with nineteen people in four ten-man rafts. Fueled by the high water, the Middle Fork became a millrace down which the parties careened in the narrow, congested gorge. The river's power was awesome, the water flowing at ten to fifteen miles per hour through ten- to twelve-foot waves. In all, forty-three people took to the Middle Fork on that June Sunday. Five days later three of them were dead.

Having reached Indian Creek, Spaulding met the remaining members of his party and continued on to Whitey Cox Hot Springs to fish and bathe in the warm waters not far from the grave, marked by a tangle of elk and deer horns, of the prospector who gave his name to the springs. The night before, Spaulding had confessed with his accustomed reticence that the river from Dagger Falls to Indian Creek was the fastest and most difficult he had ever experienced. Here at Whitey Cox Hot Springs, Couture's party passed Spaulding's and pulled ashore below, deeply concerned by the powerful force of the water and the big rapids which lay ahead downstream. Couture and Spaulding did not know that the third party upstream had already met tragedy. Sulphur Creek meets the Middle Fork just a few miles below Dagger Falls. Ordinarily a modest stream, Sulphur Creek had become a turbulent tributary. One of the boats in Don Wilson's party had flipped, and Wilson had attempted to swim across the river to assist those stranded on the other side. But the rope to which he had unwisely tied himself straightened in the powerful currents and dragged him under. He was dead by the time he was pulled to shore. Completely demoralized and leaderless, the party broke up, some walking back to Dagger Falls, others continuing with the body down twenty-six miles to Indian Creek and safety.

On Wednesday, June 24, the two remaining parties pressed down the Middle Fork. The water continued to rise, increasing its velocity and the violence of the rapids. That day both parties ran Tappan Falls, Aparejo, and Jack Creek rapids. Couture camped at Wilson Creek, while Spaulding put in a mile below at Rattlesnake Creek. A few miles beyond, Big Creek was overflowing, adding substantially to the swollen waters of the Middle Fork and the danger of the big rapids in Impassable Canyon.

As they flashed down river with incredible speed the parties were friendly, but Everett Spaulding clearly disapproved of the Couture party running without a professional guide. Outwardly insignificant, the attitude of the professional guide toward the amateur has since become an issue of great emotion and controversy in running western rivers. As the number of people permitted by government agencies has now been limited and the carrying capacity of rivers has been reached, the spaces allotted to the commercial outfitters and to the rapidly growing number of private runners has produced bitterness, hostility, and even lawsuits, as the private runners seek to gain a greater percentage of the available spaces. With the total number of people fixed, such spaces must, of course, come at the expense of the commercial outfitters. Around the campfires on western rivers the dispute rages. Commercial outfitters argue that not only is river running their livelihood, but their experience and knowledge of the river enables them to provide a safer trip than the less experienced, noncommercial runner. Unfortunately, running Redside Rapid on the Middle Fork in June 1970 did not prove to be convincing evidence for the case of the commercial outfitters. Perhaps experience and knowledge in themselves can cloud anyone's judgment. On Thursday morning, June 25, when the Spaulding party left Rattlesnake Camp, only about half wore life jackets.

Reaching the confluence of Big Creek and the Middle Fork, the river starts to enter Impassable Canyon. Here the volume of water made its difficult rapids even more dangerous. Porcupine Rapids had big waves, but Redside was worse, and a hundred yards beyond Redside were the huge waves of Weber Rapid. On that Thursday Alfred Couture liked nothing he saw at Redside. "At the head of the rapids lay an enormous hole that spelled almost sure disaster if we pulled into it. The river was curving to the right so the force of the current drove our boats to the left."

Couture studied the three slots of Redside Rapid and watched the river sweep down the center tongue to crash into and over the huge

Dee Holladay in control after the initial drop in Redside. By Ray Varley.

boulder at the bottom. In a normal water stage the run can be to the right of a rock jutting out from the left bank and then pulling left of the boulder at the bottom. In higher water the broken rocks jutting out from the base of the cliff are covered, and a rough run can be made down the right side. But the standard run is down the center, calling for frantic, hard pulling to pass right of the bottom boulder and the hole behind it. In high water the whole force of the river plunges down that center chute, and only the lucky and the strong make the pull to miss the awesome hole of Redside.

On that fateful Thursday in 1970 each party did a variation of the run in Redside. With less maneuverability in his twenty-two-foot pontoons than Spaulding's MacKenzie River boats, Couture had little choice but to hit the center chute where the full force of the flood waters were being drawn to the boulder and its hole like a magnet.

I put all my strength into the oars to avoid that treacherous hole, but I didn't quite succeed. We went down into it about 10 feet from the center, rose to the top, and hung there for a moment that seemed endless, suspended at the very crest of the wave with the river frothing around us. I had experienced that same sensation once before, at Lava Falls in Grand Canyon; a split second later we had overturned on that earlier trip.

But we were luckier this time. The pause was short-lived, and then we shot downstream again.

Plunging on through the enormous waves of Weber Rapid below Redside, Couture's rafts were big enough to negotiate the waves, but so swift and powerful was the current that they careened on down Impassable Canyon virtually out of control. They swept past Parrot Placer Camp, where despite the best efforts of the oarsmen they could not land. Down the river the pontoons hurtled, running rapid after rapid as the boatmen frantically tried to land. Not until Cradle Creek Camp were they able to work the pontoons into an eddy to pause in their flight, only to see a life jacket with its lifeless body sweep past in the current and sink into Ouzel Rapid below.

Everett Spaulding ran Redside down the center and pulled into an eddy below to wait for Gene Teague to line his MacKenzie River boat. As Teague completed lining his boat the supply raft followed, hitting the center of Redside and, like Couture, clipping the hole. Tom Brokaw has graphically described the drama at Redside and then the horror below in Weber.

The raft creaked and groaned. For a moment the wall of water was all there was to see and hear. In another instant, the wave retreated and we were safely through.

I looked up to see Teague, with Stone and Harmon as passengers, heading into Weber Falls. . . .

Suddenly I noticed that Teague's boat appeared to be stalled in the middle of Weber Falls.

It was sinking.

Later, Stone described the scene. He said a huge wave broke above them and practically filled the right side of the boat.

Teague yelled out, "Shift your weight, shift your weight," and he began frantically pulling on the oars, trying to move to calmer waters.

But it was too late. Another wave rolled over the other side. All three men were swept into the raging water. . . .

Downstream I could see Stone and Harmon neck deep in the middle of the river, racing in tandem toward another set of rapids. Teague was off to the side and behind them heading for the same rapids.

Suddenly we had our own problems. The raft flipped over when hit by a powerful wave as it plunged into Weber Falls. As I tumbled into the water I was stunned by the ferocity of the current. In a lifetime of swimming I can't recall a greater struggle to break back through the surface, even with the assistance of a lifejacket.

Scrambling on top of the overturned raft, Brokaw and his friends did not linger, but leaped as one into the water and swam to shore and safety. The others downstream were not so fortunate.

For Stone, Harmon and Gene Teague, it was a battle of survival.

When they first were washed from the boat Stone knew they were in trouble. Even with a life jacket he could barely keep his head above water as strong, deep currents insisted he join them.

Harmon, recalling Spaulding's advice, pulled himself onto the hull of the overturned boat when it surfaced. He saw the bow line trailing in the water near Stone and yelled, "Grab the line, get the line."

By pulling himself up on the rope, Stone was able to look around. He saw a small eddy off to the right. His impulse was to swim for it and he shouted the question to Harmon, "Do you want to try for shore?"

"No," Harmon yelled back. "Hang onto the boat."

Stone's impulse continued.

"Let's swim for it."

This time, from behind him, Teague yelled, "No, stick with the boat, hang onto the boat."

Stone was impressed with Teague's calm. He was wearing a life jacket and holding a seat cushion, looking as serene as a Sunday stroller. That was the last Stone saw of Teague, ever. The water quickly became much rougher and although he couldn't see more than a few feet downstream, Stone was certain they were moving into rapids again.

He was right.

He started into the rapids trailing Harmon and the hull of the boat, straining to hang onto the rope as he was sucked under water, battered by currents on every side, fighting for the surface and another breath. When he did break free, Stone still had the rope, but he was a few feet in front of Harmon who was still on the battered hull. They didn't speak, concentrating only on their private struggles for aid.

Harmon was taking wave after wave flush in the face as they washed over the hull, and the numbing effect of the 40 degree water was weakening his grip on the boat, as it was Stone's on the rope.

Stone's will also was beginning to weaken.

"This is a dream. I'm not even supposed to be here. I'm supposed to be on the raft. I'm gonna die," he thought.

Just then he was sucked under water again and the rope was torn from his hands.

When he struggled to the surface for what seemed like the hundredth time, Harmon and the boat were gone.

He had no choice. He had to swim for shore. Near death from exhaustion alone, Stone flailed against the surface currents, convinced that he was making no progress. And his tennis shoes, incredibly heavy, were dragging him down.

But gradually the water was less turbulent. Ahead of him he could make out the calm surface of an eddy.

Mustering his remaining strength, he churned out of the current and into the eddy. Totally spent, he draped himself over a boulder in shallow water, afraid he'd collapse and drown if he tried to make the final, few steps to shore.

Below Weber the remains of Spaulding's party set up a makeshift camp while Spaulding, who had successfully run Weber, pressed downriver alone looking for the lost men. At Cradle Creek Camp he came upon the Couture party and together they continued down through a series of rapids in the last seven miles to the confluence with the main Salmon. The rest of the party was taken out by helicopters the following morning, when Ellis Harmon's body was found three miles below the confluence. The river never gave up the body of Gene Teague. In the words of Everett Spaulding: "That river swallows people. Some it gives up; some it don't."

But running the Middle Fork has not always been tragic. Danger, even death, does not deter men from the love of whitewater, and for many it intensifies the attraction. Indeed the possibility of death is the price one must pay to go beyond the ordinary, the pedestrian, the dull. One will find not only danger but also exhilaration and challenge in the rocks of Redside and the waves of Weber. At the top, in the stillness of the pool above the roar and spray of Redside, there is dryness in the mouth and a queasy feeling in the pit of the stomach. No one speaks, and the boatmen strain with intense concentration to hit the slot, keeping off the boulder on the right. Suddenly the current catches the raft, which rapidly accelerates toward the tongue, the silk-like, smooth flowing water that slides into the rapid. It is in the tongue that the boatman is transformed. The dry mouth is forgotten and the queasy stomach disappears as muscles become taut digging the oars deep to make the pull right of the awesome boulder at the bottom of Redside. As the raft plows through waves, taking water and spray, the boatmen time their strokes to catch the crest, not the empty trough, as they pull away from the magnetic force of the boulder to slide into the quieter water beyond. Bail! Weber is just a few hundred yards farther downstream and the boatmen do not want to hit its huge waves out of control because of a boat loaded with a thousand pounds of water.

Weber is too close and the Middle Fork moving too fast for one to experience the tensions of the pool above Redside. Maneuvering quickly as his companions frantically bail, the boatman pulls to the right of the great hole stretching nearly the width of the river. If he is good, or lucky, he clips the right-hand corner of the hole, then plunges straight through the roller waves beyond. In the quiet water below the Redside–Weber complex there is time to bail the boats dry and to wet the throats with the magic waters of the Middle Fork.

Seven

Big Mallard

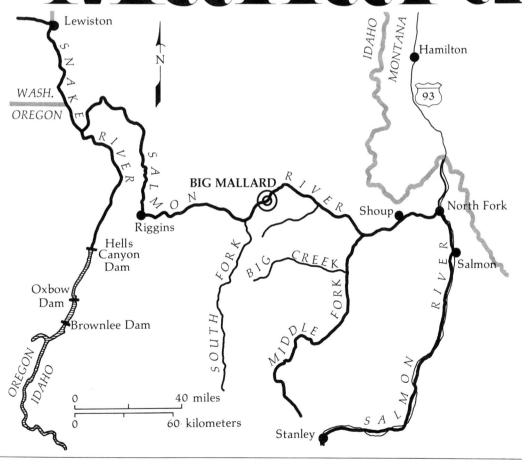

Lewiston

Hamilton

WASH.

OREGON

BIG MALLARD

Riggins

Shoup

North Fork

Salmon

Hells Canyon Dam

Oxbow Dam

Brownlee Dam

Stanley

OREGON

IDAHO

SNAKE RIVER

SALMON

SOUTH FORK

BIG CREEK

MIDDLE FORK

SALMON RIVER

IDAHO

MONTANA

93

0   40 miles

0   60 kilometers

What use are rapids?
What use are we if we remain indifferent to challenge?
What are we worth if we won't feel exhilaration?

JEFFREY INGRAM, DAVID BROWER, AND MARTIN LITTON

Having raced over a hundred miles from the upland meadows around Bear Creek, the roiling waters of the Middle Fork suddenly end in placid confrontation with the main Salmon—the fabled River of No Return. The Salmon was born millions of years ago when the intrusion of a mass of granite uplifted the great wilderness region of central Idaho, buckling the crust of the earth into a chaos of mountains and canyons. The waters which had flowed eastward, ultimately to the Atlantic, now poured out of the Sawtooth and Lemhi valleys down through the Salmon River canyon to the Snake, the Columbia, and the Pacific Ocean. The snows of the Sawtooth, White Cloud, and Bitterroot mountains feed the river as it flows 425 miles across Idaho, draining a basin of 14,000 square miles and dropping from an elevation of 8,000 feet to 905 feet where the Salmon meets the Snake. Beginning west of Galena Summit, the Salmon is a small mountain stream you can step across. It first flows north, then swings eastward as it absorbs the waters of thousands of tributaries. Then the river turns dramatically to the west and after some fifty miles disappears into the canyons of no return.

Technically the canyon of the Salmon is the second deepest gorge in the North American continent—deeper even than the Grand Canyon and surpassed only by Hells Canyon of the Snake—but the crests of the mountain ranges lie far back from the river and do not rival the sheer rock walls of the Grand Canyon. Between the river and the peaks is a land of immeasurable beauty, of blue lakes, deep forests, and alpine meadows through which bubble clear-flowing brooks.

Fed by its major tributaries, the Salmon becomes, particularly after the confluence with the Middle Fork, a big, powerful river that drops twelve feet per mile from the North Fork to the Wind River Bridge not far from Riggins, Idaho. The combination of major as well as minor tributaries and a continuous drop has produced over forty rapids, well known to river men by such names as Pine Creek, Ruby, Salmon Falls, and Gun Barrel. There are others equally known and respected, but one in particular the boatmen do not forget—Big Mallard.

Prudent boatmen always look carefully at Big Mallard. The rapid is dominated by two huge boulders situated side by side with a narrow slot between. They rest at the end of a curve in the river and so are not immediately visible. One must be alert to know they are there. In sweeping around the left-hand curve the river is forced upon the boulders by a large bar of water-polished stones on the right. Unable to drift along that outside bank of the curve, boatmen must face those two boulders with the Salmon River plunging over them into great holes and standing waves beyond.

Today's boatmen pull in on the left bank above the curve. There all is quiet, for the thick woods which crowd to the river's edge block the view and thunder of the rapid as the river swings out of sight. It is an eerie feeling, for the boatmen know the rapid is there but they cannot see or hear it. They pull their boats into the deep quiet pools by the bank. Interspersed among the rocks and pines are bunch grass and currant bushes in blossom. On the slopes and meadows above the river are yellow bell, sagebrush, and buttercups tucked among the trees. Above, golden eagles with talons locked tumble in play downward through thousands of feet of crystalline air.

The boatmen absorb all this in a glance, but they are not at Big Mallard to watch eagles. They are there to hit the slot between those two awesome boulders, so they stumble through the rocks along the bank, slipping and cursing, around the curve. There they sit or stand and stare, reading the current and watching, grim faced, the Salmon rushing through the slot. With all the precision required to run the slot on the left, the safest passage through Big Mallard appears to be on the far right. Initial instincts are to swing around the curve, run close to a rock guarding the boulder bar on the right, and pull right away from the huge holes. It seems so simple, but it seldom works. Peculiarities of the river bed and the deflecting influence of the boulder bar combine to funnel the full force of the Salmon directly into the largest hole at the bottom of the rapid. In September 1974, Gerry Hughes, hauling a jeep on a twenty-four-foot pontoon from Whitewater Ranch to Mackay Bar, rowed the right side of Big Mallard in an impressive demonstration of strength. Other boatmen, rowing with the strength of fear after having seen a boat overturn ahead of them, have "pulled" Big Mallard with power strokes. Others have not been so fortunate. In their attempt to cut to the right, they have not made the pull, and have been sucked into the hole, the river flipping their rafts like leaves before a storm.

The conclusion that boatmen reach, at least after their first encounter with Big Mallard, is to run the rapid on the left—straight down the bank and directly toward the two lower holes. This is careful calculation, not insanity. A close reading of the rapid reveals a tongue of smooth water, about three yards wide, racing between the gaping holes. Hit that tongue, and it is one of the cleanest, most satisfying whitewater runs in the West. Miss it by only a few feet, and it is one of the wettest.

Sweeping toward the tongue from upstream, a boatman's confidence tends to fail. The tongue itself is not visible. To the right and left he sees enormous mounds of water and, in low water, the rocks. Beyond that is space and the river far below the rapid. Adding to his problem are tricky waves along the left bank that kick the boat off its line. Corrective maneuvers must be delicate so close to the shoreline rocks. Strike one and the boat would spin out sideways, and there is no room for a boat in that position on Big Mallard's tongue. Finally, about thirty feet above the chaotic holes, the tongue appears: a sliver of smooth, green water laced through the white. There is time for a few corrective strokes before a properly aligned boat slices through the turbulence. Bouncing down the tailwaves, the same thought occurs to everyone: "Did you see that *hole!*" Some boatmen call it "China Hole," presumably because it is so deep.

The Big Mallard country has had a long and dramatic history of Indians, missionaries, miners, mountain men, and rivermen. The Shoshone Indians called the Salmon "Big Fish Water," for its trout, steelhead, and huge salmon. They told Meriwether Lewis and Captain William Clark that it was a river of no return, unnavigable by their canoes. Acting on the orders of President Thomas Jefferson, the explorers had started out from St. Louis in the spring of 1804 to seek the fabled Northwest Passage to the Pacific through the newly acquired Louisiana Purchase. Crossing the Continental Divide, they camped on the Lemhi River, a tributary of the Salmon, where the Shoshone chief, Cameahwait,

. . . placed a number of heaps of sand on each side which he informed me represented the vast mountains of rock eternally covered with snow through which the river passed. That the perpendicular and even jutting rocks so closely hemmed in the river that there was no possibil[it]y of passing along the shore; that the bed of the river was obstructed by sharp pointed rock and the rapidity of the stream such that the whole surface of the river was beat into perfect foam as far as the eye could reach. That the mountains were also inaccessible to man or horse.

Dismayed that Cameahwait's information "fell far short of my expectations," Captain Clark nevertheless continued down the Salmon, passed the North Fork just above the present settlement of Shoup, named after the first governor of the State of Idaho, Colonel George L. Shoup. Here Clark turned back. He wrote in his journal on August 23, 1805:

The River from the place I left my party to this Creek is almost one continued rapid, five very considerable rapids . . . the passage of either with Canoes is entirely impossible, as the water is Confined between huge Rocks & the

Bob Collins, with Jan Collins in the bow (right), slices down Big Mallard. By Rod Nash.

Current beating from one against another for some distance below . . .my guide and many other Indians tell me that the Mountains Close and is a perpendicular Clift on each Side, and Continues for a great distance and that the water runs with great violence from one rock to the other on each Side foaming & roaring thro rocks in every direction, So as to render the passage of anything impossible.

Convinced that the Salmon could never be the Northwest Passage, Lewis and Clark returned to make their way over Lost Trail Pass and Lolo Pass to the Clearwater River and the Columbia. The canyon of the Salmon, which in the words of an old-timer many years later, "seems like the Creator chopped it out with a hatchet," remained inviolate.

After Lewis and Clark came the missionaries. In 1855, twenty-seven Mormons established a mission among the Indians on a tributary of the

Salmon which they called Lemhi, after a character in the Book of Mormon. They constructed a fort, farmed, and preached to the Bannock and Shoshone Indians. Life was hard on the Lemhi. Crops were decimated by grasshoppers and frost, and to sustain the mission supplies had to be hauled from Salt Lake City, four hundred miles to the south. In fact, the great distance from Salt Lake brought criticism from Brigham Young himself. In 1857 when he visited the post he told the missionaries they had gone too far from the Mormon heartland, and he preached in a sermon upon his return to Salt Lake City about the probable failure of the mission. Nevertheless, he renewed his efforts to keep the Lemhi mission intact by sending sixty more missionaries to bolster the original group of settlers. By the autumn of 1857 over a hundred Mormons were actively working to turn Lemhi into a substantial Mormon community, but within six months the effort was abandoned and the settlers returned to the Salt Lake valley.

Although well-intentioned, the missionaries were not particularly successful in converting the Bannock and Shoshone. After some initial conversions they found the Indians unwilling to abandon their traditional ways for those of the Mormon. Dissension within the community over the harsh living conditions at Fort Lemhi only exacerbated the frustrations of the missionaries at their failure to convert large numbers of Indians. Moreover, relations between the missionaries and the mountain men who trapped in the Salmon River country had become increasingly strained. Mountaineers have traditionally not been enthusiastic for religion, and the arrival of the Mormons appeared a direct threat to trade with the Indians. Indeed, the growth of the settlement disturbed the Indian and mountain man alike, for the coming of farmers threatened the manner of life and livelihood of both. Supposedly incited by the mountaineers, the Bannock and Shoshone Indians attacked Fort Lemhi, driving off the stock and killing two Mormons. Brigham Young closed the mission and the Salmon River country returned briefly to the Bannock, Shoshone, the Nez Perce, and a handful of mountain men. But the times were changing, and within three years men motivated not by God but by greed and gold were pouring into the Salmon River valley and its tributaries.

For some decades before the first big strike at Pierce, it was common knowledge that there was gold in the streams of Idaho. Father De Smet, an early pioneer Catholic priest, had reported its presence in the 1840s, and French Canadians had discovered a small site in 1852 on the Pend d'Oreille River. There were other rumors of gold, but it was not until 1859, when Captain E. D. Pierce discovered gold in Canal Creek near Orofino, that gold was to be had in appreciable quantities. By 1861 word had spread of Pierce's find, and in August there were seven thousand men and women in what was called Pierce City. From Pierce the miners swarmed up the creeks and valleys looking for the precious metal, and mining towns sprang up at Orofino, Elk City, and ultimately in the Salmon River country. On the tributaries of the Salmon, strikes were recorded at Pioneer Gulch, Miller Creek, and elsewhere. And after the miners came the traders who supplied them with food, equipment, whiskey, and women. By the autumn of 1861 a tent city of some ten thousand inhabitants had spread out at the head of Baboon Gulch, which was renamed Florence. The miners kept working into the winter, but as the snow piled deep in the uplands the town found itself completely isolated until May. Food prices soared, and many became ill and debilitated from surviving on flour and pine bark. But the lure of plentiful gold was too great to discourage the miners. Some were making $100 a day by panning in the streams, while the machinery of the placers sucked up the metal from the tributaries of the Salmon. Others were taking out gold valued at $400 a day with box shaped rockers operated by hand. By 1863, however, the richest workings were denuded and the bonanza days were over. In the spring of 1864 Florence was virtually deserted, and the Chinese who had labored on the Central Pacific Railroad were permitted to settle there, where they worked the abandoned claims with patience and persistence until the 1880s. Ten years later a new gold strike brought fleeting prosperity back to the

Salmon River country, but by the turn of the century Florence consisted only of a hardy few who remained to earn a meager living from the remnants of the boom days.

There were other strikes on the Salmon tributaries. Thunder Mountain and Roosevelt were producing gold south of the Salmon until destroyed by landslides. Warren's Camp, also south of the Salmon, produced $50,000 in just one gold shipment. Farther to the east and only fifteen miles from the town of Salmon, gold was discovered in July 1866 in Napias Creek, which flows into a tributary of the Salmon. The rush began, and Leesburg, a town of seven thousand miners, tradesmen, and sporting ladies, boomed with well-paying placers until 1874, when, like Florence, the gold was exhausted and the inhabitants drifted off, their places taken by the ubiquitous Chinese. Leesburg survived into the twentieth century until the last inhabitant left in 1946; it had produced $16 million in gold before becoming a ghost town.

The Salmon River country abounds in legends of those who came to the canyon. There was Johnny MacKay, who is credited with running the rapids of the Salmon over twenty trips in a wooden flatiron boat. MacKay carved his name at Barth Hot Springs, but it is better known in association with one of the largest flat areas or "bars" along the mountain river. Another Scot named McKay was famous for supposedly uprooting cotton trees with which he smacked the Devil himself, scattering his teeth across the river to create Devil's Teeth Rapids. Other men came to the canyon of the Salmon and, as in the other canyons of the West, chipped their names on the boulders above the waters. In 1827 P. Flapper was one. Much later, after the gold was gone, some men stayed on living as hermits: men like Andy the Russian and, perhaps the most famous hermit of them all, Buckskin Billy. Andy lived in isolation for twenty-five years, fishing and raising vegetables and fruit. He was over eighty when he died. Buckskin Billy is of more recent vintage. Born Sylvan Hart, he first came out to the Salmon in 1916, returned to West Virginia for a few years, then came back to the land where he wanted to live out his life. Like the other hermits, he lived off the land and the animals for thirty-five years in his cabin at Five Mile Creek, regaling river runners with tales of his many adventures.

After the abortive Mormon settlement in mid-century, gold brought not only prospectors but many others to pack in the supplies and equipment so necessary to carry out the diggings. There were others who brought the materials down the river. Many of these were river men from the Middle West and the calmer waters of the Ohio, the Missouri, and the Mississippi who had little understanding of the rocks, rapids, and log jams on the Salmon. Some learned to navigate the Salmon, but most did not. Among the Salmon River boatmen the most renowned was Harry Guleke.

Harry Guleke was a huge man of great strength and agility. Bold-speaking in the fashion of frontiersmen, there was little he feared, except perhaps Big Mallard. He later ran with David Sandilands, a slender, wiry Scot with a quiet reserve not uncommon to boatmen. He was the younger brother of George Sandilands who had accompanied Guleke on his first trip in 1896, only later to drown in Pine Creek Rapids. With Guleke, David made many successful runs down the river. They did not run for sport, but were in great demand by the mining companies to bring down machinery weighing thousands of pounds to mine Salmon River gold.

Harry Guleke designed and built his own boats, the prototype of the famous Salmon River sweep boat used today on the main Salmon and the Middle Fork. Guleke's boat was a shallow-draft scow with sweeps at the bow and stern. It was thirty-seven feet long, five feet high, and eight feet wide, but the sweeps were its distinctive characteristic. Each sweep was enormous, twenty-five feet long, and had huge, ten-foot blades maneuvered by two boatmen standing bow and stern to guide the boat downstream through the rapids.

Guleke hauled hundreds of tons of machinery, 90,000 pounds alone for the Salmon River Mining Company under the direction of John R. Painter. He also brought down coffee, dynamite, sugar, flour, tobacco, bacon, and other goods for the miners. His first run in 1896 was widely heralded. With their big sweeps, he and George Sandilands snaked down through the rapids of the Salmon and the Snake rivers to Lewiston, where they were wined and dined as the guests of the city. For the next forty years Harry Guleke made a career of transporting goods and people down the River of No Return.

Today boatmen argue around the campfire about which rapid on the Salmon is most to be feared. Some say Pine Creek. Others will claim that Gun Barrel, Groundhog Bar, Chittam, Salmon Falls, and Ruby are the trouble spots, particularly at high water. As for Harry Guleke, there was nothing to dispute. For him Big Mallard presented the greatest challenge on the Salmon. And he feared it the most the night beaver gnawed through his bow and stern lines above Big Mallard and, out of control, the boat went with the current to shoot miraculously between the two great holes, bouncing off rocks but emerging at the bottom of Big Mallard right side up. In the words of Harry Guleke, when the top of Big Mallard is in sight, "We always go ahead here and look out a trail."

Perhaps the best description of Big Mallard was made by Caroline Lockhard, who accompanied Guleke in 1912 on a trip carrying mining machinery.

Interesting? It was terrifying. I looked in a horror I made no effort to conceal. It is no disgrace to be scared at the Big Mallard. In fact I wish to say that the person who is not afraid at certain places in the Salmon River has not sense enough to be afraid. I have met rapids before—shot them and poled over them—but never anything like the rapids of this river, and he who makes the trip can assert with truth that he has taken the wildest boat ride in America.

Words seem inadequate and colorless when I think of describing the Big Mallard. As we stood among the boulders, looking up at it in nothing less than awe, I could well understand the dread it inspired even in such men as Captains Sandilands and Guleke.

The river, running like a mill race, came straight but comparatively smooth until it reached a high, sharp ledge of rock where the river made a turn. Then it

Rod Nash strains for a slot in Big Mallard; the Collins raft follows. By Ray Varley.

made a close swirl and the current gave a sudden rush and piled up between two great rocks, one of which it covered thinly. Behind this latter rock the water dropped into a hollow that was like a well and when it rose it struck another rock immediately below that churned it into fury.

It was Cummings, the third boatman, no longer swaggering, loud-mouthed, and boastful, but white as paper to his ears, who finally said in a strained, subdued voice:

"It's a whole lot worse than the first trip."

Captain Sandilands and Guleke continued to regard it with grave faces. Guleke shook his head.

"We can't make the other side of the rock; we've got to come through here."

I could not believe he was in earnest. I had not thought they had even considered this narrow passageway. The space was not wider than twice the width of the boat and the masses of rock so close to the surface on one side, that yawning hole on the other, the turn around the ledge giving so little time to act and get results in the tremendous current that it looked like deliberate suicide to attempt it. It seemed sure and utter destruction.

No one spoke as we returned to the boats. My feet dragged and I had a curious goneness in the region of my belt buckle. I even considered howling until they let me walk, although it was not possible to make a landing for several miles below. I lost faith in my life-preserver, past achievements in the water were no consolation; we were all going to drown then and there and I knew it! It was in this frame of mind that I crawled limply into the boat.

Nothing could exceed the caution with which the pilot worked the boat into the current that it might catch it in the proper way and place. He watched the landmarks on either shore, measuring distances and calculating the result of each stroke like a good billiard player placing his ball. He knew and we all knew that the error of a single stroke too much or too little in such close quarters meant death to one or all of us.

We were full in the current now. The turn was just ahead. Was it possible that Guleke with all his great strength and marvelous skill could place the boat so that in the final rush between the rocks it would cut the current diagonally? Too far to the left meant the submerged rocks, too far to the right meant the yawning green hole, which looked to be bottomless from the shore. It did not seem within the range of human possibilities to do so.

As we whipped around the point I forgot something of my fear in looking at the pilot. The wind blew his hair straight back and the joy of battle was gleaming in his eyes as he laid down on the sweep. His face was alight with exultation; he looked a monument of courage, the personification of human daring. Fearlessness is contagious, and a spirit of reckless indifference to consequences filled me as we took the final rush. It lasted only a second or two, but the sensations of many years were crowded into the tense moment when on that toboggan slide of water the boat shot past the rocks on the left and cut the hole on the right so close that half the stern hung over it and the bailer stared into its dark depths with bulging eyes.

The boat leaped in the spray but our nerves relaxed, for we knew that we were safely through.

There are many tales old and modern of disaster in Big Mallard. Even the redoubtable Guleke failed on occasion to make the slot and lost his boat in the hole. The old-timers still tell the story of Floyd Dale's encounter with Big Mallard, recounted by Robert Bailey.

He had bought the old Churchill ranch and as there was a small sawmill at the Sam Myers place, some ten miles up the river, where lumber could be had, Floyd decided to have a real home just like city folks. So up the river he hiked and made arrangements for the cutting of 10,000 feet of lumber as the preliminary load he was going to float to his old home. Floyd was used to river travel, and a little thing like the peaceful Salmon River wasn't going to hinder him. After the lumber was cut he secured the services of Charlie Guffel to help him raft it. All the lumber was made into one raft and on a quiet, peaceful morning the journey was begun. Everything went so well that the raftsmen almost went to sleep on the monotonous voyage. But hark! That roaring doesn't sound so good. Neither does the accelerated motion of the raft. Faster and faster the unwieldy craft moves and much louder becomes the river's roar. Ol' Man River just keeps rolling along and the raft is now travelling at a speed that no self-respecting raft should. Those treacherous Big Mallard rapids, where the veteran pilot Captain Guleke has several times met misfortune, are looming big and angrily in sight. The end comes quickly. In the narrow passage there is no room for the large raft, and it hits with tremendous impact on a big boulder in the center of the river. Charlie lost no time in deserting the stricken raft. At the first shock, he leaped for shore and was fortunate enough to be where he could make it without trouble. Floyd was more deliberate. He sat himself down and calmly unlaced his shoes, removing them so that the passage to shore could be made in more leisurely and less laborious manner. But Ol' Man River was working fast, and by the time Floyd was ready the raft had broken up into single boards. He made a dive overboard, but a giant hand seemed to be holding him back. Try as he would he couldn't shake the giant's hold. Over and over he rolled in the white-capped, rock-strewn waters, but somehow he always seemed to remain near the surface and couldn't sink. And then calm and placid waters gave him time to take an inventory. The whole story was clear. He had chained the lumber raft together as best he could, and in some places had used large nails or spikes. One of these spikes had become bent, and as Floyd jumped from the raft the hook caught in his shirt (some of his friends were unkind enough to say elsewhere) and he was impaled on the board as an Indian mother fixes her baby on a "tecach" when she is about to strap the infant to her back. But the board served the purpose in this case of saving the life of [Floyd] Dale. The Mallard rapids are wicked, and it would have been a miracle for anyone loose among the timber of the broken-up raft to have survived death or serious injury.

The old-timers who pioneered running Big Mallard and the rest of the main Salmon have died or left the canyons for calmer waters. Harry Guleke's tombstone in Salmon City, Idaho, bears a river man's simple epitaph: "Captain Harry Guleke, 1862–1944. River of No Return."

About the time Guleke ended his long river-running career, new types of boats arrived on the scene to disprove the idea of a "no return" river. Motors made the difference. Shortly after World War II Paul Filer began to make upriver runs in large fiberglass boats driven by seventy-horsepower engines. Along with Don Smith, Filer found he could make a living transporting supplies and mail upriver to the ranches, mines, and sportsmen's camps scattered throughout the roadless Salmon gorge. To make the job easier, the powerboaters dynamited several boulders out of Dried Meat Rapid, a short but rock-choked drop below Big Mallard. At the time, the deed was cause for local celebration. By creating a channel through which the big boats could roar, the explosives marked one more step in man's conquest of nature.

Inexplicably, Filer and Smith did not attempt to defuse Big Mallard as they had Dried Meat. That rapid remained the most dangerous for boatmen, whether propelled by power or oars. And Filer remembered that his closest call came there. He was following Smith upriver, attempting to hit the same slot between the rocks that the raftsmen seek. The moment of truth was over in seconds, and though Filer had made the run frequently without a problem, this time the river made him pay. As he shot into the slot his boat suddenly broached, slipped sideways, and crashed into the center rock. The impact tossed Filer into the river and his boat began to sink. With Smith safely above Big Mallard, there was no immediate rescue; and Filer bounced, half drowned, from rock to rock in the lower rapid. Finally Smith realized he was alone, spun his boat, and shot back downstream through the slot to pick up his companion. "I thought I was a goner," Filer admitted. Later he turned philosophical: "You can't fight this river, she'll beat you every time."

Rivermen of the 1940s and 1950s had more success in transporting goods and people up and down the Salmon. Few ran the river for fun; it was just a way of getting through rough, roadless country. But the age of recreational river running was not long in dawning in Idaho. Among the first to see the Salmon's whitewater as a recreational resource in its own right, not just as transportation, was the veteran Utah river outfitter Bus Hatch. Initially running rapids for his own enjoyment, Hatch saw he could make a living taking paying passengers on river trips. But it was not all fun and games, particularly where Big Mallard was concerned. On one occasion Hatch and the three other boatmen in his party spotted a black bear and her cub eating berries along the shore. Thinking they could separate the pair and catch the cub, two boats rowed ahead to find a landing spot. Instead they found themselves heading directly into Big Mallard. There was no chance to stop in the strong current. Hatch, who stayed behind, watched horrified as both boats flipped. With his customers floundering in the lower rapid, Hatch raced ahead to assist, but Big Mallard flipped him too. The fourth boatman, amply warned, managed to begin his pull early enough and skirt right of the holes. Finally reunited, the party could count one broken leg, one head stuck in a five-gallon pitch bucket, and two escaped bears.

In recent years commercial and private recreational boating on the main Salmon has boomed, and the river is being studied for inclusion in the National Wild and Scenic River System. Several thousand persons each summer negotiate the rapids that turned back Lewis and Clark, but Big Mallard remains the most respected drop in all but the highest water stages. It still fools first-timers. Each season a number of boatmen, some very experienced, land above the Big Drop, walk down the left bank, take their look, shrug, and return to their boats with the intention of pulling right of the holes. They untie, push off, row right as hard as they can for one hundred yards, and slam straight into those seething cauldrons. The next time, sadder but wiser, they go left and thread the needle.

Eight

Granite Creek

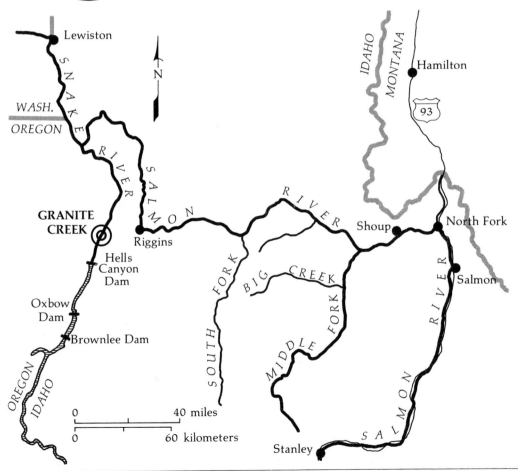

Rapids are very beautiful, especially from above. They start with a tongue of smooth oily water that breaks up into waves. Almost always you go down the middle of the tongue, or a little to one side in the main flow. Often the boatman goes sideways down the tongue and at the last second turns the boat into the first wave, and then tries to hit the wave head-on and avoid the deepest holes between the waves as well as any rocks that may be around. At the edge of the rapid are eddies and whirlpools that sometimes move upstream. The boatman tries to keep out of these for he loses time and control. When waves are too high or close to each other, the boat does not have time to come up for each one; then it is very wet in the boat. When waves come from different angles, perhaps bouncing off the canyon walls, it is hard to run them at the right angle. If these erratic waves are big and the boatman loses control, the boat may flip over.

ERNEST BRAUN

By any standard, one of the most unlikely first descents ever made of a Big Drop was the steamboat *Shoshone's* successful navigation in 1870 of Granite Creek Rapid in Hells Canyon of the Snake River. This great gorge, which defines the Oregon–Idaho border for over one hundred miles and averages 6,500 feet vertically from rim to river, presented a formidable barrier to river transport from the earliest days of westward exploration, but the dream of using the Snake as a commercial highway from the interior to Columbia River ports persisted. In 1866 the Oregon Steam Navigation Company built a triple-decked, stern-wheeled steamboat on the Snake some distance upstream from Hells Canyon.

The *Shoshone* was nearly one hundred feet long and fully outfitted to supply the needs of southern Idaho's mining camps. Business, however, diminished with the gold, and the big boat never carried a payload down the Snake. Finally, in 1870 its owners dispatched veteran steamboat captain Sebastian "Bas" Miller and engineer Dan Buchanan with instructions to bring the *Shoshone* through Hells Canyon and down to the Columbia or wreck it trying. Miller knew what he was about on rivers. He waited for the high, rock-covering water of April to start his run, and he chose to float downstream with his engines in reverse to slow his speed and provide steerage. This was the same concept Nat Galloway later applied so successfully to smaller, oar-powered boats on the Colorado.

The trip began inauspiciously. At the very first rapid the cumbersome steamboat smashed against rocks that shortened its bow by eight feet. Repairs required only a day, but a rolling log struck Miller, knocking him unconscious for another day. Once back on the river, the steamboat somehow survived the big rapids of upper Hells Canyon. At Granite Creek Rapid the *Shoshone* took a terrific pounding. Too wide to run either of Granite's tongues, the ninety-two-foot boat wallowed right through the center hole. Bridging the Snake's huge waves rather than rising and falling with them, the *Shoshone* was torn and wrenched. Planks broke loose; the safety valve came open and steam shrieked. Down in the engine room, Buchanan found himself alternately slammed against one wall and then the other. His steady stream of profanities flew up the speaking tube to Miller who was wrestling with the wheel.

When Miller and Buchanan tied up a few days later at Lewiston, Idaho, the townspeople could not believe their eyes. In one of the rapids in Hells Canyon a plank bearing the boat's name had torn loose and floated downstream. Retrieved from the lower Snake, it seemed conclusive evidence that the *Shoshone* would never be seen again. A memorial service was already being planned when Miller and Buchanan steamed around the bend.

Cleaving the high country of western Idaho and eastern Oregon on its way to the Columbia and the Pacific, the Snake River has cut, in Hells Canyon, the deepest gorge in the American West. Statistically, if not in terms of drama, it surpasses even the Grand Canyon of Arizona. The Snake has an elevation of 1,300 feet in the approximate middle of Hells Canyon. On the Idaho side of the gorge the Seven Devil Mountains rise to a maximum height of 9,393 feet, and the western or Oregon rim averages 7,000 feet above sea level with isolated peaks in the Wallowa Mountains attaining 10,000 feet. One of the first Europeans to see this place, Robert Stuart, noted in 1812 how the river "enters the mountains, which become gradually higher. . . . The whole body of the river does not exceed forty yards in width, and is confined between precipices of astonishing height." Although he did not run the river, Stuart also observed how "cascades and rapids succeed each other, almost without intermission." The fury of this water, the blackness of the basalt and granite lining the inner gorge, and the stifling heat of summer combined in time to pin the name "Hells" on the Snake's handiwork.

The canyon has indeed been hell for explorers and travelers for a century and a half. Although the Snake is logically the best route west from the Continental Divide, the ruggedness of Hells Canyon prevented its development as a transportation corridor like the Missouri or the Ohio. Lewis and Clark avoided it in 1805. Wilson Price Hunt and Donald McKenzie, leading John Jacob Astor's transcontinental expedition in 1811, lost boats and boatmen in the upper Snake, then almost perished traversing the country east of Hells Canyon on foot. Captain Benjamin L. E. Bonneville could not penetrate the gorge on his way to Oregon in 1833. Setting a precedent for subsequent travelers, Bonneville left the Snake at Farewell Bend and struck out across the dry, rough country of eastern Oregon on his way to the lower Columbia and the valley of the Willamette. The Oregon Trail followed this route, and the engineers responsible for Interstate 80N made the same sensible decision a century later. To this day Hells Canyon remains roadless and railless.

Before 1967, when Hells Canyon Dam drowned the upper reaches of the gorge, the Snake was a strong contender for producing some of the toughest whitewater in the West. In a stretch of fifteen miles there were as many formidable rapids as in any comparable distance in the Grand Canyon. Amos Burg, who pioneered small inflatable boat running on both rivers in the 1920s and 1930s, rated Hells four times harder than the Grand, although he may not have seen the rivers at comparable flow levels.

In the predam Hells Canyon the first of the fearsome rapids occurred at Kinney Creek. It had a runnable tongue but huge waves in the high water that seasonally boomed down the Snake. Les Jones, the pioneer mapper of western rivers, rated Kinney a seven on a scale of difficulty extending to ten. A mile and a half downstream, Squaw Creek confronted river runners with an extremely sharp initial drop and then yards of rocks. Squaw drew a rating of nine from Jones, and so did Buck Creek Rapid, a mile farther down. Buck was widely regarded as the toughest rapid in Hells Canyon by those fortunate enough to run it before it died under a reservoir. Its drop was an incredible twenty-two feet in fifty yards, and there was no easy way around an awesome hole in the center with a backwave that could toss boats like toothpicks. A photograph from the 1950s of Buck Creek Rapid shows a pontoon raft, about thirty feet long, totally airborne and upside down, equipment and bodies raining from the boat into the rapid. Only a mile after Buck early Snake River boatmen faced Sawpit Rapid. Les Jones compared it to Hance Rapid, a boulder-choked monster in the Grand Canyon, and gave it an eight on his rating scale.

Hells Canyon Dam is the concrete tombstone of Kinney, Squaw, Buck, and Sawpit. But the final two major rapids in the sequence remain. Wild Sheep comes first, five miles below the dam. At 55,000 cubic feet per second, a flow the Snake still regularly attains, Wild Sheep is a strong candidate for a Big Drop. But two more river miles bring boats to the most difficult remaining rapid in Hells Canyon, high flow or low: Granite Creek.

The name as well as the run of Granite Creek Rapid presents a problem. There is indeed a Granite Creek entering Hells Canyon, and it is a beautiful trout stream, but it is not the location of the rapid that bears its name. Granite Creek drains a major watershed on the Idaho side of the canyon, including the heart of the Seven Devil Mountains; it is a major tributary with an impressive canyon of its own. But this means that in its lower reaches Granite Creek is a relatively mature watercourse characterized by a mild angle of descent. Big rocks, the kind that cause big rapids, do not move readily down such a drainage. Only a small riffle marks the confluence of Granite Creek and the Snake. Passing it, first-time river runners have been lulled into a false sense of security by assuming that the notorious Granite Creek Rapid is really nothing at all.

A half mile farther the real Granite Creek waits in ambush. It is actually located below and caused by Cache Creek, which has all the credentials for making a Big Drop. Cache's drainage is very short and very steep on the Oregon side of the Snake. Black and Bear mountains, both over 6,800 feet, are only two lateral miles up the side canyon. That works out to a rate of descent of something over two thousand feet per mile! Given the flow produced by sudden heavy storms, Cache Creek can move rocks the size of houses and tons of smaller boulders. Such a storm may occur only once in a hundred years, but the Snake has been very patient. The result is apparent to people who read the land. A long grassy terrace, criss-crossed with game trails, hangs a full fifty feet above the confluence of Cache Creek and the Snake. Big rocks have thundered through the terrace to land in the river and form the Big Drop.

Although it is possible to scout the illogically named Granite Creek Rapid from the terrace below Cache Creek, boatmen usually land on the Idaho side of the Snake and walk a horse trail to a vantage several hundred feet above the whitewater. For people who will proceed on boats rather than horses, the view is not comforting. Large rocks, and correspondingly large holes, guard the sides of the river, preventing boats from sneaking down the shoreline. The center of the Snake is a seething cauldron, fully thirty feet across, and below it the water reverses, moves back upstream against the flow. An enormous rock, brought down by Cache Creek, explains the cauldron.

To the right and left of the big rock are smooth tongues that would seem to offer an easy passage through Granite Creek. But they are very deceptive. Unusual angled waves can funnel boats directly into the seething center pit. An error of only a foot or two in the positioning of a raft almost guarantees an upset. In that case there are only three hundred yards of very rough water (rocks in low flows) to swim through. The terror of being upset in Granite Creek is the possibility of being trapped, held, and probably drowned in the giant hole.

Granite Creek is tough enough at its rocky, low-flow stage, when the left tongue can be followed into a narrow slot between exposed rocks and the center hole. In medium flows the tongues are as steep as any found on western rivers. At high water, which on the Snake means 35,000 to 70,000 cubic feet per second, a right-side run is mandatory, and the waves are enormous. At more than 70,000 cubic feet per second, which the Snake occasionally reaches in the spring runoff, stay home.

There is some question about when Granite Creek was first run. In 1862 a Lewiston, Idaho, newspaper published an account of a boat trip up and down the Snake River through Hells Canyon. According to the story, the three men in the party ran every rapid and returned to town glowing with enthusiasm and predicting a golden age of river trade on the Snake. But the 1862 trip is suspect in several particulars. The reported distances between locations along the Snake are so inaccurate (by hundreds of miles) that they throw into doubt the credibility of the reporters. Furthermore, the alleged 1862 conquerors of Hells Canyon state that they "found nothing in the river to impede navigation." If that was their conclusion after actually running the rapids from Kinney Creek to Granite Creek, the three men were either the best boatmen or the best liars in the Pacific Northwest.

It would appear, then, that the voyage of the *Shoshone* in 1870 stands as the first proven run of Hells Canyon and Granite Creek Rapid. The difficulties Miller and Buchanan encountered might have scared off even the most daring, but the hope of steamboating Hells Canyon died hard. Twenty-five years after the *Shoshone's* wild caper, the *Norma* challenged the Snake. Considered in relation to a rocky, powerful river that

Standing to read tailwaves near the end of a run. By William Morgan.

narrows in places to 60 feet, the *Norma's* dimensions are astonishing: overall length, 185 feet; width, 40 feet; deckhouse, 120 feet; cabin deck, 80 feet; pilothouse, 12 feet.

The *Norma's* run began May 17, 1895. Anticipating trouble, the crew sealed off the boat's multiple bulkheads and filled the front compartments with cordwood to buffer collisions; despite these efforts one rock ripped a hole in the hull 40 feet long. The crew at this point made clear their reluctance to continue the trip, and reluctance turned to near rebellion when a ferry operator reported that he had seen "a drift log a hundred feet long up end and go under one cliff and it never came up."

Captain W. P. Gray had a problem on his hands. In the tradition of Christopher Columbus, he dealt with it by assuring the men he would turn back shortly, all the while knowing that once committed to the current of Hells Canyon there was only one way out. So the *Norma* pressed on, racing down channels only a few yards wider than her hull. In the big waves of Granite Creek she nosed down so sharply that her stern paddle wheel came completely out of the water to spin wildly in the air. On May 24 the *Norma* docked at Lewiston, the many stove pipes jammed as caulking in holes in her hull giving the appearance of a gunboat. There was good reason to be proud. Never before or since has so large a boat successfully run such formidable rapids anywhere in the world. However, the final victory belonged to the river: the *Norma's* run marked the end of the steamboat era in Hells Canyon.

After the *Norma's* 1895 effort, runs of Hells Canyon were few and far between. A railroad survey crew navigated the gorge in 1911, but lined almost all of its big rapids after breaking a boat in half the first day out. Another group of surveyors carried their boat around Granite Creek Rapid in January 1920, only to have the unsettling experience of traveling through the lower canyon as part of an ice flow that blanketed the river from shore to shore. These were the last people to give serious consideration to using the Snake for freighting. Only one economic bonanza remained untapped. The same wilderness and whitewater that broke the dreams of empire builders enticed recreational river runners. The future of boating in Hells Canyon would belong to those who coveted rather than cursed the rapids. In due course, companies outfitting vacationing tourists would wring more money out of the Snake than all the early miners, trappers, steamboaters, and railroad builders combined.

The era of running Hells Canyon for fun began in 1928, when Amos Burg and John Mullens negotiated it in Burg's boat, *Song of the Winds*. A few other sportsmen followed: Jack Vandenburg and Harold Thomas in 1932 and Haldane "Buzz" Holmstrom a few years later. In July 1940 two reporters from the Lewiston *Morning Tribune* made the first detailed record of a run of Granite Creek Rapid. Clarence Moore and Paul Jones used two wooden, oar-powered boats, cleverly named *Snake Charmer* and *Hells Belle*. John Olney, a local Oregon boatman, led the party. Also on the trip was Kyle McGrady, who had begun to win a reputation as an operator of the motor-powered mail boat that served the ranches below Hells Canyon.

Putting their boats on the river a few miles below Homestead, Oregon, the Olney party proceeded cautiously. They lined Kinney Creek Rapid and, by their account, lined or portaged the next three big ones: Squaw, Buck, and Sawpit. The first night's camp was at Deep Creek, just below the present site of Hells Canyon Dam. Early the next day they encountered a rapid where, according to Moore, "the water . . . poured over a large rock and then plunged directly toward the river bottom." This was Granite Creek, and it punished Moore and some of his companions.

John Olney, rowing the first boat, proceeded directly into the whitewater and somehow made it through upright. Seeing Olney's boat bobbing in the tailwaves, Moore slid down the right-side tongue.

Seaworthy as our boat was it could not stand being pushed upward on one side and sucked down on the other. It flipped over so quickly that I was still in a sitting position when I tumbled out, head first and bottom up. An undercurrent caught the three of us . . . and swept us under the river. It must have been more than fifteen feet [deep] because my ears ached from the pressure for about six hours. I recall the changing current turning me about in the water in slow motion as some "amazing stories" report that men do in mythical space ships, and all the time I was wondering if I was apt to hit any rocks.

Moore finally surfaced in the tailwaves, still beneath his overturned boat. Almost unconscious from lack of air, he barely extricated himself and floated to shore. Yet he had the river in his blood; his final statement in the newspaper was a vow that he would make "another trip tomorrow if I could."

Other early recreational river runners also met their match in Granite Creek. R. J. Wood, the postmaster of Weiser, Idaho, became sufficiently curious about the canyon he lived near that he decided to float the Snake with five friends. They scouted Granite Creek's two tongues in an effort, Wood stated, to pick "the lesser of two evils." After much deliberation, Oren "Mac" McMullen, who weighed 230 pounds, started his run with two passengers while Wood watched from shore. As the current above the rapid quickened, the powerful McMullen rowed so hard that he broke one oarlock and lost his hold on the other oar. It was low water, and the huge center rock loomed directly ahead. For Wood, on shore, "seconds seemed like hours." Then:

The prow of the boat rose as she stood on end as the water hit the rock. Mac grabbed the tow rope as it dropped past him. Pledger fell off into the water. Parker grabbed a hand rope and hung on—put his foot out and the next second Pledger grabbed it and before you could say it, he had his arms around Parker's neck. [The boat] stood on end—how long I do not know. I do know that two still cameras [on the shore] set and ready to push the button were forgotten entirely . . . and . . . the crucial moment remains unrecorded. Finally, a backwash brought the boat to an even keel and it slowly backed up into the stream and on down the river. We all drew a sigh of relief.

It was several miles and two more, smaller rapids, however, before the oarless boat could be dragged by swimmers to the shore.

The 1940s also found Kyle McGrady, the garage mechanic who had flipped in Granite Creek on the John Olney trip, pushing his fifty-eight-foot powerboat farther and farther up Hells Canyon. McGrady's philosophy of river running was simple and forthright: "You gotta keep lettin' that river know who's boss or you're a goner sure." But he never tested his method against Granite Creek, electing to run only the lower portions of Hells Canyon. The first powerboatman to run Granite Creek from the bottom up was Bob Smith of North Fork, Idaho. In 1952 Smith climbed Granite's staircase in an open aluminum craft powered by two thirty-five-horsepower outboard engines. Smith also ran up through Buck, Sawpit, and the other predam monsters. His feat remains one of the most impressive in the history of boating on the Snake.

By the time of Smith's run, the frequency of river trips in Hells Canyon was on the rise. Ray Holt of Homestead, Oregon, began scheduling commercial recreational trips in 1952. In the same year the

Facing page: The calm, glassy tongue of a major rapid and the violent whitewater below create a dramatic contrast. Badger Rapid, Grand Canyon.

Rocks, here worked down from two tributary canyons, cause rapids. View of Badger from the canyon rim.

The speed of this twelve-foot raft as it breaks through a wave gives its riders the sensation of flying. Lava Falls.

Lunch stop at Redwall Cavern in Marble Canyon, Grand Canyon.

How it looks from the boat
during a right-side run of Lava Falls.

Crystal smothers a pontoon.

A quiet moment on the Snake River in Hells Canyon after a run of Granite Creek.

Entering the left side of Hance Rapid, Mile 77, Grand Canyon.

legendary kayaking physician, Walt Blackadar, rafted Hells Canyon, flipping in Buck Creek Rapid. Having proved her ability in the Grand Canyon of the Colorado, Georgie White brought her act to the Snake River in the mid-1950s. Along with Hatch River Expeditions and Western River Expeditions, Georgie found sufficient interest among her clients to run several trips a year. In 1957 Les Jones concluded the pioneering era, in a sense, by making a detailed scroll map of the river and a guide to its rapids. To his credit, Jones changed the erroneous label of Granite Creek Rapid to "Cache Creek Rapid," but the correction made no headway against custom and tradition. The name remains Granite Creek Rapid today and is still a source of confusion and consternation for the uninitiated.

A major river like the Snake magnetizes dam builders. In 1941 a group of engineers ran Hells Canyon on a business trip. Asked by reporters if they had experienced any "thrills" on the trip, their spokesman coolly replied, "We were impressed by the rapids rather than thrilled." What did thrill the engineers was the abundance of dam sites in the canyon. In the ensuing years some in the upper gorge were utilized: for Brownlee Dam (1958), Oxbow Dam (1961), and Hells Canyon Dam (1967). Drowned under reservoirs were most of the original Big Drops of Hells Canyon, including Buck Creek Rapid. Indeed, only eighty-five miles of free-flowing river remained after the dam builders finished their work. Then, seizing on a Federal Power Commission recommendation that more dams in Hells be authorized, utility companies made plans to complete the taming of the Snake. If these plans had been implemented, Granite Creek Rapid would have gone the way of Buck Creek and the others. But a 1967 Supreme Court decision, spearheaded by a longtime friend of wilderness, Justice William O. Douglas, forced reconsideration. The Court simply asked if the Federal Power Commission had considered the option of building no more dams at all on the Snake, and sent the case back for further study.

The 1967 decision encouraged friends of a wild Snake. Citizen conservationists brought forward the fact that no less than eighteen dams already impeded the river's flow. Of the Snake's entire thousand-mile

Facing page: The river runner's reward: floating in slow current at day's end, lower Grand Canyon.

course only the eighty-five miles below Hells Canyon Dam and a few miles in Wyoming remained free-flowing. This was becoming a matter of concern to more and more people, among them Senator Robert Packwood of Oregon. On April 14, 1971, he addressed the United States Senate on the subject of saving Hells Canyon. A few weeks later Packwood ran the river. At Granite Creek Rapid he became so excited that he kayaked the next five miles under the tutelage of Walt Black-adar.

With the question of more dams in Hells Canyon becoming a major national environmental issue, more politicians wished to see firsthand what all the fuss was about. On August 14, 1972, three United States congressmen arrived at the top of Granite Creek Rapid with Jim Campbell, a commercial river trip outfitter. Already nervous because of the congressmen's presence, Campbell's boatmen paled when they walked up the horse trail to scout Granite Creek. The Snake's flow was about 14,000 cubic feet per second, and at that level Granite's tongues were extraordinarily steep and narrow. Normally the boatmen would have opted for the left side, but they were anxious to give the congressmen an exciting ride. They would go for it. Cort Conley was running the lead boat, and his positioning was perfect. His twenty-seven-foot pontoon slipped between boiling holes on either side of the right tongue. Conley later admitted, however, "It was the steepest tongue I've ever dropped off in a boat."

As he bucked through Granite's tailwaves it occurred to Conley that if the following boats missed their entry into the rapid by as little as a yard on either side, they would flip. He had no time to land and run back along the shore with his warning, and the roar of the rapid prevented shouting. He could only watch in horror as the second pontoon dipped down the tongue, caught an edge in a hole, and turned bottom side up.

The unfortunate boatman climbed on top of his inverted raft and looked frantically for his passengers. Spotting Congressman James Kee, who was elderly and in poor health, he hauled him onto the

A dory entering the left side of Granite Creek. Photo courtesy of Martin Litton's Grand Canyon Dories.

overturned boat. Meanwhile Jim Campbell brought the third and last raft down the rapid with no special trouble. Rowing furiously, Campbell caught up with the flipped pontoon and seized its bow line. Then began the struggle to land both boats before the next rapid, already audible downstream. Annette Tussing, reporting for the Lewiston *Morning Tribune,* recorded the moment:

Rowing with extreme effort [Jim Campbell] finally fell from his seat amidships in exhaustion.

Congressman Mike McCormack, D-Wash., who had been taking his turn at the oars in milder rapids upstream, leaped to the oars now, bracing almost horizontal as he strained to pull the big raft swinging at the end of the ropes, out of the fierce grip of the fast current and toward shore.

Almost there he gave out and James Olson grabbed the oars, also extending himself with unbelievable stamina to move both rafts.

If we missed a small jut of rocks just downstream both craft would be swept into the next rapids.

We were only two feet from the rocks when our raft began losing ground, slowly sliding back toward the ponderous pull of the big craft.

McCormack and Campbell leaped into the deep water bounding the abrupt jut of boulders. Both of them clawing at the smooth slippery boulders, lost holds and slid under our raft, briefly.

Olson still pulled at the oars to prevent us from sliding away from shore again.

Finally, scrambling and clawing, the men in the water got the bowline around a rock. It gave way. Another, and it loosened and tumbled out of place.

A third rock held. The rest of us scrambled ashore on the huge rocks, to help pull the big raft in and tether it to the jumble of boulders which pitched sharply into the deep water.

After a number of deep breaths the party unloaded and righted the flipped pontoon. Congressman Patrick T. Caffery of Louisiana poured water out of the suitcase he had ill-advisedly brought on the river. Several members of the U. S. Army Corps of Engineers along on the trip observed almost in unison that if more dams were built on the Snake such things would not happen. Congressman McCormack replied that the opportunity to challenge, and maybe lose to, a rapid was precisely its value for an increasingly overcivilized society.

A few hours behind the congressional party the same August day in 1972 Verne Huser and Hank Miller had charge of another Jim Campbell trip. They had just finished scouting Granite Creek Rapid when a member of the congressional trip panted up the horse trail with news of the upset. The messenger was supposed to tell Huser and Miller not to try the right-hand tongue, but something was lost in the translation and the boatmen headed directly for the trouble spot. Not wishing to create anxiety among their passengers, they had kept the news of the upset to themselves. But Huser felt considerable apprehension as he drifted toward the roar of Granite in his twenty-five-foot pontoon. Just before the tongue he reminded himself that he had run Granite successfully on ten previous occasions. "I know how to run it," he thought. "Hit the haystack at a slight angle to the right so the angular wave will set us up for the tail waves—no sweat." As it turned out there was plenty!

"Somehow," Huser remembers, "I misjudged the angle and hit the haystack too straight so that the angular wave turned us to the left and instead of riding lightly over the wave, we were at the perfect angle to ride up onto the long curler and be driven right back into that horrendous hole. I had my left oar in the water, and the force of the rollback drove us down into the hole so hard that the oar, which was twelve feet long, hit the bottom of the river and broke in two." Huser believes that before breaking the oar acted like a brace, keeping the boat upright long enough to wallow out of the hole. He also credits getting out to his boat's low center of gravity, the result of carrying fully packed provision boxes. Perhaps the river, having already eaten one boat that day, just decided to let him through.

At the time of the congressional river trip in 1972, the future of Granite Creek Rapid and the remaining wild stretch of Hells Canyon was undecided. But the pressure of environmentalists and the changing mood of the nation were inexorable. On December 31, 1975, President Gerald R. Ford signed into law a bill adding 101 miles of the Snake to the National Wild and Scenic Rivers System. The same act created a 650,000-acre Hells Canyon National Recreation Area and, within it, a 193,000-acre addition to the National Wilderness Preservation System. Many Big Drops on the Snake had been stilled, but in Granite Creek's case the nation opted to let one remain dancing and alive.

Nine

Crystal

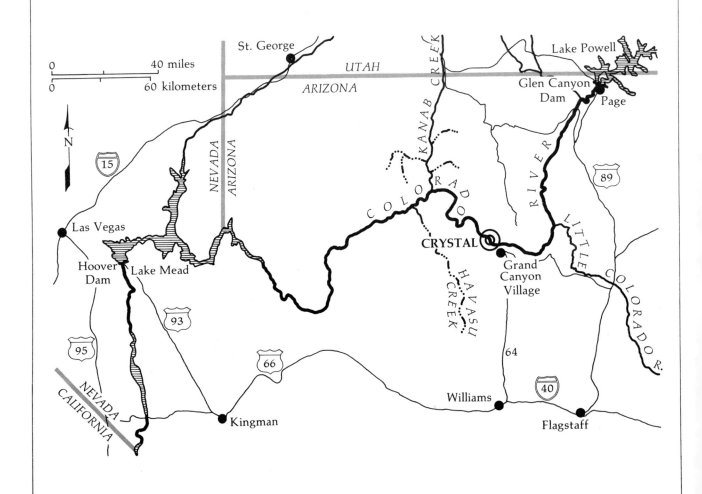

The great tailwaves were all that anyone remembered of that run, grand, glassy mountains of water with swooping valleys between them; climbing for three boatlengths or more until it seemed we'd lost all power to climb; perching then on a crest as sharp as an alp and wondering whether we'd pitch forward into the next trough or back down the slope onto another boat (everyone saying later they looked up and saw the whole bottom of the next boat out of the water above them on the crest ahead); pitching down into another trough nearly as deep and soaring up to another crest nearly as high, and after four or five crests finally being sure we would carry over the next, not fall back. And looking around at each other when we reached the still water, almost amazed to see all boats right side up: it was supposed to work that way, but it still seemed incredible.

GAYLORD STAVELEY

Rain began to fall over northern Arizona in the grey morning hours of December 4, 1966. An unseasonal, but extremely intense, low pressure system drew saturated air from the Gulf of California and the Pacific Ocean north and east toward the snow-dusted Kaibab Plateau. As the warmer air from the sea rose over the nine thousand-foot Kaibab, it cooled and condensed as precipitation. Such winter storms over the Grand Canyon are common, but this one was different: *fourteen inches* of water fell in a period of only thirty-six hours. One consequence was the almost instantaneous creation of a Big Drop.

Earth scientists and meteorologists speak of fifty- and one-hundred-year storms and floods. They mean a phenomenon that only occurs on an average of once every fifty or one hundred years. The storm of December 4 and 5, 1966, over the Crystal Creek drainage is given at least a one-thousand-year rating. There are no historical records of comparable precipitation for the plateaus north of the Grand Canyon. Indian ruins known to date from the twelfth century and located over forty feet above normal water level in the creek were carried away by the high waters of December, 1966.

In December the north rim of the Grand Canyon is one of the more isolated places in the American West. The road that carries summer tourists forty-five miles from U.S. 89A to the lodge at Bright Angel Point closes after the first snow. Thereafter only the rare snowmobiler or cross-country skier traverses the pine-dotted meadows to stare into the abyss. Almost certainly the great rain of 1966 fell unobserved, but we can imagine it hammering the frozen ground, then quickly collecting in rivulets and moving southward into the canyon. This seemingly obvious fact merits some attention. Had the big rain fallen above the south rim of the Grand Canyon, on the Coconino Plateau, there would be no Big Drop at mile 98 on the Colorado River. The slope of the land on the south rim is, somewhat illogically, away from the Canyon. The explanation is that the ancestral Colorado River cut through the uplifted northern part of Arizona south of its highest point. The Kaibab Plateau is a full two-thousand feet higher than the Coconino. Water runs into the Canyon on the north side and away from it on the south.

The Crystal Creek drainage is one of the longest north of the central section of the Grand Canyon. The December 1966 runoff began among the aspen and pine of Lower Little Park, twenty-five air miles from the Colorado. At the eight-thousand-foot level the water dropped over the north rim. The Colorado was almost six-thousand feet below, and in the course of winding toward it, Crystal Creek gathered the waters of a dozen major side streams. But a rainfall that covered every square foot with fourteen inches of water turned each fold in the canyon walls into a torrent. By the time Crystal Creek curled past a long, twisting ridge known as The Dragon and descended into the vast Hindu Ampitheater, it was a raging brown beast. At this point Dragon Creek, almost as long as Crystal, joins it from the east. The combined flow must have been awesome. Powered by a steep rate of descent, lower Crystal Creek moved thousands of tons of gravel and small rock at speeds close to fifty miles per hour. Boulders three feet in diameter were suspended in the flow. Larger ones rolled along the stream bed with a low, ominous rumble. Occasional earth slippages and mud flows gave the swollen stream the viscosity of molasses.

Lashing from wall to wall like an enraged serpent, Crystal finally powered into the Colorado. The rocky delta of Crystal Creek quadrupled in size. That pushed the Colorado southward toward Slate Creek, which enters directly opposite Crystal. Steep cliffs downstream from Slate constricted the river, forcing it to rampage through the new obstacle course.

The old Crystal Rapid had a moderate drop of about fifteen feet, and the few sizeable rocks in the rapid could be easily avoided in low water. At higher flows there were regular waves of unremarkable size for the Grand Canyon. Not one of the early accounts of running the Colorado even mentions Crystal Rapid. Why should they? In the preceding ten miles the pioneer river parties had to deal with extraordinary rapids such as Horn, Granite, and Hermit; by comparison the old Crystal seemed easy indeed. After December 1966, however, no one ignored Crystal. Overnight it became one of the most dreaded rapids in the West.

Although no one saw the transformation of Crystal Rapid into a Big Drop, what took place there has been deduced from documented events in the Bright Angel Creek drainage a dozen miles to the east. Bright Angel also begins on the Kaibab Plateau above eight-thousand feet, and its watershed received approximately the same amount of precipitation in the 1966 storm. Dan Doherty, the manager of Phantom Ranch, was living on Bright Angel at the time. Located a mile from the Colorado, Phantom has served hikers and riders since early in the century. Normally it is a cottonwood-shaded oasis. Bright Angel Creek, usually a little hop-across stream, gurgles along below the guest cottages. Doherty recalled the change caused by the torrential rains. The flood struck Phantom Ranch "with the noise of a dozen locomotives." Immediately marooned by the rising water, the few persons at the ranch began to fear for their lives, and the mules bolted so high on the

Before and after Crystal became a Big Drop. Extreme low-water conditions reveal the anatomy of the rapid in both aerial photographs. Note the tremendous increase in the size of the gravel "fan" after the flood. Bureau of Reclamation photo by Al Turner.

canyon walls they later had to be assisted down with ropes. Doherty recalled that the ground trembled under his feet—the result of boulders bounding down the creek bed. "It wasn't just the size of the flood," Doherty remembered, "but the duration of it. It rose up and didn't drop an inch for three days."

Among the casualties were scores of 150-year-old cottonwoods,

stone walls, buildings, irrigation works, and the sewer system of the ranch. One bunkhouse ended up in Lake Mead, two-hundred miles down the Colorado. The greatest loss along Bright Angel, however, was the brand new water pipeline that ran from Roaring Springs, high on the north wall, down the creek, across the Colorado, and up to the tourist facilities on the south rim. The project cost $2 million, and it was an engineering marvel. In a few hours the creek ripped out the work of two years. Pipe, bridges, and sections of the new North Kaibab Trail disappeared down the Colorado. As mute evidence of the cause, a rock measuring three feet by two feet by two feet was found in the flood's aftermath poised on one of the few remaining bridges, a full thirty feet above the normal level of the creek. It had been carried like a grain of sand in the raging water.

National Park officer Frank Betts saw Bright Angel Canyon soon after the flood. He also noted the hundreds of cubic yards of raw earth ripped from the canyon walls and the devastation of the Bright Angel delta at its confluence with the Colorado. In Betts' view, "It looked as if the whole Colorado River had come down Bright Angel Creek." The topography showed the result. The trail and pipeline were not reopened for four long, expensive years.

The discharge of Bright Angel Creek did not create a major rapid in the Colorado but rather a series of sharp, swinging bends peppered with gravel bars. It is a totally different story ten miles downstream. The principal way the great flood of 1966 altered Crystal Rapid was by doubling its drop. The outwash from Crystal Creek literally dammed the Colorado with a fifteen-foot layer of rock and gravel. Some of the rocks, particularly those that lodged against the left, or southern bank, are enormous, and at high water they cause holes as large as any in the Grand Canyon, including Lava Falls.

From a boatman's perspective the run of Crystal begins innocently enough on a lush bed of grass on the right bank above the rapid. Carefully, boats are tied to the trunks of tamarisk. Some boatmen walk down along the river, but many elect to climb the one-hundred-foot cutbank left by Crystal Creek. It always seems oven-hot among the cactus on the trail, and the heat increases with each step away from the river. From the top of the rise the Colorado sweeps around Crystal's huge fan-shaped delta in a seething white arch. The tailwaves of the rapid disappear beyond a bend a half mile downstream. Taken as a whole, Crystal is one of the Grand Canyon's longest rapids.

From this distance a rapid cannot be read properly, so the boatmen scramble down the steep slope to Crystal's floodplain, where they vanish in the head-high vegetation that has become established since the high water of 1966. Thrashing through it, they come to a small, clear stream; the innocuous trickle is notorious Crystal Creek. At the edge of the Colorado the temperature drops fifteen degrees and the ominous roar peculiar to really big rapids fills the air. River runners stand like herons on beautifully rounded pink and orange rocks brought down by Crystal Creek from cliffs thousands of feet above. Looking up the Colorado, the tongue of Crystal Rapid appears broad and silky, but the smoothness is deceptive. The water actually powers down Crystal's initial drop at speeds approaching twenty miles per hour. Grand Canyon boatmen know how hard it is to row or motor across such water. Prior positioning becomes crucial.

Along the tongue small rocks and their ensuing holes pock the right side of the river. Increasing in frequency and size, they funnel the Colorado inexorably toward a truly unbelievable hole. Regardless of how they walked down to scout the rapid, boatmen invariably find themselves standing shoulder to shoulder, silently contemplating this dark, seething pit that could swallow a school bus. It exists because of several enormous rocks directly at the end of Crystal's long, racing tongue. Most of the Colorado River plunges over the rocks and down twelve feet into the hole. Rebounding, the water shoots twenty feet into the air. It is this mountain of water that fills boatmen's nightmares.

If Crystal Rapid ended with the big hole, it still might qualify as a Big Drop. In fact the hole is only a quarter of the way through the whitewater. Below it and slightly to the right is a rock that many Grand Canyon veterans think of as the worst on the river. Actually it is rather pretty: orange in color and nicely smoothed, a block of Supai sandstone. The problem with this rock is its location. Boats slamming off the right side of the big hole will, if the boatman loses control, wash directly onto the orange rock and then career onto a barely submerged island of large boulders.

The walk back to the boats at the top of Crystal is never pleasant. Minds focus on the big hole, the orange rock, and the "pull" off the tongue needed to miss them. The commercial trip leader who once proposed lunch after scouting Crystal almost had a mutiny on his hands. It is a time to run, not relax.

Untied from the tamarisk, the boats at first barely move. Then the pace of the current quickens, the roar of crashing water increases, and the battle is joined. The whole point in running Crystal is to counter the force of the water moving into the big hole by powering to the right off the tongue. Motor-powered rigs commonly drift down the left side of the tongue backwards, motors downstream. At the proper moment, the boatman allows his bow to swing to the right, guns the motor, and attempts to reach the narrow band of smoother water to the right of the hole.

Oar-powered boats take a different approach. Swinging wide to the left on the main tongue will guarantee a view of the hole from its bottom. Instead oarsmen and paddlers hug the right bank and then the right side of the narrowing tongue, pulling right, right, right. The smaller and lighter the boat, the better the chances of success in this maneuver. Tiny inflatable canoes and seven-foot Sportyaks can duck off the tongue early, slalom through the top rocks and skid into a small eddy on the right bank just below the hole. It is not too hard, in the way that walking a six-inch plank one hundred feet above the ground is not too hard. The problem is not physical so much as psychological.

With heavier rowed boats, the ones that carry five people and a thousand pounds of equipment, for instance, there is less chance of a quick, clean pull to the right. The waves on the right side of the tongue are surprisingly large and so angled that boats striking them are bounced back toward the center of the river. Bumping a rock with the stern will also cause the boat to ricochet onto the speeding tongue. Breaking an oar is another distinct possibility on the rocky right side. And Crystal is unforgiving. One false move and you eat the hole.

"Pull" rapids like Crystal pose a special problem for triple rigs—three sixteen-foot inflatable boats lashed together side to side and controlled by two boatmen, each with a long sweep oar. Commonly a triple rig will carry twelve persons and a ton of gear. It is a stable craft in big waves,

A fifteen-foot inflatable raft skirts the big hole in Crystal. By Art Vitarelli.

but its weight and size make precise maneuvering difficult. In Crystal, for example, the speeding tongue tries for two hundred yards to spin the triple rig out into the main current. The bow or downstream oarsman must be aware of the position of the rear boat; if it starts to slide left into the fast current, he must actually row left to prevent a spin and give his partner in the rear a chance to regain proper position. It is unnerving in the extreme to row *toward* the big hole in Crystal, but paradoxically this is the only way to avoid it in a triple rig.

The rowers of heavier boats must be philosophical about the big hole, particularly at lower water levels. Try as they may, they never miss it entirely. A good run is one that only catches a corner of the gaping monster. That, however, is good enough when the stakes are survival.

Once past the hole, there is exhilaration but no relief. The next decision is the most crucial in running Crystal. To which side of the orange rock and the head of the boulder island should the boat be directed?

Two factors must be fed into the computer of the boatman's mind immediately upon passing the hole. The first is his position relative to the rock. Did the hole kick his boat far enough right to miss the rock on that side? Or should he try to cut behind the big hole and make a left-side passage? The second factor is the condition of the boat and passengers. Is it swamped with tons of water, making any maneuver difficult? Are the oars still functional? If a triple rig, is the rear oarsman still in the boat, or did the hole rip him off his oar? Are any passengers clinging to the sides of the boat, making steering difficult? One glance and one split second are all the river permits. Right or left? The orange rock is an uncompromising judge of the boatman's decision.

In 1967 and 1968, the first two boating seasons after the creation of Crystal Rapid, a second enormous hole gaped downstream and slightly left of the first one. No small boat could come through that combination upright, and it even rolled thirty-three-foot pontoons. Since 1968 a shift of rocks on the bottom of the river has greatly reduced the size of the second hole, and some boatmen today plan on cutting back sharply to the left below the big hole and above the orange rock. For them running the rest of the rapid is "only" a matter of negotiating five hundred yards of big waves. In low water this lower left side is sprinkled with exposed, boat-tearing rocks.

The lower right side of Crystal also has its difficulties. Immediately below the orange rock there are holes capable of overturning small boats. Even a third of a mile later such holes are found. Avoiding them would not be difficult under ordinary circumstances; a boat filled with several tons of water is not ordinary.

In marked contrast to Lava Falls, there is a way to run Crystal Rapid without hitting any holes or even shipping much water. But such perfect runs are rare, especially for heavier boats. In its relatively brief history, Crystal has generated its share of river horror stories. A number of boats have capsized in the big hole, leaving their occupants feeling, as one put it, "like a mouse being flushed down a toilet." Sometimes Crystal strips a boat of its boatmen and passengers, but lets the boat through right side up. On one trip for high-ranking National Park Service personnel, the boatman managed to steer his pontoon directly into the hole. The boat hit the big wave head on, slowing it from approximately twenty miles per hour to a standstill in one second. The boat's occupants continued forward—swimming. They were lucky. At certain water levels a hole like Crystal's can trap and hold bodies and boats, recycling them furiously. It is that prospect which pumps the adrenalin as boatmen start down the long, fast tongue of the rapid.

Crystal has, on occasion, "folded" triple rigs. This occurs when the front boat of the three-boat lash-up rises so sharply on a wave that it folds on top of the middle boat. The resulting rubber sandwich with people and equipment in the middle is difficult to untangle. Fortunately, there is usually an air pocket between the folded boats permitting people to breathe until the rapid ends. A variation finds the rear boat folded under the first two, which have been stopped by the steep face of a wave. The river tears loose the passengers in the underfolded boat, washing them under the entire rig and on down the river. Good life preservers are special friends in such a situation.

Dozens of boats hit Crystal's notorious orange rock every season. The lucky ones spin off it to pound down through the boulder field beyond. The less fortunate are punctured or splintered and limp downstream. And a few boats wrap around it, and stay there. Wrapping is, in the estimation of many, the worst fate that can befall a riverboat. In an upset, at least, the boat washes downstream where it can be recovered and righted. But a wrapped boat is bent around a rock and pinned there by the force of moving water. Some boats can be freed using lines from shore, but often they remain wrapped until the river shreds them into rubber ribbons or wooden or metal splinters.

The most famous wrap on the orange rock in Crystal involved the thirty-foot inflatable pontoon of a prominent river guide. It was motor-propelled and carried about a dozen people. Out of control after wallowing through the big hole, the pontoon struck the orange rock

Kevin Gallagher kayaks Crystal. By Art Vitarelli.

sideways. The speeding Colorado immediately bent both ends downstream. The boat was securely wrapped. Floundering out of the swamped side of their boat, passengers and crew perched on the exposed upper tubes like turtles on a log while Crystal Rapid raged around them.

There was no assistance from shore, and the boatmen soon determined that they could not dislodge four thousand pounds of firmly pinned rubber. It then became necessary to tell the frightened passengers some good news and some bad news. The former concerned the water level of the Colorado: When the wrap occurred it was low, the result of curtailed nighttime water releases from the Glen Canyon Dam 112 miles upstream. The river could be expected to rise and wash the boat free. Now the bad news: high water would not occur until the next day. It would be necessary to spend the night in the middle of the rapid.

As darkness descended the boatmen secured lines to the orange rock to prevent the boat from coming loose during the night. Then, in a commendable show of poise, they served dinner. One of the supply cans was fished from the whitewater racing through the boat, and cold food was distributed to those who had stomachs for it under the circumstances. There was little rest in "camp" that night. As expected, the Colorado began to rise about midnight. The boat might have been released from the rock, but the boatmen were afraid of a night run of the lower part of Crystal and kept the lines in place. The first light of morning found the orange rock nearly submerged, the rising river tearing at the pontoon, and its occupants cowering on the small area that was not awash. The mooring lines, normally an inch in diameter, were reduced to the thickness of a pencil under the strain. Simultaneously three persons touched knives to the taut ropes, which parted with a sound like pistol shots. Then the pontoon continued on the longest run of a Big Drop ever made.

The rise in the river that freed the wrapped pontoon is a reminder that the flow of the Colorado in the Grand Canyon is now artificial. The water in the river is not a result of natural processes but rather a gift from the engineers who control Glen Canyon Dam. Completed in 1963, Glen's water release schedule is, in turn, a function of the hydroelectric power needs of metropolitan centers in the Southwest. A sweltering day (and the need for air conditioning) in Phoenix and Los Angeles means a high-water day in the Grand Canyon.

For some river runners this artificiality is disturbing. It detracts from the wilderness experience many enter the Canyon to find. Although obviously not visible at Crystal Rapid, Glen Canyon Dam is a psychological factor, an unseen presence. Its importance cannot be dismissed since, in the last analysis, wilderness is a state of mind. But the full balance sheet must be read. The dam gives as well as takes away. It has, for example, created the opportunity to catch trout in the cold waters released from the bottom of Lake Powell. Trout habitat now exists all the way down to Crystal. Glen Canyon Dam also extends the river running season. In the predam days it was either feast or famine, too much water or too little. During the floods of late spring and early summer, the Colorado normally reached flows of 100,000 cubic feet per second and at least once in recorded history (in 1884) topped 300,000.

The low flows of late summer were less than 2,000 cubic feet per second. The Colorado still has these low flows, but only in the winter months, when the need for Glen Canyon power is reduced. From April to October, river runners can usually count on flows in the 10,000 to 30,000 range, ideal for boating.

The closing of the gates at Glen Canyon in 1963 means that the new Crystal Rapid, formed in 1966, has never been subjected to the high water of the predam era. This is a fact of some consequence in Crystal's present status as a Big Drop. At very high flows the Colorado, like Crystal Creek itself, is capable of moving very large rocks and enormous masses of gravel. If Glen Canyon Dam did not exist, it is probable that the high water of the spring of 1967 would have scoured away many of the rocks Crystal Creek deposited in the Colorado the previous December. The result, in time, would have probably been a rapid resembling the old Crystal Rapid.

Unquestionably this process of flash flood and debris removal has occurred over and over again in the geologic past of the Grand Canyon. Assuming the periodic occurrence of high water, the big river is a good housekeeper, carrying its dirt to the ocean. Glen Canyon Dam, however, is capable of releasing a maximum flow of only 30,000 cubic feet per second. At rare intervals tributaries like the Paria and the Little Colorado add enough water to bring the flow at Crystal to perhaps twice that amount. But this is still five times less than the known high water of the last century, which itself may have been unimpressive compared to flows over the past thousand years. The inescapable conclusion is that side-canyon runoffs comparable to the one that created the new Crystal Rapid could in the future dump so many large rocks in the Colorado as to create an unrunnable waterfall. Crystal comes close to being in this category. One more house-size rock to the right of the tongue would eliminate the chances of safe passage through the rapid.

Occurring simultaneously with the great rain that brought the rocks down Crystal Creek, another storm threatened to have a profound effect on Crystal and the whole Grand Canyon. This one was political, its "drainage" the halls of Congress, and its subject dams. Soon after the completion of Glen Canyon Dam in 1963, federal agencies announced plans for more dams on the Colorado, and this time the Grand Canyon itself was the target. The two-thousand-foot drop of the Colorado River through its largest canyon was too much for the Bureau of Reclamation to resist. To wring the most hydroelectric power from the river, they proposed two dams. One in Marble Canyon (actually the first part of the Grand Canyon) would have created a reservoir fifty-three miles long, extending right to the base of Glen Canyon Dam. This was the kind of total utilization of a river efficient engineers relish despite the deathblow it deals to diversity of environment and experience. A second dam in the lower reaches of Grand Canyon would have backed water up almost a hundred miles and claimed Lava Falls as one of its victims.

Crystal Rapid, located between the proposed upper dam and the intended head of the lower reservoir, would have been spared. But to what fate? Along with the dams, engineers developed plans for a diversion tunnel under the Kaibab Plateau that would carry water from the upper reservoir into the Kanab Creek drainage to spin the turbines of yet another powerhouse. Since Kanab Creek is downstream from Crystal, had the tunnel been built the flow in the Colorado at Crystal would have seldom been more than a trickle. For all practical purposes river running in the Grand Canyon would have ended.

Few realize how close these projects came to being approved by Congress and the Johnson administration in 1965 and 1966. At that time the sport of running rivers was in its infancy, and few knew the Grand Canyon's rapids firsthand. Dams, on the other hand, were objects of national celebration. They made possible the growth and development that until the 1960s had been unquestioned American gods. Fortunately for the river there were a few iconoclasts. One was David R. Brower, then the powerful executive director of the Sierra Club. The advertisements he placed in nationally prominent newspapers in the summer of 1966 elicited the public outrage that ultimately defeated the dams. Important, too, was the 1967 journey through the Grand Canyon of Secretary of the Interior Stewart L. Udall and his family. For two weeks Udall ran with veteran outfitter Jack Currey, and his mid-June trip was among the first to negotiate the recently remodeled Crystal Rapid. It is not hard to imagine the dryness in Currey's throat as he found a Big Drop in place of the minor rapid he was accustomed to seeing at the mouth of Crystal Creek. Having a cabinet member in the boat only added to the tension of the moment. But Currey, using an outboard motor for power, slipped through unscathed. Udall came away from his Grand Canyon experience convinced that a wild river was its own best argument for existence. "The burden of proof," Udall declared in a subsequent article, " . . . rests on the dam builders. If they cannot make out a compelling case, [Grand Canyon National Park] should be enlarged and given permanent protection." That the Grand Canyon dams were intended only to make money to pay for pumping water to Phoenix was not, for Udall, a persuasive argument.

Under continued pressure from a citizenry which felt there were already enough dams on the Colorado, Congress gradually retreated from the brink of a pro-dam decision. In the summer of 1968 a bill authorizing the Central Arizona Project was approved without either of the Grand Canyon dams. Except for a few die-hard western congressmen and rabid developers, Americans agreed that the nation was not yet so poor that it had to fund development by damming the Grand Canyon. Conversely, it was no longer so rich that it could afford to sacrifice environmental treasures like Crystal, Lava Falls, and the free-flowing Colorado.

No sooner had the Grand Canyon dam controversy been settled in favor of whitewater rather than kilowatts than another problem loomed over Crystal. Ironically, this one was the product of too many friends rather than too few. Rivers, it was becoming apparent, could be loved to death. From the standpoint of wilderness values too many river runners posed the same problem as too many dams. The issue centered on the concept of carrying capacity, the number of persons who could enter and enjoy a wilderness without disrupting its wilderness qualities. The impact of visitors on wildlife, beaches, and vegetation was comparatively easy to calculate. More tricky, and ultimately more crucial, was the impact of people on each other. Clearly there was a point (the psychological carrying capacity of a wilderness) at which the admission of more people ended anyone's chance of having a wilderness experience. It still might be fun in the sense that Disneyland is fun, but it would not be the kind of pleasure associated with being in wild country.

Although it is hard to believe in view of the expeditionary character of early Grand Canyon voyages, the Colorado River was actually becoming overcrowded by the early 1970s. Statistics tell the story:

Travel on the Colorado River Through the Grand Canyon

Year	Number of People	Year	Number of People
1867	1?	1958	80
1869–1940	73	1959	120
1941	4	1960	205
1942	8	1961	255
1943	0	1962	372
1944	0	1963–64	44
1945	0	1965	547
1946	0	1966	1,067
1947	4	1967	2,099
1948	6	1968	3,609
1949	12	1969	6,019
1950	7	1970	9,935
1951	29	1971	10,385
1952	19	1972	16,432
1953	31	1973	15,219
1954	21	1974	14,253
1955	70	1975	14,305
1956	55	1976	13,912
1957	135	1977	11,830

Tony Stearns catches air midway through Crystal. By Art Vitarelli.

As a consequence of the limited access points for the Grand Canyon river trip these figures are very accurate. The possible single passage in 1867 was that of James White (see pages 191–194). In 1963–1964 the closing of the gates of Glen Canyon Dam so Lake Powell could fill precluded running the Grand Canyon for all but forty-four individuals willing to drag their boats from pool to pool. After the 1972 season the National Park Service began to limit the number of persons permitted to make the run to that year's level, and unforeseen cancellations kept use below the limit in the succeeding years. The drought of 1977 in the West compelled the Bureau of Reclamation to cut releases from Glen Canyon Dam drastically and thereby eliminate several months of river travel through the Grand Canyon. Management proposals based on extensive research into visitor impact allow for a maximum annual use of 15,000. The number of people who want to run the river, particularly those who want non-commercial trips (in their own boats, without guides), has risen every year, but less than eight percent of the total use is allocated to do-it-yourselfers. The resulting competition for permits is one of the unhappy consequences of the growing popularity of white-water boating. Proposed revisions would change the ratio to thirty percent non-commercial and seventy percent commercial.

The big story in these statistics is the astonishing growth of river running after 1965. This is, of course, related to the increased interest on the part of many Americans in temporary alternatives to their largely urbanized way of life. Far from being the adversary it was to pioneers, wilderness is a refreshing novelty to the modern American, whose normal existence might be characterized as overcivilized. Solitude, challenge, danger, self-sufficiency, and humility in the face of natural forces are, at any rate, increasingly rare and increasingly coveted. The search for them brings people to Big Drops.

Another factor that changed river running from a daredevil stunt to a family sport is the equipment revolution. Just as backpacking benefited from the advent of lightweight pack frames, food, stoves, and tents, the river runner's world changed radically with the availability after World War II of inflatable rubber boats. Capable of bouncing off rather than smashing on rocks, the inflatables are also unsinkable, maneuverable, and comfortable. They are the reason why a rapid like Crystal is run rather than lined or portaged as it surely would have been by the early runners (and was, on occasion, by wooden boat operators like Gaylord Staveley and Martin Litton). The new boats are magic carpets that take people easily, perhaps too easily in view of the numbers, into the wilderness.

In the case of the Grand Canyon the publicity surrounding the dam controversy proved a direct stimulant to river travel. The Sierra Club distributed magnificent films and books that allowed millions to see what the canyon had to offer. In the space of a few years after the struggle against the dams began in the mid-1960s, the Grand Canyon river trip became the classic American wilderness experience, a "must do" for the growing number who prized wild places. Responding to and in some ways accelerating this demand, commercial river outfitters sprouted overnight. By 1971 twenty-one companies had obtained licenses to conduct trips in the Grand Canyon. Their color brochures and promotional films created long waiting lists, even for a product currently costing over $400 to $800 per person.

Amid all the issues surrounding its management, the Colorado still runs free through Crystal Rapid. At the present level of visitation it is common on the typical summer day to find another party or two inspecting or running the rapid. Watching other boats may lessen the sense of pioneering, but it does nothing to diminish the need of each boatman to execute his task perfectly. The wilderness setting is, of course, important, but were a Big Drop located on the Hudson River adjacent to New York City, it would still be a Big Drop. The challenge of controlling a boat on fast water remains. And on the long, curving tongue of Crystal Rapid there is still the quintessence of man and boat vying against one of the natural world's most awesome forces.

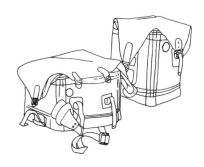

Ten

Lava Falls

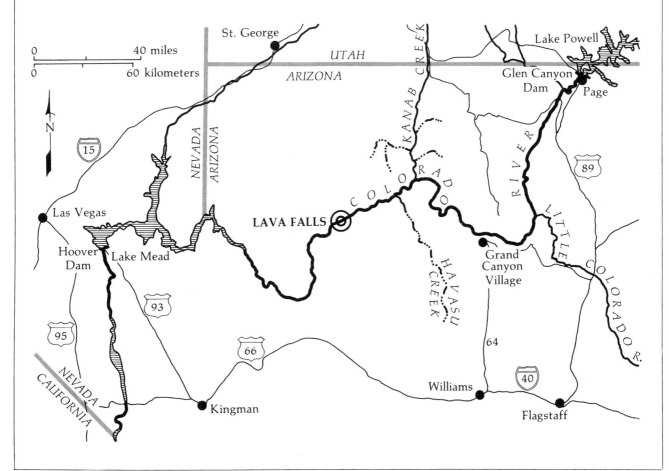

Once on the tongue, I faced downstream and braced myself, as my boat gathered speed with every yard. Then with a great hiss the first wave was upon us. The boat reared skyward, perched on top for an instant like the cap on a mushroom, then plunged into the trough beyond. Up, down, up, down, we hurtled. Jets of spray stung our faces; the roar of the rapid drowned out our voices. I strained at the oars to keep the boat headed into the waves and avert a broach which could lead to an upset. Gradually, I pulled to the right, out of the main current; and at last, my lungs heaving from the effort and my arm muscles knotting with cramps, I reached the eddy and rowed triumphantly to the beach. Between hitting the tongue and hitting the beach, perhaps a minute had elapsed.

FRANÇOIS LEYDET

You never really finish running Lava Falls. Asked on the river the night before Lava if he was ready for the rapid, a Grand Canyon boat-man said he hoped so because he had run it four hundred times that winter—driving to work every morning and before sleeping each night. Few rapids in the world grip the mind that way; few have the ability to condense a year, a lifetime on moving water into forty-five pounding seconds. Lava does. It is the *undisputed* Big Drop. Season after season, high water and low, kayaks to pontoons, Lava has a strong claim to being the most difficult stretch of runnable whitewater in the West, maybe in the world.

The climax of every trip in the Grand Canyon is Lava Falls. A veteran boatman says, "There is only one rapid on that river," and no one who has run the Colorado through Grand Canyon asks "Which one?" The length and rhythm of the Grand Canyon river trip only reinforces this perception. From the put-in at Lee's Ferry, Arizona, the trip is either 225 miles to the take-out at Diamond Creek or 279 miles to Lake Mead. The Colorado crashes through Lava Falls at mile 179.2, near the end of any trip. It is the last major rapid, a final showdown with the river.

Upstream, of course, are awesome rapids, including Crystal, and for a time the business of running them obscures what is waiting just below mile 179. But Lava has a way of creeping into the consciousness and conversation of people on the river. "You think that's big?" a boatman will shout over the screams of passengers in the tailwaves of a rapid in the upper canyon, "Wait until we get to Lava!" Or he thinks to himself after a sloppy run, "I better not do that in Lava." Someone quietly puts aside a cigar or a can of beer for "after Lava." So the reputation grows, and even those who are new to the Colorado quickly sense that Lava Falls is something special. "How big is this rapid compared to Lava?" they invariably ask. Or, "When do we get to Lava?" Or, more to the point, "Can you walk around Lava?"

Sometimes humor covers the anxiety. "I'll bet you can't keep that cigar lit through Lava," someone challenges. Once a group finds out that you can walk around the falls, there are endless jokes about chickening out. But behind the comic facade every river runner begins to sense the necessity of a personal confrontation with the big one. And he wonders, secretly, if he *will* want to walk around.

Occasionally a person new to the Grand Canyon will get fed up with the steady diet of Lava talk. Lava Falls cannot be much tougher than what they have seen in the many miles from Lee's Ferry; it is just the boatmen's way of keeping up interest until the end of a long trip. But things look different on the downstream side. As one upstream doubter who had just been through Lava Falls exclaimed, "I believe, baby, *I believe!*"

So it is that a Grand Canyon river trip unfolds with Lava Falls looming over the minds of river runners as the Redwall limestone looms over the river itself. Tension builds once Crystal, at mile 98, has been passed. The next few days are not so tough, and there is time to think ahead. Some groups plan Lava parties and relish what they will eat and drink and smoke after getting through. Some compose songs about the rapid. Others write poetry. Jack Reynolds' "The Hole" commemorates the time "late in May/When I approached Lava Fall/in the heat of the day." The water, we learn, was very low, but from the end of the rapid issued an "unusual roar." When Jack went to look:

> My jaw dropped down in disbelief
> for there it was in awesome relief
> A monstrous hole ten feet wide
> And one mile deep!

Sandy Nash takes the familiar Christmas fable and turns it into :

> 'Twas the night before Lava
> And all through the camp
> The boatmen were pacing
> Their armpits were damp.
> Their life vests were hung
> On their bow lines with care
> In hope that the river gods
> Would answer their prayers.

Her poem goes on and on. In truth, though, most boatmen try to appear nonchalant above the rapid. Occasionally you catch them staring into space. In their minds they are rehearsing, like a springboard diver, the moves and decisions they will have to make at Lava Falls.

It is hard to think of much else than the rapid the night before Lava. After an afternoon playing in blue-green Havasu Creek, most parties camp near National Canyon, mile 166, just as John Wesley Powell did on August 24, 1869. This leaves twelve miles to Lava Falls. They are slow miles with no whitewater; in places there is little surface current to move the boats downstream. Motor-powered rigs blast through the lakes above Lava. Oarsmen slog it out, stroke after stroke.

There never seems a great deal to say on Lava Day. The boatmen turn inward, absorbed in their own thoughts, tinkering with knots and equipment. They know that a Grand Canyon trip with oars requires about seventy hours of time on the river. Almost anyone can handle a boat safely except for ten minutes of this time. But in those ten minutes—minutes spent positioning above or maneuvering in the biggest rapids—boatmen earn their pay. There are only a few tongues or slots you have to hit in the Grand Canyon, but, in the carefully measured words of veteran outfitter Ron Smith, "You better hit them!" Lava Falls is one such moment, one such place. The boatmen, who at other times might be tour guides, cooks, comedians, lovers, and naturalists, become boatmen. It is time to concentrate on basics. The passengers seem to understand this. After a week on the water they tend to take the boatmen for granted, but Lava creates new respect born of new anxiety.

At Cove Canyon, five miles above Lava Falls, the Colorado makes a gradual swing to the west and slows still more. Here the canyon walls are three thousand feet high. From the Toroweap overlook it is possible to toss a stone directly into the river. And here begins one of the world's most dramatic displays of volcanic activity. About one million years ago, long after the Grand Canyon had been cut nearly to its present depth, eruptions of molten rock along the structurally weak Toroweap fault caused radical topographic transformations. Lava poured from a number of vents, chiefly to the north of the Colorado, and covered thousands of acres, some of it flowing down to the river. Looking at the lava cascades, long since cooled into basalt rock, that blacken the cliffs like thick paint, John Wesley Powell wrote in 1869: "What a conflict of water and fire there must have been here! Just imagine a river of molten rock running down into a river of melted snow. What a seething and boiling of the waters; what clouds of steam rolled into the heavens!"

One result of this awesome geologic spectacle was a dam—really a series of them corresponding to the several lava flows—that effectively plugged the Colorado River. Estimates of the height of the lava dams vary from six-hundred to fifteen-hundred feet. A block of the larger size would have created a lake in the Grand Canyon extending all the 179 miles back to Lee's Ferry. After the initial flows, the new lake gradually filled, and in view of the volume of water carried by the prehistoric Colorado it probably did not require many years. There then commenced one of earth history's great confrontations of rock and

Lava Falls can flip any boat on the river, even five-thousand-pound pontoons. By Ken Klementis.

moving water. When the rising lake reached the top of the natural dam it began to pour right over and to wear away the dam. For thousands of years the Colorado raged through 70 miles of lava debris in a Big Drop to end comparison. Basalt is extremely hard, but time always favors the river. Little by little the Colorado scoured its lava-blocked channel in the same way it had cut through a mile of rock to form the Grand Canyon. By the time the first man peered over the rim, perhaps five-thousand years ago, the million-year battle was almost over. All that remained was Lava Falls.

Thinking about the prehistoric lava dam at mile 179 always brings to mind man's efforts to control the river with lesser dams of concrete and steel. Several have been proposed within the last decade for this section of the Grand Canyon. One, Bridge Canyon, at mile 237, would have transformed ninety-three miles of river into a flatwater impoundment. Had it been built, Lava Falls would have become a jumble of rocks on the bottom of a lake. In terms of longevity, man-made dams have one advantage over natural ones: spillways. Engineers plan for water to go through, rather than over, dams and turn turbines in the process. But the axiom still holds: the river always wins. Especially in a watershed of high siltation such as the Colorado, the dams eventually fill up with the powdered rock remains of continental erosion. No one has figured out how to keep the silt from filling the reservoir, building toward the top of the dam, and choking the spillways. Finally, as the basin silts in, a wave slightly larger than the rest washes over the lip. It is the beginning of the end for a dam, the start of the same process that wore down the old lava plug. Big dams like Hoover and Glen Canyon look eternal but they are doomed. In the long run of geologic time the river will triumph. These monuments to man's drive to control nature will be a tangle of concrete and metal debris through which the liberated river roars. And then, to use Edward Abbey's vision, our far-removed descendants will come to the edge of the canyons to look over and wonder at the origins of tremendous rapids. Of course *their* distant descendants will not see more than a scoured canyon and placid river. The debris will be mud on the floor of an ocean. The river always wins.

Vulcan's Forge—some call it his Anvil—rises directly out of the Colorado about a mile above Lava Falls. A pinnacle about 100 feet high, it is all that remains of the central core, or neck, of an ancient volcano. The lava broke to the earth's surface directly beneath the river. The clouds of steam Powell imagined must have been enormous. Now the river grinds away at the black basalt of Vulcan's Forge, its erosive action aided by the roots of a few cactus that have managed to find a liveable niche among the lumps of solidified lava. On the north rim, to the right, towers Vulcan's Throne. A mile-wide cinder cone, it was the source of much of the lava that spewed out along the Toroweap fault line.

As Vulcan's Throne disappears behind the towering north rim of the inner gorge, the river slows still more. Big rapids exert a damming effect on moving water, pooling it for as much as a mile upstream and the Colorado takes on a lake-like quality above Lava. You try to sit, relaxed, at the oars, but it's a nervous time. Few boatmen do not eventually turn and row methodically to the right (north) bank above the rapid.

There is a little welcome shade under the tamarisk, and the boatmen tie their bow lines to the trunks of these small trees. The path to the viewpoint winds up through the lava rubble and across talus slopes to a level spot several hundred feet above the river. It is always hot here, the black basalt radiating the absorbed heat of the desert sun. You hear the rapid before you see it. The deepest and most ominous of the river's many voices surges up to tear at your confidence. No one says very much at first.

From the viewpoint almost directly over the top of Lava Falls you can see the black boulders littering the right bank. Similar rocks under water are the main cause of the astonishing behavior of the river here. But there is another factor at work in creating Lava. From the south a major canyon, Prospect, cut along the Toroweap fault line, joins the Grand. In its times of flood, Prospect Canyon has pushed a gravel fan into the Colorado and scattered the quarter-mile of boulders that cause problems on the left side of the rapid.

At Lava Falls the Colorado drops thirty-seven vertical feet; twenty feet of this occurs in an astonishing hundred yards at the top of the rapid—a rate of descent that Robert B. Stanton, with his engineer's eye, extrapolated at 352 feet per mile on his 1890 Colorado River survey. From above you watch the smooth, slick water gather speed as it approaches the lip. In a boat, floating toward the main falls, all you see is a line across the river and, beyond, the tops of tailwaves. It is these falls that prevent Lava from being a simply structured rapid like Upset or Crystal. Take away the fall, and boats could run Lava close to the Prospect Canyon gravel fan, pulling away from the holes and waves along the right shore.

You look down the tongue of smooth water funneling at an impossibly steep angle down the right side of the falls toward two sets of enormous V waves. A hundred yards of irregular ten-foot waves follows. Then comes the biggest standing wave most boatmen will ever see. Among printable descriptions, it is most commonly called "the big hole in Lava." The hole–wave complex occurs where the strong flow from the left of the falls meets the right-hand current caroming off an enormous lava block jutting from the right bank. Periodically, in a cycle of five to seven seconds, this wave "explodes." The energy of the moving water within it becomes so great that the wave breaks backwards on itself in a fury of whitewater. On the United States Geological Survey's 1923 trip, boatman Lewis R. Freeman reported that at a flow of 125,000 cubic feet per second this upstream breaking wave compressed air which jetted out from its sides in the manner of a blowhole in the rocks on an ocean shore. These unusual conditions were the result of unseasonal rains that raised the river level twenty-one feet in twenty-four hours. In 1957 P. T. Reilly encountered a flow of about the same magnitude. The lower wave in Lava was cycling at about twelve-second intervals, and it covered nearly half the swollen river. The periodic explosion sent spray flying over both banks of a river 100 yards wide! Curiously, between the explosions, there are intervals when the huge wave is relatively smooth and regular in shape. It is a question of timing, an element over which the river runner has no control. If the wave explodes in your face, too bad. The next boat could sail right over. The river gods have the last word.

After the exploding wave, Lava's tailwaves taper off to fifteen feet, twelve feet, eight feet. But that is at a flow of less than 30,000 cubic feet per second, the normal maximum since the placement of Glen Canyon Dam upstream. It was different during the great runoffs of the predam era such as the estimated 300,000 cubic feet per second flow of 1884. Huge coffee-colored tailwaves must have continued right down to the cliff on the left a quarter-mile below the end of the modern rapid. Indeed the possibility of being pounded against that cliff would have been the most terrifying part of running a high-flow Lava Falls before the upstream dam. Across the river, just upstream of the cliff, there is a flash of sunlight as hot springs gush through a thicket of head-high sawgrass and plunge over the bank into the Colorado. Their presence is a reminder that the earth fires which created this place still burn deep under the Toroweap fault.

After a time alone the boatmen ritually gather on a large flat-topped hunk of lava directly above the start of the rapid. "Where're ya' goin'?" someone grunts, and the group begins to compare possible routes, pointing and gesturing in an effort to identify waves that in the surprising scale of the Grand Canyon are still a quarter-mile away.

Study of the rapid reveals several possible runs. For small boats there is the possibility of the far left side, the "chicken run." It is an exercise in rock dodging, the whole purpose of which is to avoid being swept out into the main, right-moving flow of the rapid or dumped by holes behind larger rocks in the Prospect Canyon outwash. The far left is also the route for lining and portaging boats.

The main falls present several options. By following a line of bubbles on the left, a precise oarsman can catch a wave angled at forty-five degrees to the falls and slide down it to their base. The jolt is neck-snapping, but assuming oars and people are still in the boat, there is a chance for four or five pulls hard right with the object of missing a very sharp hole that has the potential of holding boats and bodies. Still angling right through large waves, the full force of water will frequently turn boats completely around. The alert boatman then simply confronts the huge lower wave stern first. To wash up on it sideways is an almost sure flip. The left is a nice run, but the margin for error in positioning at the top is very small. So is the so-called "dory slot" to the right of the falls. If a boatman misses these slots and goes over the main falls, he usually dumps. The same is true for the other little tongues that, at certain water levels, boatmen sometimes think they can see in the main falls. The major problem with them all is that you do not run the rapid from a 200-foot-high vantage on the shore where the slots were visible. At river level, even standing on the seat of a boat, all the boatman can see is space and an occasional blast of spray. Until the last few yards there is no way to know if the boat is heading for the tongue or the fall.

And by that time the boat is committed. "Keys" become crucial. You try to remember how far to place your boat from this shoreline rock or that recurring swirl in the current, aiming always for something you cannot see.

On one occasion a boatman missed the angled wave and dropped straight over the left side of the main falls. From below, the boat appeared to hang in midair, upside down, raining people into the river. Thirty seconds later a girl hurtled over the top of the big wave in the lower rapid. Her long blond pigtails, tied with bright blue ribbons, streamed straight out behind her. But when we fished her out of the river, she was smiling. Getting through Lava does that to people.

You think about this sort of thing as you walk back across the lava and down through the shoreline brush to the boats. Little things suddenly become big. You tie the laces of your tennis shoes and tie them again. You tug for the twentieth time at the belt of your life preserver, check the lines securing gear on the boat, reseat the oars in their locks. It is no time for banter. Most boatmen ask their passengers not to talk as they float back into the current. It is an agonizingly slow float toward the lip of Lava Falls. Only in the final few yards does the river gather speed. It also veers sharply to the right, directly into a series of gaping holes. Experienced boatmen have prepared for this, positioning themselves much farther left than appears safe. A perfect entry, in fact, seems to the unknowing to be carrying a boat straight over the main falls. The last few seconds make the difference.

A properly positioned boat rises and falls over a set of smooth, but surprisingly large entrance waves. It is a delicious fluid moment of calm before the storm. Rising over these first satin waves, the whole rapid is finally visible, that huge black rock near the end seeming very far away. Immediately in front is the steep tongue. Now everything happens fast. The first V waves lie at the downstream end of the tongue. Some boatmen think they can "crash" the left side of this wave, but the attempt usually ends in a sideways position and a flip. The better course is to plow into the very point of the V. Being light (you should not have shipped much water to this point), most boats will rise quickly on the side of the wave and push through it. But in the process they take on hundreds of pounds of Colorado River. That makes positioning for the second, larger V wave more difficult.

The lower V packs one of the hardest hits in whitewater boating. It has flipped every kind of boat from kayak to thirty-foot pontoon. But sometimes the wave simply stands a boat on its side and strips it of its occupants. It is also possible, of course, to punch through in relative control of an upright boat. The next hundred yards are a confused jumble of irregular waves. You slant the bow left, right, left in an effort to meet them head on. Water continues to cascade over the sides, filling boats to the gunwales. It is important to understand that you don't get splashed in Lava Falls; you get inundated. Eating a solid wall of water is one of the quintessential experiences of running this rapid. Not a few river runners have distinctly recalled being in the boat but completely underwater and unable, for several tense seconds, to breathe. In one astonishing run a boat flipped over on one wave and back, right side up, on another. It required a film, taken from shore, to convince its confused occupants, who never left their seats, that they went completely around.

As you pound down the middle section of Lava Falls, you become increasingly aware of the black lava block, big as a house, on the right shore. Awareness turns to terror as the view from the tops of the waves makes it appear that the current you are riding is pounding directly against it. Boatmen know, however, that it would be hard to hit the rock if they wanted to. A "buffer wave" rolling off its upstream side will carry boats around. If you have sufficient courage and control to point your boat squarely at the big rock, it is sometimes possible to slide between it and the giant wave immediately to its left. The price paid for trying this is the possibility of rolling not to the left of the rock but to its right and into a deep, angry whirlpool surrounded on three sides by jagged rock. A wooden dory went into this potato peeler once and came out splinters. The boatman, luckily, gained the left buffer and escaped downstream in one piece.

Most boatmen choose not to play tag with the black rock and instead line up as best they can for the biggest wave in the West. When you see it from the crest of the wave immediately upstream, it seems absolutely inconceivable that a boat could climb anything so high and so steep. Grand Canyon veterans learn to "push" on their oars in this situation, adding a little more momentum to the twenty miles per hour provided by the current. Combined with the weight of a nearly swamped boat, the force is enough to drive boats through the top of the wall of water—usually. It is also possible, especially if the wave decides to "explode" in your face, to remain in the hole, caught in a dynamic balance of forces generated by the downstream current and the backward-breaking wave. Boatmen have reported starting up the wave again and again only to slide back down it into the hole. Sometimes this frightening minuet ends with the boats being squirted out the side of the hole. More often they finally catch an upstream edge, roll, and wash through. The big wave's explosion cycle is the key. You cannot time a run to catch the unpredictable moment when the hole "fills in," offering a relatively easy passage. You take your chances, and you say your prayers.

No one will ever know for certain who was the first to run Lava Falls. Perhaps it was James White. White did not really take a boat down Lava; he floated through on a tangle of huge logs. The year was 1867, two years before John Wesley Powell's first planned expedition. White's story is astonishing. It is based entirely on the oral reports of this unlettered and unassuming frontiersman, a fact which has made it easy for subsequent river runners to dismiss the whole affair. But if we take James White's word for where he started and ended his 1867 trip, it is hard to deny that he did indeed pass through the Grand Canyon and over Lava Falls.

White's ordeal began in the spring of 1867 when he left Colorado City, Colorado, on a prospecting venture with two other men. Somewhere in the San Juan River drainage, considerably north of the Grand Canyon, Indians attacked the party and one of White's companions

A seventeen-foot raft with five aboard (two are under the wave) dumps in the big hole at the bottom of Lava. By Bart Henderson.

was killed. The remaining two fled down a dry streambed to the Colorado River, where they constructed a makeshift log raft. White later remembered that they floated four days on a big calm river through yellow rock—a perfect description of Glen Canyon. After drifting past the future site of Lee's Ferry, the character of the river changed. Rapids repeatedly broke their raft apart and finally claimed the life of White's remaining friend. By this time he was well into Marble Canyon and there seemed no alternative but to continue riding the river. He tied himself to logs, gnawed two rawhide knife scabbards for food, and went on floating twelve to fourteen hours a day. At night he tied his raft to the shore and slept. Finally on the fourteenth day of his ordeal,

September 7, 1867, he was pulled half-dead from the river by Mormon settlers at Callville, Nevada, sixty miles downstream from the Grand Wash Cliffs, which mark the end of the Grand Canyon.

In his recollections of the trip White recalled one rapid, bigger than all the rest. It could have been Lava Falls. And he almost certainly floated through it. White, after all, was not scouting rapids in an effort to bring boats and equipment through the Canyon. He was just trying to get out as fast as he could to save his life. If he lost one log in a rapid, he found another. There was no reason to line or portage.

White's detractors maintain he simply could not have done what he claimed, the journey was impossible, and White was a liar. But such opinions were voiced by the pioneers of Grand Canyon river running, who tended to exaggerate the difficulty of their journey to accentuate their own achievement. Reconsidered in the light of present experiences on the Colorado, White's feat seems much more plausible. What he claimed to have done is clearly possible. Men have deliberately swum the entire length of the Grand Canyon. Empty boats have floated along for miles, sometimes upside down. Driftwood regularly floats through the canyon; so could a man holding on to it. The speed of the descent of a log, allowing for time caught in eddies, would have been just about what White remembered having taken—two weeks from Glen Canyon to Callville. It would have been inconceivable to have taken that amount of time floating the sixty miles from the Grand Wash Cliffs to Callville. White could and would have walked that far over the open desert bordering the river in two or three days. So the controversy returns again to White's memory and his honesty. If he in fact spent so long a time floating the Colorado as he claimed, then he must have passed through the Grand Canyon. Moreover, 1867 was a year in which the Colorado carried exceptionally high water. Many of the rocks that might have killed White were covered while the current pushed along his logs at top speed.

Still, it is pointless to celebrate James White as the first man to run the Grand Canyon. John Wesley Powell's reputation is well deserved. His was a planned achievement. White's journey was just blind luck, but remains to tantalize the imagination. Think of a weakened, dazed man, looking up from his logs at the line across the river, listening to the boom of Lava, and thinking, in desperate condition, that he might as well hang on and hope for the best. Then the sickening first drop and the brown water tearing at his body and smashing it against the wood and, finally, the calm below and the wondering how much more could he take before death. He took enough to get out barely alive and tell a tale nobody would, at first, believe. We do.

John Wesley Powell did not run Lava on his 1869 exploratory descent of the Colorado. His journal is quite clear. After camping the night of August 24 near National Canyon the nine men and three boats floated the twelve miles to Lava Falls. They noted the evidence of volcanic activity and imagined the lava dam that had temporarily blocked the river. Landing on the less precipitous left bank, Powell made his decision after a quick glance at the rapid. "We have to make a portage here," he wrote in his journal, "which is completed in about three hours; then on we go." And go they did. The last entry for August 25 reads: "Thirty-five miles today. Hurrah!" Subtracting the three hours spent portaging Lava, it was a remarkable day.

If the Powell party "cheated" Lava Falls, they made an unexpected run three days later of a rapid that may well have been a greater challenge. Lava Cliff Rapid, as Powell named it, had the same physical characteristics as Lava Falls, but it is now drowned under Lake Mead. The lava was on the north side in a cliff a hundred feet high with huge rocks at its base. The tributary canyon, Spencer, came in from the left side as at Lava Falls, but for some reason Powell crossed back to the right thinking he could lower the boats from a 100-foot line off the top of the cliff. This meant confronting the main fall of the rapid. It was a difficult moment. That very morning, six miles upstream at Separation Canyon, Powell and five followers had left three men who had determined to desert the expedition and climb out of the canyon. Now, above Lava Cliff, it appeared that the deserters' doubts about getting out alive by the river route were well founded. Persisting with the right-side lining, Powell put one of his best boatmen, Civil War veteran George Bradley, in the first boat to fend off from the cliff. The others started to lower him down the rapid. Meanwhile Powell went ahead to check on the downstream end of the cliff. To his horror he found a waterfall. Rushing back to order the men to stop, he found them already committed. The boat had been lowered to where it could not be retrieved against the current. To make matters worse, the rope Powell had thought would reach to the top of the cliff was too short. Now the boat, held stationary in the current by the rope, began to veer in and out. Each inward lurch smashed it against the cliff despite the efforts of the desperate boatman to hold off with an oar. It was time for quick decisions. Bradley, feeling it better to risk the rapid than be splintered by the cliff, moved to cut the tethering line with his knife. Just at that moment the whole fixture to which the line was tied broke away. Powell describes the consequences:

With perfect composure Bradley seizes the great scull oar, places it in the stern rowlock, and pulls with all his power (and he is an athlete) to turn the bow of the boat downstream . . . rather than to drift broadside on. One, two, strokes he makes, and a third just as she goes over [the main falls] and the boat is fairly turned, and she goes down almost beyond our sight . . . Then she comes up again on a great wave, and down and up, then around behind some great rocks, and is lost in the mad, white foam below. We stand frozen with fear, for we see no boat. Bradley is gone! So it seems. But now, away below, we see something coming out of the waves. It is evidently a boat. A moment more and we see Bradley standing on deck, swinging his hat to show that he is all right.

Returning to his second boat, Powell and two boatmen prepared to run. Their course was almost certainly farther left than Bradley's who, after all, had been directly against the cliff when he tore loose from his line. At any rate, the first wave at the base of the fall swamped Powell's boat and the second rolled it over. The men tumbled through the tailwaves, and Powell's next recollection was being lifted from a whirlpool by Bradley. But their agony was almost over; the next day, August 29, 1869, the boats floated past the Grand Wash Cliffs and out of what they called "our granite prison." The three deserters were never seen again.

Powell's second Colorado River expedition ended at Kanab Creek in September 1872, and he did not see either Lava Falls or Lava Cliff Rapid. The next river runner to pass that way was Robert B. Stanton, the engineer who dreamed of constructing a railroad along the Colorado through the Grand Canyon. He portaged Lava Falls in late February 1890. This suggests that the first men to run Lava in boats were George F. Flavell and Ramon Montos. These trappers started without fanfare at Green River, Wyoming, on August 27, 1896. Flavell, at least, was an excellent craftsman who rebuilt his skiff twice on the upper river in anticipation of the rapids in Grand Canyon. Trapping beaver and taking their time, they reached the Little Colorado on October 20. Then, anxious to end the trip, Flavell and Montos blasted through to the Grand Wash Cliffs, arriving just eleven days later. They were able to accomplish this stunning feat by running the rapids rather than lining or portaging them. Flavell reported their philosophy: "If we had lowered over all the bad places, it would have taken a month." He fully expected to turn over and hit rocks in his flat-bottomed boat, the *Panthon*, but he was confident about getting through. "There is only one stone we must not hit," Flavell noted, " . . . our Tomb Stone!" Since Flavell and Montos were unschooled trappers, as opposed to scientists like Powell and Stanton, had no idea where they were in the Grand Canyon, and left no journal, it is impossible to reconstruct their possible run of Lava Falls.

The next boatman to see Lava Falls was Nat Galloway, first in the winter of 1896–1897 and then as the guide of Julius Stone's expedition in the fall of 1909. In the low-water conditions of fall and winter when Galloway ran, the rocks of Lava would have been perilous for his light wooden boats, so the Stone party portaged their boats around Lava

Falls. Sixty-six miles below they reached Lava Cliff Rapid. Stone reports Galloway's opinion that this was "the worst rapid in the whole series of canyons" beginning in Wyoming. Confident with the experience of many rapids, they had hoped to run it, but the spectacle of the now vanished Lava Cliff Rapid changed their mind. Stone recounted in his journal for November 13: "If fear has any message for us or disaster any threat, here is where we should hear it on the quivering air. The shock of the angry water actually makes the air pulsate." The baggage was carried around the whitewater and the boats lined and, for a short distance, portaged.

Ellsworth and Emery Kolb ran the Grand in the winter of 1911-1912 and found Lava Falls "so filled with jagged pieces of black rock that a portage was advisable." They completed it in near-freezing conditions made tolerable only by periodic soaks in the hot pools below the rapid. Like Galloway and Stone, the Kolbs thought Lava Cliff Rapid worse than Lava Falls. They lined and portaged it, using log skids for their boats. So did the United States Geological Survey trip of 1923. Clyde Eddy and his improbable crew of inexperienced college boys, a dog, and a bear cub followed suit. Their account of a 1927 trip simply stated that "Lava Falls Rapid cannot possibly be run." And when the alternative is portaging a twelve-hundred-pound boat, one does not come to such a conclusion without much reflection.

In November 1937 Haldane "Buzz" Holmstrom ran the Colorado from Green River, Wyoming, to Lake Mead—alone. He built his fifteen-foot boat with painstaking care from Port Orford Cedar which was native to his southern Oregon home. It did a splendid job, but when he came to Lava Falls, Holmstrom noted "vicious waters twisting between great blocks of lava" and portaged—one of only five carries he made on the eleven-hundred-mile run.

If not Flavell and Montos in 1896, the first to run Lava Falls was almost certainly Norman Nevills. Nevills, who pioneered commercial river running in the Grand Canyon, began taking paying passengers down the Colorado in 1938 in his specially designed cataract boats for a fee of $1000, and he usually ran Lava. Nevills was to dominate commercial running in the Grand until his tragic death in a plane crash near Mexican Hat in 1949.

On their 1940 trip down the Colorado, Barry Goldwater recalled that Nevills carried food and gear around Lava on the left bank. Then, while Goldwater waited impatiently, Nevills deliberated for hours whether to run or line the rapid. He finally elected to run down a slot on the left that, according to the annoyed Goldwater, "he must have seen the first minute he looked at the falls." The politician's impatience indicated little understanding of the boatman's psychology. Nevills, running alone, putting it all on the line, had to be sure.

The next year, 1941, Nevills was back with the first kayaker to attempt the Grand Canyon: Alexander "Zee" Grant of the Appalachian Mountain Club. His boat was a rather flimsy seventeen-foot canvas-covered craft which he had dumped in Badger, House Rock, and, improbably, 164 Mile Rapid, all above Lava. Grant wanted to run the big one, but after seeing it he lined his boat around the left side. Not until 1960 did Walter Kirschbaum take a kayak through Lava Falls. Today, expert kayakers relish the rapid, often running it several times on the same trip. They frequently flip—often several times in the same run—but roll up and continue on their way. Real virtuosi can "surf" on the upstream side of Lava's huge waves and in this manner actually move upstream for short distances.

The big inflatable pontoons, the baloney boats, are at the other end of the scale of watercraft negotiating the Grand Canyon. They carry a big payload for commercial operators but have difficulty maneuvering at the critical point above Lava Falls. If they fail to straighten out by the time they reach the second V wave and plunge into the big holes on the right, Lava can toss the tons of rubber, metal, and people like a cork. Usually the big pontoons are simply pounded, raked by a huge volume and weight of water. Sometimes there are interesting variations. Giant "G-rigs" (three pontoons tied together) have "sandwiched" in Lava, the side pontoons folding over upon the center one, trapping the thirty scared passengers in a rubber envelope until help arrives below the rapid to untangle things.

The wooden boats that the early runners used are still seen at Lava Falls. Lacking the cushioning effect and bending ability of inflatables, the hard boats get tossed around more. Robert Wallace tells the following story of a 1971 dory run with Martin Litton:

Litton assembled his passengers at the head of Lava Falls and made a brief speech. He would never, he said, take a boat through this stretch of water if he could avoid it. Lava Falls Rapid was a beast. I glanced at him, looking for his customary half-smile, but it was not there. Previously he had not offered his passengers a choice between riding through rapids and walking around them, but now he did. Indeed he urged them to walk, and the great majority took his advice. However, a half dozen of them remained to try the boats.

I got into Litton's dory and we pushed off into quiet water above the rapids. He steered close to the right bank. Neither of us spoke; the noise of the water would have drowned our voices in any case. We entered Lava Falls at what seemed to me the perfect place and angle; but suddenly the boat plummeted headlong into a deep hole and then pitched upward at an angle of nearly 90 degrees. As the water closed over my head I had a glimpse of Litton still rowing, his oars sweeping the air. In a moment the boat righted itself; then a huge wave broke over it and tipped it so far over on its port side that it seemed certain to capsize. My head was submerged again, and when I could see daylight Litton had disappeared. The wave had swept him overboard.

The oars were still fastened in the rowlocks. I moved into Litton's place and took them, glancing hopefully left and right to find him. In a moment he bobbed up near the boat. I held out an oar and he seized it, pulling himself up to the gunwale. His bulky life jacket prevented him from climbing back into the boat, even though it was swamped and riding very low in the water; so he hung onto the gunwale as we wallowed along in the rapids. At length he said, "I'll be all right. I'll float down the river, and you try to beach the boat on the right bank."

There were two small sandy beaches on the right, separated by a half-sunken peninsula, a stoneyard of scattered rocks. On the left side of the river there was a heavy torrent of water with four-and five-foot waves: Lower Lava Falls, a continuation of the big rapids. I could scarcely move the boat, which weighed over 500 pounds empty and a ton when full of water. The current shoved it broadside against the rocks, pounded it over them, and carried it into quiet water near the second of the beaches, where I pulled it ashore and tied it to the roots of a big tamarisk. Almost 10 minutes later Litton came walking slowly up the riverbank toward me, grinning. "Pleasant day," he said.

The other wooden boats in the party also had trouble that day. People were washed from two of them, as Litton had been, while two others flipped over. Everyone, however, rode out the rapid safely and joined in towing the boats into the eddy below the falls. The only casualty was a passenger who had elected to walk around Lava Falls and sprained his ankle in the rocks.

Sometimes the margin of safety is a little thinner. Photographer Ernest Braun reports that on one hard-boat trip he watched Clyde Childress overturn with two passengers in Lava. In the aftermath, one of them could be seen swimming for shore and another head appeared in the tailwaves far downstream. But there was no sign of Childress for a minute, two minutes! Finally he struggled out onto a rock close to where the boat had flipped. The story emerged later. Instead of riding with the main flow through the rapid, Childress swam to the right to rescue a floating camera. The tricky, powerful right-side currents sucked him under and forced him into a rock tunnel. The current flowing through the tunnel pinned him firmly. Childress struggled to force his way back out, upstream. At length, his lungs bursting, he gave up, resigned to drowning. It was his salvation. His half-conscious, relaxed body popped through the downstream end of the tunnel and into the sunlight. Such experiences make the decision of one 1958 river party understandable: After seeing Lava in high water, they turned their boats loose and hiked out of the canyon. Later they retrieved two of the boats floating peacefully in Lake Mead.

Motor-powered hard boats are also battered in Lava. In 1949 Otis "Dock" Marston pioneered downstream travel on the Colorado in motorboats. With the speed of the motors added to that of the river, his runs in Lava were more like ski jumps. Photographer Bill Belknap was with Marston in 1954. Scouting Lava, he remarked:

Funny thing about that rapid. Each time you come to it on a river trip you wonder why you didn't have sense enough to stay home. The landscape swims before your eyes . . . a boat simply couldn't take that kind of punishment. You get down to the serious business of picking a course. The wet fact stares you in the face. There's no turning back.

Dock Marston made a beautiful run in 1954. At full throttle he roared into the right-side tongue, was clobbered, and cut left of the big wave at the bottom. Then it was Belknap's turn. As he walked to his boat he thought, "You're sure of one thing. It'll be quick. Three seconds after the first drop you'll know whether you did it right or wrong. It'd better be right. Missing the entrance by a few feet could mean disaster for men and boat."

His dual Evinrude outboards roaring, Belknap made a practice run upstream, then eased off, turned downstream in the current, and stood up to pick his entrance.

The current was swift and the seconds few. I picked the spot and leaned on the throttles with everything I had. The bow rose sharply and plunged down. We were in it.

It seemed as though there was water over us, under us, and on all sides. I remembered it'd be necessary to fight left in order to avoid "the big hole." As I turned the wheel a mountain of water hit us from behind and both motors died. "Hang on, we're going in the hole!" I yelled at Willie and Jorgen [his passengers], taking a deep breath. The bow dropped and we plunged deep under the big wave. Tons of water came down on us. Even clinging to the wheel it was hard to stay in the cockpit.

Suddenly we slipped out into the air again. The cockpit was full. Jorgen asked, "Are we sinking?" "I don't know," I told him, "wait a minute and I can tell you better."

In 1960 New Zealander Jon Hamilton came to the Grand Canyon with the propeller-less "jet" boats his family invented for the shallow rivers of their island nation. First, the four-boat expedition made a downstream run. At Lava the driver of the lead boat hit a standing wave so hard his boat was catapulted into the air in a near vertical position. The resulting impact shattered his leg and he was flown out of the canyon by helicopter. The other boats were more successful, and all four ultimately reached Lake Mead. Then they turned around to attempt for the first time running upstream through the Grand Canyon. Lava was the rapid they most feared. Hamilton, the lead driver, made three abortive attempts to climb it. His wife describes the next try:

He comes at it a fourth time, faster, his white jet plume flying. This time he is in earnest. *The battle is on!* Right up the side he comes, then darts suddenly out into the rough, fighting hard, forcing his way diagonally across, bobbing like a tiny orange cork in the white water, sometimes vanishing from sight in the wild waves to re-appear, nose still pointing upstream, still seeking a loophole in Vulcan's defences. He has swung right across towards the north bank. Now he crabs over center again, over to the right, he has found the tongue— he's going to make it!

The boat hesitated for a moment, swaying, feeling for a hold. Then it gripped the solid water of the tongue and leapt forward, up and over the top into the smooth water beyond.

And then disaster almost struck. The motor in Hamilton's jet boat failed, and he began to slide, backwards, towards the lip of the falls. Only at the last possible moment did it catch, enabling Hamilton to crawl up and away from the rapid.

On the next two attempts, with Hamilton driving, Lava lured the boats almost to the base of the falls. Then freak currents slammed them onto half-submerged rocks. Hamilton wanted to get one more boat over the rapid before nightfall, and for forty minutes he pounded against the waves while remaining essentially in the same place. Bill Belknap, who watched the attempt from shore, observed that

photographs can only hint at the violence of the struggle between man and river. One moment the boat teeters on a wave top. Another instant and nothing shows above the crests but the driver's head. Always the river roars and thunders, drowning every human sound.

In the morning they tried again. Joyce Hamilton watched her husband's run from the canyon rim, a half-mile above Lava:

the boat looked so small and helpless as it thrashed around in the great angry river. Over and over again it was sucked down among the white waves and spewed out at the tail of the rapid. Once it came right up almost to the tongue and we waited breathlessly, and almost wept when we saw it being dragged back and back, the yellow nose leaping up as it dropped stern first into a hole.

At last Hamilton surmounted Lava, taking advantage of the surges and pauses characteristic of moving water. He literally waited for the river to relax its force for an instant; then powered ahead. With two boats up, Hamilton walked back to try the third. Halfway up the fall he was bounced into the air by waves and landed high and dry on three protruding rocks. The Colorado raced by on all sides, but the water was shallow enough to permit men to pry the boat off with logs. Once free, Hamilton fired his engine and again soared up the tongue. The final boat failed miserably on its first attempt at Lava's tailwaves, and Hamilton beached for a mechanical overhaul. It was almost dark when he finished, but, lights glowing, he challenged the rapid and won.

No one will have a chance to attempt to duplicate Hamilton's incredible feat of boatmanship. Present National Park Service regulations make upruns of the Colorado in Grand Canyon illegal, and a proposed management plan calls for the phasing out of motorized travel on downstream runs. It is better that way. To travel down a river is to go with the flow. It is to accept and be a part of natural processes. Upruns go against the current and natural flow of rivers. They symbolize man's attempt to overpower nature—to shape and control it rather than to accept his and its limitations. The consequences of this point of view are manifest today in many of our most critical environmental problems. Conversely, going with the flow symbolizes a philosophy of harmony with the environment, the importance of which far transcends the walls of the Grand Canyon.

The smaller, oar-powered inflatable boats that have followed Amos Burg's 1938 lead in the Grand Canyon have their share of Lava stories. Riding relatively low, they receive a terrific beating in the waves and holes. Fred Eiseman, one of Georgie White's early boatmen, recalls a 1956 run that underscores the wide gap between intention and reality in Lava Falls:

I'll bet Dan Davis and I studied the damn thing for two hours. We had every rock and hole spotted, and there were lots of them since the flow was only 7,400 cubic feet per second. We had our routine down pat. First pull this way. Avoid that big black one. Then that way around the hole, then a stroke and a half right past the big lateral, and so on. Well, we got into it, and it wasn't one second before we were totally out of control, ass over teakettle. We didn't flip or pancake, but we were so full of water, both externally and internally, that we couldn't take a single stroke. Luckily the boats were so full of water that riding up on that big black bastard at the bottom right didn't turn us over.

The next season, in June, Eiseman returned, vowing to do better. But 1957 was a year of exceptionally high water on the Colorado with flows varying between 90,000 and 125,000 cubic feet per second at the time he was on the river. No one had ever faced Lava Falls at this volume, and upstream there was much discussion about how the rapid would look. Arriving at the normal scouting point above Lava, Eiseman stared in astonishment:

There was nothing but slick water. The entire rapids had moved downstream several hundred yards. Where Lava normally is, there was a tongue, smooth as glass from wall to wall. About where Lower Lava is, perhaps starting a bit upstream from it, there was the most god-awful collection of tailwaves that I ever saw in my life, making Hermit [a Grand Canyon rapid with 15-20 foot waves in normal water levels] look like a pup-tent. But, just down the left side of the tailwaves there was a nice little narrow slick spot.

Georgie rode right down the middle. Discretion was surely our better part, and we pulled in so close to the left bank that we scraped all the way down. We were actually almost in an eddy, even at the left of the tongue, because the water in the center was going so fast. It seemed like an eternity before we dropped off on the smooth tonguelet, ran past those skyscraper tailwaves, and made it through without a single drop of water in the boat.

Sometimes Lava is generous.

One of the most remarkable runs of Lava ever recorded was that of Bill Beer and John Daggett. College students casting about for a new way to spend spring vacation in 1955, they hit upon the idea of swimming the length of the Grand Canyon. Mae West life vests and swim fins were part of their gear, as well as four rubber river packs that floated when sealed. Beer and Daggett did well on the upper river. Then, on their twentieth day, they came to Lava Falls. Beer describes their run, or swim:

The water churned, twisted and leaped into the air worse than in any rapids we had seen so far. We tossed innumerable sticks and even a log into the foaming stream, trying to find the safest course. The currents were confusing, but I finally fixed in my mind what I believed would be the best passage, and worked back upstream to where I'd left my rubber boxes.

Firmly grasping the boxes, I pushed into the river and began to drift slowly toward the stormy rapids. Then the current—and I—picked up speed. I looked for the course I had mapped, but all I could see were big brown waves. Then I dropped fast and hit bottom—hard; I had gone over a four-foot waterfall. Before I could catch my breath, the stream picked me up and began rolling me over and over until I no longer knew which way was up. I just gasped for breath whenever I saw sky above. Then I was thrown high and clear by a wave and caught a glimpse of John on a rock just a few feet away. As I went under again, I braced myself to hit the rock, but another wave knocked me sideways. When I came to the surface again, the way was clear. I bounced through the rough tail of the rapids into the calm waters below and shouted triumphantly at the canyon walls.

John came down farther to the right than I had, and although he avoided the waterfall I had hit, his course put him in more dangerous waters. He narrowly missed the rock on which he had been sitting only a few minutes earlier.

Few people since have chosen to swim Lava; a number have done so unintentionally, and at least one has died.

It is hard to remember much about the end of a run of Lava Falls. There are the diminishing tailwaves, the overpowering sense of relief, the hugs and shouts, the endless bailing. In the exultation of the moment it is tempting to think you have conquered the rapid. Old hands know better. You never beat the big one. The river gods just decide to let you through. As you sit on the small beach below Lava with a last, precious beer, stashed for days for this moment, you look back upstream at the white staircase and think, gratefully, "One more time."

Man always kills the thing he loves, and we the pioneers have killed our wilderness. Some say we had to. Be that as it may, I am glad I shall never be young without wild country to be young in. Of what avail are forty freedoms without a blank spot on the map? ALDO LEOPOLD (1949)

HONOR ROLL

The following rapids, all of them Big Drops, have given their lives in the service of a civilization that, some feel, has yet to prove fully worthy of their sacrifice.

LAVA CLIFF RAPID, GRAND CANYON
COLORADO RIVER, ARIZONA

SEPARATION RAPID, GRAND CANYON
COLORADO RIVER, ARIZONA

DARK CANYON RAPID, CATARACT CANYON
COLORADO RIVER, UTAH

GYPSUM RAPIDS, CATARACT CANYON
COLORADO RIVER, UTAH

BUCK CANYON RAPIDS, HELLS CANYON
SNAKE RIVER, IDAHO-OREGON

KINNEY CREEK RAPIDS, HELLS CANYON
SNAKE RIVER, IDAHO–OREGON

SQUAW CREEK RAPIDS, HELLS CANYON
SNAKE RIVER, IDAHO–OREGON

ASHLEY FALLS, FLAMING GORGE
GREEN RIVER, UTAH

THE PINBALL
TUOLUMNE RIVER, CALIFORNIA

CELILO FALLS
COLUMBIA RIVER, WASHINGTON

GREAT FALLS
MISSOURI RIVER, MONTANA

SELECTED BIBLIOGRAPHY

Adney, Edwin Tappan and Howard T. Chapelle. *Bark Canoes and Skin Boats of North America*. Washington, D.C.: Government Printing Office, 1964.

American River Touring Association. *River Guides Manual*. Oakland, Calif.: ARTA, 1973.

Arighi, Scott and Margaret S. Arighi. *Wildwater Touring: A Guide to Extended Tripping By Canoe, Kayak, Drift Boat, or Raft*. New York: MacMillan, 1974.

Ashworth, William. *Hells Canyon: The Deepest Gorge on Earth*. New York: Hawthorne, 1977.

Bailey, Robert G. *Hells Canyon*. Lewiston, Idaho: R. G. Bailey Print Co., 1943.

––––––– *The River of No Return*. Lewiston, Idaho: R. G. Bailey Print Co., 1947.

Baker, Pearl. *Trail On the Water*. Boulder, Colo.: Pruett Pub. Co., 1969.

Beal, Merrill D. *Grand Canyon: The Story Behind the Scenery*. Flagstaff, Ariz.: KC Publications, 1967.

Belknap, Bill and Buzz Belknap. *Canyonlands River Guide*. Boulder City, Nev.: Westwater Books, 1974.

Belknap, Buzz. *Grand Canyon River Guide*. Boulder City, Nev.: Westwater Books, 1969.

Brokaw, Tom. "That River Swallows People. Some It Gives Up; Some It Don't." *West* (Los Angeles *Times* Sunday Magazine), 1 November 1970, pp. 12–19.

Carrey, Johnny and Cort Conley. *The Middle Fork and the Sheepeater War*. Riggins, Idaho: Backeddy Books, 1977.

Clark, Georgie White, and Duane Newcomb. *Georgie Clark: Thirty Years of River Running*. San Francisco: Chronicle Books, 1977.

Crampton, C. Gregory. *Land of Living Rock: The Grand Canyon and the High Plateaus*. New York: Knopf, 1972.

––––––– *Standing-up Country: The Canyon Lands of Utah and Arizona*. New York: Knopf, 1968.

Dellenbaugh, Frederick. *A Canyon Voyage: The Narrative of the Second Powell Expedition down the Green-Colorado River from Wyoming, and the Explorations on Land in the Years 1871 and 1872*. New Haven, Conn.: Yale University Press, 1962

––––––– *The Romance of the Colorado River*. New York: Putnam, 1909.

DeRoss, Rose Marie. *Woman of the Rivers: Adventures of Georgie White*. Costa Mesa, Calif.: Gardner, 1967.

Eddy, Clyde. *Down the World's Most Dangerous River*. New York: Frederick A. Stokes Co., 1929.

Evans, Laura and Buzz Belknap. *Dinosaur River Guide*. Boulder City, Nev.: Westwater Books, 1973.

Goldwater, Barry. *Delightful Journey Down the Green and Colorado Rivers*. Tempe, Ariz.: Arizona Historical Foundation, 1970.

Hamblin, W. Kenneth and J. Keith Rigby. *Guidebook to the Colorado River: Part 1 and 2.* Provo, Utah: Brigham Young University, 1968.

Hamilton, Joyce. *White Water: The Colorado River Jet Boat Expedition, 1960.* Christchurch, N. Z.: Caxton Press, 1963.

Hayes, Philip T. and George C. Simmons. *River Runners' Guide to Dinosaur National Monument and Vicinity with Emphasis on Geologic Features.* Denver: Powell Society, 1973.

Hogan, Elizabeth, ed. *Rivers of the West.* Menlo Park, Calif.: Lane, 1974.

Hughes, J. Donald. *The Story of Man at Grand Canyon.* Flagstaff, Ariz.: KC Publications, 1967.

Jenkinson, Michael. *Wild Rivers of North America.* New York: Dutton, 1973.

Kolb, Ellsworth L. *Through the Grand Canyon from Wyoming to Mexico.* New York: MacMillan, 1914.

Lee, Weston and Jeanne Lee. *Torrent in the Desert.* Flagstaff, Ariz.: Northland Press, 1962.

Leydet, François. *Time and the River Flowing: Grand Canyon.* San Francisco: Sierra Club, 1964.

Lingenfelter, R. C. *First Through the Grand Canyon.* Los Angeles: Dawson, 1958.

Martin, Charles. *Sierra Whitewater: A Paddler's Guide to the Rivers of California's Sierra Nevada.* Sunnyvale, Calif.: Fiddleneck Press, 1974.

McGinnis, William. *Whitewater Rafting.* New York: Quadrangle–New York Times, 1975.

McKee, E. D. et al. *Evolution of the Colorado River in Arizona.* Flagstaff, Ariz.: Northland Press, 1968.

Midmore, Joe. *Middle Fork History.* Reno: Harrah's Club, 1970.

Nash, Roderick, ed. *Grand Canyon of the Living Colorado.* New York: Sierra Club–Ballantine, 1970.

Nash, Roderick. *Wilderness and the American Mind.* Rev. ed. New Haven, Conn.: Yale University Press, 1973.

Nash, Roderick and Robert Hackamack. "Picking Up the Pieces of the Tuolumne." *Sierra Club Bulletin* 61 (November-December 1976): 7, 8, 16.

Northwest Cartographics. *Middle Fork Salmon River: Map and Guide.* Eugene, Ore.: Northwest Cartographics, 1977.

Northwest Graphics. *Rogue River Canyon: River and Trail Guide.* Eugene, Ore.: Northwest Graphics, 1976.

Norton, Boyd. *Snake Wilderness.* San Francisco: Sierra Club, 1972.

Powell, John Wesley. *The Exploration of the Colorado River and Its Canyons.* New York: Dover, 1961.

Pringle, Laurence. *Wild River*. Philadelphia: Lippincott, 1972.

Rabbit, Mary C. et al. *The Colorado River Region and John Wesley Powell*. Geological Survey Professional Paper 669. Washington, D. C.: Government Printing Office, 1969.

Schwind, Dick. *West Coast River Touring: Rogue River Canyon and South*. Beaverton, Oreg.: Touchstone Press, 1974.

Simmons, George C. and David L. Gaskill. *River Runners' Guide to the Canyons of the Green and Colorado Rivers with Emphasis on Geological Features*. Flagstaff, Ariz.: Northland Press, 1969.

Smith, Dwight L. "The Engineer and the Canyon." *Utah Historical Quarterly* 28 (1960): 262–273.

Stanton, Robert Brewster. *Colorado River Controversies*. Edited by James M. Chalfont. New York: Dodd, Mead, 1932.

―――― *Down the Colorado*. Edited by Dwight L. Smith. Norman, Okla.: University of Oklahoma Press, 1965.

Staveley, Gaylord. *Broken Waters Sing: Rediscovering Two Great Rivers of the West*. Boston: Little, Brown, 1971.

Stegner, Wallace. *Beyond the Hundredth Meridian: John Wesley Powell and the Second Opening of the West*. New York: Houghton Mifflin, 1954.

Stegner, Wallace, ed. *This Is Dinosaur: Echo Park Country and Its Magic Rivers*. New York: Knopf, 1955.

Stone, Julius Frederick. *Canyon Country: The Romance of a Drop of Water and a Grain of Sand*. New York: Putnam, 1932.

Strung, Norman, Sam Curtis, and Earl Perry. *Whitewater!* New York: MacMillan, 1976.

Tejada-Flores, Lito. *Wildwater: The Sierra Club Guide to Kayaking and Whitewater Boating*. San Francisco: Sierra Club Books, 1978.

United States Forest Service. *Proceedings: River Recreation Management and Research Symposium*. General Technical Report NC-28. St. Paul, Minn.: North Central Forest Experiment Station, 1977.

Urban, John T. *White Water Handbook for Canoe and Kayak*. Boston: Appalachian Mountain Club, 1973.

Wallace, Robert. *The Grand Canyon*. American Wilderness Series. New York: Time-Life Books, 1972.

Waters, Frank. *The Colorado*. New York: Rinehart, 1946.

Watkins, T. H., ed. *The Grand Colorado: The Story of a River and Its Canyons*. Palo Alto, Calif.: American West Pub. Co., 1969.

Whitney, Peter Dwight. *White-Water Sport: Running Rapids in Kayak and Canoe*. New York: Ronald Press Co., 1960.

SELECTED INDEX OF NAMES AND PLACES

Alsek River, 5
Aparejo (Rapid), 118
Applegate River, 36
Ashley Falls, 48, 52, 88
Ashley, William Henry, 42,
   47–49, 53, 67, 106
Astor, John Jacob, 145
Atlantic and Pacific Railway,
   81

Baboon Gulch, 132
Badger Rapid, 85, 198
Bailey Falls–Staircase
   complex, 4
Bailey, Robert, 138
Bannock Indians, 110, 130,
   131
Bannock War, 109, 112
Bear Creek, 115, 126
Bear Valley, 106, 114, 115
Beckwourth, Jim, 48
Beer, Bill, 205
Belknap, Bill, 201–202
Bernard, Captain Reuben S.,
   110–112, 116
Best, James S., 85–86
Betts, Frank, 164
Big Creek, 107–108, 110–112,
   116, 118–119
Big Drop, the, 77, 80, 85–90,
   93–94, 96–101. See also
   Satan's Gut
Big Mallard, 4, 58, 64,
   126–129, 134–135, 137–141
Big Meadows, 28
Bitterroot Mountains, 126
Blackadar, Walt, 61, 153–154
Black Bar Falls, 29
Blossom Bar, 29–30
Boise, Idaho, 111–112
Bonneville, Captain Benjamin
   L. E., 145
Boulder Dam, 98
Boulder Falls, 55–58
Bradley, George Y., 79,
   195–196
Bridge Canyon, 184
Bridger, Jim, 48
Bright Angel Canyon, 164
Bright Angel Creek, 161–162
Brokaw, Tom, 117, 121–122
Brower, David R., 126, 173
Brown, Baptiste, 48
Brown, Frank M., 82–84,
   86–87, 94

Brown Betty (Rapid), 83, 99
Brownlee Dam, 153
Brown's Park, 40–42, 47–48,
   59
Buchanan, Dan, 143–144, 148
Buck Creek Rapid, 146,
   151–153
Buckskin Billy, 133
Bureau of Land Management,
   36
Burg, Amos, 94, 115, 145,
   150, 204

Cache Creek, 147
Cache Creek Rapid, 153
Caffery, Congressman
   Patrick T., 156
Callville, Nevada, 192–193
Cameahwait (Shoshone
   Chief), 129
Camp Howard, 110–111
Campbell, Jim, 7, 154–156
Canal Creek, 132
Canyon of Lodore, 39–40, 42,
   50, 52
Cascade Range, 25
Cataract Canyon, 43, 77–80,
   83, 85–92, 94, 96–99, 101,
   114
"The Cataract of Lodore," 40
Catley, First Lieutenant
   Henry, 110–112
Central Arizona Project, 174
Chattooga River, 5
Chenoweth. W. E., 90
Chilko River, 5
Chittam (Rapid), 135
Churchill Ranch, 138
Clark, Captain William,
   129–130, 141, 145
Clavey Falls, 9, 11–23, 58
Clavey River, 12–13
Clavey, William, 12
Clearwater River, 106, 130
Clover, Dr. Elzada U., 91, 94
Coconino Plateau, 160
Coffee Pot, 30
Colorado Basin, 40, 50
Colorado Plateau, 48
Colorado River, 3, 5, 9, 20, 39,
   45, 56, 58–59, 68, 77–78,
   82–83, 86–88, 90, 92–94, 99,
   101, 112, 114–115, 117, 144,
   153, 160–161, 163–165,
   169–175, 178, 181, 183–186,

188, 190, 192–193, 196–198,
   201, 203
Colorado River Storage
   Project, 70, 72
Columbia River, 126, 130,
   143–144
Congo River, 5
Conley, Cort, 113, 154
Continental Divide, 41, 67,
   103, 129, 145
Corkscrew (Rapid), 104. See
   also Weber
Cougar Dave, 107
Couture, Alfred E., 117–121,
   123
Cove Canyon, 183
Cradle Creek Camp, 121, 123
Cross Mountain, 3
Crystal Creek, 159–161,
   164–165, 172, 174
Crystal Rapid, 3, 159, 161,
   164–174, 178, 181–182, 186
Cucumber (Rapid), 5
Currey, Jack, 174

Dagger Falls, 3, 103, 117–118
Daggett, John, 205
Dale, Floyd, 138–139
Dandy Crossing, 85–86
Dark Canyon, 77
Debord, Knoel, 16
Deep Creek, 151
Deerlodge Park, 62
Deliverance, 5
Dellenbaugh, Frederick S.,
   39, 45, 50, 59, 79
Denver, Colorado Canyon,
   and Pacific Railroad Co., 82
DeSmet, Father, 132
Desolation Canyon, 4, 53
Devil's Teeth Rapids, 133
DeVoto, Bernard, 70–71
Dimple, the, (Rapid), 5
Dinosaur National
   Monument, 69–72
Disaster Falls, 42–43, 53, 88
Doherty, Dan, 161–162
Dolores River, 4
Double Z (Rapid), 5
Douglas, Earl, 69–70
Douglas, Justice William O.,
   153
Dragon Creek, 160
Dried Meat Rapid, 127, 140

Dubendorff, S. S., 87
Dubendorff Rapid, 94

Eagle Rock (Rapid), 104. *See also* Redside
Echo Park, 62–63, 66, 68, 70 72
Echo Park Dam, 70–72
Eddy, Clyde, 91–94, 96, 197
Egan, Private Harry, 110
Eggert, Charles, 71
Eiseman, Fred B., Jr., 55–56, 96–99, 204
Ellington, "Moki-Mac", 95, 101
Explorers Club, 45

Farewell Bend, 145
Farrow, Lieutenant Edward S., 112
Federal Power Commission, 153
Filer, Paul, 140
Flaming Gorge, 48
Flavell, George F., 50, 196
Fleming, India, 17
Florence, Idaho, 132–133
Fort Lemhi, 131
Frazier, Dr. Russell G. "Big Joe", 114–116
Freeman, Lewis R., 187

"G-rigs", 198
Galice, Oregon, 28, 33
Gallenson, Art, 7
Galloway, Nathaniel T., 6, 50–53, 68, 86–87, 89, 92, 95, 144, 196–197
Galloway, Parley, 68, 92, 114
Ganges River, 5
Gates of Lodore, 41–42
Gauley River, 5
Glen Canyon, 52, 77, 85, 192–193
Glen Canyon Dam, 170–173, 176, 185, 187
Gold Beach, 34
Golden Creek, 104–105
Goldwater, Senator Barry, 94, 198
Goodman, Frank, 42
Grand Canyon, 2–3, 5, 9, 19, 43, 53, 77–79, 87, 91, 94, 96, 114, 121, 126, 144–146, 153,
159–161, 164–165, 171–178, 180–181, 183–184, 186, 188, 191–194, 196–198, 202–205
Grand Canyon National Park, 174
Grand Junction, Colorado, 82
Grand River, 78. *See also* Green River
Grand Wash Cliffs, 192–193, 196
Granite Creek, 143, 146–148, 150–152, 154
Granite Creek Rapid, 143–144, 146–148, 150, 153–154, 156–157
Granite Rapid, 3, 161
Grant, Alexander "Zee", 198
Grants Pass, Oregon, 25, 33
Grave Creek, 28, 36–37
Grave Creek Rapids, 28, 33
"Graveyard of the Colorado", 78, 88. *See also* Cataract Canyon
Gray, Captain W. P., 149
Great Falls of the Potomac, 5
Green River, 4, 39–41, 43, 48–49, 51, 56, 58–59, 66–68, 70–71, 77–78, 81, 88, 92, 99, 112, 114
Green River, Utah, 2, 52–53, 82–83, 91–92, 99
Green River, Wyoming, 45, 51–54, 81, 86, 88, 196–197
Grey, Zane, 33–35, 37
Greyhound Bus Stopper (Rapid), 5
Griffith, Dick, 95
Groundhog Bar, 4, 135
Guleke, Captain Harry, 113, 134–140
Gun Barrel Rapid, 127, 135

Hall, Andrew, 39–40
Hamilton, Jon, 202–203
Hance Rapid, 3, 146
Hansborough, Peter, 85
Harmon, Ellis, 121–123
Harper, S. S., 81–82
Hart, Sylvan, 133. *See also* Buckskin Billy
Hastings, Langford W., 27
Hatch, Bus, 95, 101, 114, 141
Hatch Brothers, 113

Hatch River Expeditions, 62, 153
Havasu Creek, 182
Hells Canyon, 126, 143–146, 148–154, 157
Hells Canyon Dam, 145, 151, 153–154
Hells Canyon National Recreation Area, 157
Hellsgate, 34
Hell's Half Mile, 39, 42–45, 47, 50, 52–59, 64, 66, 68, 88, 99
Henry, Andrew, 47
Henry's Fork, 51
Hermit Rapid, 3, 161, 204
Hetch Hetchy Dam, 11, 72
Hetch Hetchy Valley, 10, 22, 70
Hindu Amphitheater, 160
Hite, Utah, 86, 89, 91
Hite, Cass, 85
Holladay, Dee, 64, 95
Holland, Al, 63–64
Holmstrom, Haldane "Buzz", 54, 150, 197
Holt, Ray, 152
Hoover Dam, 54, 185
Horn Rapid, 3, 161
House Rock Rapid, 3, 198
Howland, Harry, 94
Howland, O. G., 42, 44
Howland, Seneca, 42
Hudson River, 178
Hudson's Bay Company, 27, 47, 82, 106
Hughes, Gerry, 128
Hunt, Wilson Price, 145
Huser, Verne, 156–157
Hyde, Bessie, 91
Hyde, Glen R., 91

Idaho Primitive Area, 103
Impassable Canyon, 103, 112, 116, 118–119, 121
Indian Creek, 22, 117–118
Indus River, 5
Iron Ring (Rapid), 5

Jack Creek Rapid, 118
Jackson, David E., 48
Jawbone Ridge, 12
Johnson, "Trapper", 107
Jones, Les, 146, 153

Jones, Paul, 150
Jotter, Lois, 91, 94

Kaibab Plateau, 51, 159–161, 173
Kanab Creek, 173, 196
Kee, Congressman James, 155
Kendrick, Frank C., 82
Kimball, Edith, 113
Kinney Creek Rapid, 146, 148, 151
Kirschbaum, Walter, 198
Kolb, Ellsworth, 44, 52–53, 87–90, 197
Kolb, Emery, 44, 52–53, 87–90, 93, 197

La Framboise, Michel, 27
Lake Mead, 162, 181, 194, 197, 200, 202
Lake Powell, 77, 171, 176
Land of Standing Rocks, 78–79
Lava Cliff Rapid, 194–197
Lava Falls, 3, 19, 58, 66, 91, 121, 164, 168, 173–174, 180–187, 189–192, 194, 196–206
Law, W. J., 86
Lee's Ferry, Arizona, 51, 85, 91, 94, 181, 184, 192
Leich, Harold H., 91
Lemhi Mission, 130–131
Lemhi River, 129
Leopold, Aldo, 207
Lewis, David, 107. *See also* Cougar Dave
Lewis, Meriwether, 129–130, 141, 145
Lewis and Clark, 47, 145
Lewiston, Idaho, 134–135, 144, 148, 150
Lewiston *Morning Tribune*, 150, 155
Lightfoot, Austin, 114
Little Colorado River, 172, 196
Little Creek, 108
Little Hole, 51
Little Porcupine (Rapid), 104
Litton, Martin, 7, 71, 126, 177, 199–200

Lockhard, Caroline, 135
Lodore Canyon, 43, 48–50, 53–54, 78, 88, 99
Loin of Pork (Rapid), 104. *See also* Weber
Lolo Pass, 130
Loper, Bert, 86, 89
Lost Paddle (Rapid), 5
Lost Trail Pass, 130
Lower Lava Falls, 200, 204
Lunch Counter Rapid, 4

Mackay Bar, 128
MacKay, Johnny, 133
MacKenzie River boats, 117, 120–121
Malone, Pat, 86
Manly, William, 49–50
Manti La Sal, 79
Marble Canyon, 83, 85, 192
Marston, Otis "Dock", 200–201
McCloskey, Michael, 22
McComkie, Wayne, 94
McCormack, Congressman Mike, 155–156
McGrady, Kyle, 150, 152
McKenzie, Donald, 145
McMullen, Oren "Mac", 152
Meral, Gerald, 16
Middle Fork (Salmon River, Idaho), 3, 9, 103–107, 109–112, 114–119, 124, 126, 134
Mile Long Rapid, 80, 86–88, 92, 99
Miller, Hack, 115
Miller, Hank, 156
Miller, Sebastian "Bas", 143–144, 148
Mississippi River, 9, 40, 134
Missouri River, 40, 134, 145
Mist Falls, 105
Moab, Utah, 51, 82
Monnette, Edmund, 86–87
Montos, Ramon, 50, 196
Moore, Clarence, 150–151
Moose Creek, 4
Morehouse, Jim, 17
Mormons, 130–131, 133, 192
Mount Lyell, 9
Muir, John, 10
Muir Gorge, 10

Mule Creek Canyon, 30
Mullens, John, 150

Napias Creek, 133
Narrow Canyon, 77–78, 85
Nash, Sandy, 182
National Canyon, 182, 194
National Park Service, 64, 69, 168, 176, 203
National Wild and Scenic Rivers Act, 36
National Wild and Scenic Rivers System, 22, 36, 116, 141, 157
National Wilderness Preservation Act, 72
National Wilderness Preservation System, 73, 157
Needles, California, 51, 81, 89, 94
Nevills, Norman, 94–95, 113, 197–198
New River, 5
Nez Percé, 131
Niagara Falls, 3
Niagara River, 4
Nile River, 5
North Fork (of the Salmon River), 127, 129
North Fork of the Payette, 3
Northwest Passage, 129–130

Ogden, Peter Skene, 27
Ohio River, 134, 145
Oldham, Les, 63–64, 66
Olney, John, 150–152
Olson, James, 156
Oregon Steam Navigation Company, 143
Oregon Trail, 145
Orofino, Idaho, 132
Oro Grande, Idaho, 109
Ouzel Rapid, 121
Oxbow Dam, 153

Packwood, Senator Robert, 154
Paria River, 172
Parrot Placer Camp, 121
Pathe–Bray party, 91
Pend d'Oreille River, 132
Phantom Ranch, 161
Pierce, Captain E. D., 132

Pierce City, Idaho, 132
Pillow Rock (Rapid), 5
Pine Creek (Rapid), 127,
  134–135
Pistol Creek Rapid, 104,
  114–115
Platte River, 41
Porcupine Rapid, 104, 119.
  See also Redside
Powell, John Wesley, 2, 4,
  39–40, 42–45, 47–50, 52, 56,
  59, 66–68, 78–81, 83, 87,
  89–90, 94, 99, 112, 182–183,
  185, 191, 194–196
Powerhouse Rapids, 104
Prospect Canyon, 186, 188
Pruitt, Bob, 34

Railroad (Rapid), 5
Rainie Falls, 25–37, 58
Ramey (Reamy) (prospector
  30
Rattlesnake Canyon, 119
Rattlesnake Creek, 118
Red Gorge, 48, 88
Redside Rapid, 103–105,
  114–115, 117, 119–121, 124
Reilly, P. T., 187
Reiner, Doug, 25, 99
Reynolds, Jack, 182
Richards, H. C., 85
Richmond, William Chesley
  51
Rio Grande (River), 3, 81
Rio Grande and Western
  (Railroad), 81
"River of No Return", 126,
  135, 139
Roaring Springs, 162
Rogue River, 25–26, 29–31,
  33–37, 58
Rogue River Canyon, 28
Rogues (Indians), 26–28
Ross, Kenny, 95, 100–101
Rubber Rapid, 104
Ruby Rapid, 4, 127, 135
Russell, Charles, 86–87, 89

Salmon Falls, 135
Salmon Falls Rapid, 127
Salmon River, 4, 43, 58, 103,
  106, 109, 113–116, 123,
  126–131, 133–135, 138

Salmon River Mining
  Company, 134
Salmon River Mountains, 103
Salmon River sweep boat, 134
Salt Lake City, 49, 131
Sanderson, Rod, 95, 101
Sandilands, David, 134
Sandilands, Captain George,
  134–136
San Francisco Public Utilities
  Commission, 21
San Juan River, 94, 192
Santa Fe Railroad, 81
Satan's Gut, 66, 77–78, 80,
  85–88, 90–91, 93–95,
  98–101
Sawpit Rapid, 146, 151–152
Sawtooth Mountains, 103,
  107, 114, 126
Sayre, Joel, 97
Seeds-ke-Dee (Green River),
  48
Selway River, 4, 9
Separation Canyon, 194
Seven Devils Mountains, 107,
  144, 146
Sevy's Rock, 104. *See also*
  Redside
Sheepeater Indians, 109–112,
  116
Sheepeater War, 112
Shoshone, 143–144, 148
Shoshone Indians, 109, 129,
  131
Shoup, Colonel George L.,
  129
Shoup, Idaho, 129
Sierra Club, 16–17, 22, 71,
  173, 177
Skull Rapid, 4
Slate Creek, 161
Smith, Bob, 152
Smith, Charles, 88–89
Smith, Don, 140
Smith, Jedidiah, 48
Smith, Ken, 117
Smith, Ron, 183
Snaggletooth (Rapid), 4
Snake River, 4, 106, 126, 134,
  143–148, 150, 152–154,
  156–157
Soap Creek, 85
Soap Creek Rapid, 85

Soldier Bar, 110, 116
Solitude Bar, 26
Southern Pacific (Railroad),
  81
Spaulding, Everett, 117–121,
  123
Spencer Canyon, 194
Split Mountain, 49
Sportyaks, 166
Squaw Creek, 146
Squaw Rapid, 151
Stanislaus River, 4, 17, 22
Stanley, John, 106
Stanton, Robert Brewster,
  80–81, 83, 85–87, 186, 196
Staveley, Gaylord, 55–58
  99–100, 159, 177
Steer Ridge Rapid, 4
Stegner, Wallace, 72
Steward, John F., 45
Stikine River, 5
Stone, Julius, 44, 50, 52, 68,
  86–87, 94, 115, 121–123,
  196–197
Stone, Martin, 121
Stuart, Robert, 145
Sublette, William L., 48
Sulphur Creek, 118
Sunderland, Richard, 16
Susitna River, 5
Swain, Frank "Limber,"
  114–116

Takelmas (Indians), 26
Talmalamne (Tuolumne), 9
Tappan Falls, 104, 114,
  117–118
Teague, Gene, 117, 121–123
Teapot Canyon, 99
Thomas, Harold, 150
Thomas Creek, 108
Thompson, Almon H., 45
Toom'-pin wu-near' Tu-weap
  ("Land of Standing
  Rocks"), 78
Toroweap Fault, 185–186, 188
Toroweap Overlook, 183
Triple rig, 95
Triplett Falls, 43, 53, 88
Tukuarika (Indians), 109
Tuolumne Electric Company,
  22
Tuolumne River, 9–12,
  14–18, 20–23, 58, 70

Tussing, Annette, 155
Tyee Rapids, 29

Udall, Stewart L., 173–174
Uinta Basin, 69
Uinta Mountains, 40–41, 43, 48, 67
Umatilla Indians, 110–111
U.S. Army Corps of Engineers, 156
U.S. Bureau of Reclamation, 68, 70–71, 117, 173, 176
U.S. Cavalry, 109–110, 112
U.S. Forest Service, 11, 30, 36, 104, 116
U.S. Geological Survey, 53, 80, 90, 104, 187, 197
Upset (Rapid), 3, 186
Utah Power and Light Company, 53
Utah State University, 74

Vandenburg, Jack, 150
Vasey's Paradise, 85
Velvet Falls, 104, 114
Vernal, Utah, 50–51, 114
Vulcan's Forge, 185
Vulcan's Throne, 185

Wallace, Robert, 199
Wallowa Mountains, 144
Warm Springs, 62–64, 75
Warm Springs Cliff, 64, 66
Warm Springs Draw, 61, 63, 67
Warm Springs Rapid, 65–66, 68, 73–74
Weber Falls, 121–122
Weber Rapid, 104–105, 115, 119, 121, 123–124
Western River Expeditions, 153
Westwater Canyon, 4
Whirlpool Canyon, 49
Whiskey Creek, 28, 37
White, Georgie (Clark), 95–96, 98, 101, 153, 204–205
White, James, 176, 191–194
White Cloud Mountains, 126
Whitewater Ranch, 128
Whitmore, Bryce, 17–18, 22–23
Wild and Scenic Rivers Act, 116
Wild Sheep Rapid, 146

Wilderness River Trail, 71
Wilderness Society, 71
Willamette Valley, 27, 145
Wilson, Donald, 117–118
Wilson Creek, 118
Wind River Bridge, 127
Wind River Range, 67
Winkle Bar, 33
Wood, R. J., 151–152
Wooldridge, Glen, 30, 33
Work, John, 106

Yampa Canyon, 49, 72
Yampa River, 3, 61–62, 64, 66–68, 70–71, 73–75
Yangtze River, 5
Yosemite National Park, 10–11, 70
Yosemite Valley, 11
Youghiogheny River, 5
Young, Brigham, 131

Zaire River, 5

24½ Mile Rapid, 3
164 Mile Rapid, 198
232 Mile Rapid, 3